1979

AN OVID READER

Allan G. Gillingham
Eric C. Baade

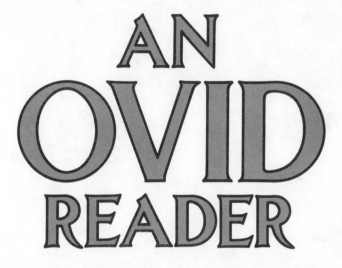

CHARLES E. MERRILL PUBLISHING CO.
A Bell & Howell Company
Columbus, Ohio

ISBN O-675-06212-8

Copyright © 1969 by
Charles E. Merrill Publishing Co.
A Bell & Howell Company
Columbus, Ohio 43216

Printed in the United States of America

PREFACE

Ovid is an attractive and important author who deserves a larger place than we commonly provide in the Latin curriculum; hence this *Ovid Reader*, which takes as its point of departure the selections from the *Metamorphoses* given in *Latin: Our Living Heritage, Book II.*

Ovid's influence on world literature has been greater than that of any other Latin author, and he is also our chief source for classical mythology. His style is lively, his subject matter interesting; and (most important of all for young readers) his works can be read rapidly, so that there is no time for interest to flag. Ovid can be read with ease after three semesters of High School Latin. The only difficulties which will confront a second-year student in reading Ovid are a few constructions which are more common in poetry than in prose, and the new vocabulary which he will encounter. These difficulties are met in this book by the running vocabulary and notes.

The running vocabulary supplies all words which the student is not likely to have learned in three semesters. Each selection is regarded as an independent unit, and new words are listed in each selection when encountered for the first time; for although the readings are given in chronological order, we assume that the teacher will not necessarily wish to follow this sequence. The asterisk indicates a word which we feel is worth memorizing, either because it will recur in the particular selection or because it is regarded as basic in the acquisition of an Ovidian vocabulary. The student will thus be able to read a greater amount more readily than would be the case were he expected to consult the end vocabulary for each new word encountered.

Unfamiliar grammatical constructions are pointed out in the notes, and suggestions offered for translation; those which occur frequently are listed in the Introduction, along with the more common rhetorical figures and the principles of Latin versification. The notes also provide enough information about proper names to make the reference comprehensible; the Index of Proper Names offers background details about persons and places.

For those readers who would like to be informed on Ovid's influence on later literature and on the arts, we would recommend especially W. Brewer: *Ovid's Metamorphoses in European Culture* and M. Grant: *Myths of the Greeks and Romans.*

A.G.G.
E.C.B.

▨▨▨▨▨ CONTENTS ▨▨▨▨▨

INTRODUCTION

MAPS

AMORES

ARS AMATORIA

FASTI

METAMORPHOSES

TRISTIA

Life of Ovid

Publius Ovidius Naso, whom we call Ovid (or sometimes Naso), was born at Sulmo, a little town some ninety miles east of Rome, in 43 B.C.; he died in A.D. 17 or 18. His lifetime therefore spanned the reign of the Emperor Augustus; and he came of age about the time that the Roman Revolution, which had been going on more or less violently for nearly a century, was ended by Augustus' establishment of a new imperial constitution. Augustus, when the vicissitudes of civil war had left the supreme power in his hands, was faced with a tremendous task, the re-establishment of order out of chaos. The government of the republic was rotten to the core: the old ruling families had destroyed their country in their struggles for power. Their custom of cementing political alliances by dynastic marriages between the powerful families had made a mockery of the marriage vows: divorce and adultery were common, and the birthrate among the aristocracy had declined sharply.

Augustus' attempts at reform.

Augustus took from the hands of the senatorial nobility those administrative functions which they had shown themselves incapable of performing, and at the same time he attempted to strengthen the Senate by recruiting into it members of the aristocratic families of the smaller towns of Italy.

Ovid's family was just such a family: good, respectable, well-to-do country stock or local gentry; and Ovid's father sent his two sons to Rome to be trained for political careers. They studied under the best teachers of the day, acquiring a thorough grounding in literature and rhetoric. Ovid's brother took to his political training with enthusiasm and would have pursued a career as a lawyer-politician if he had not died in 24 B.C. at the age of twenty; but Ovid's first interest, from boyhood on, was in poetry. His father pointed out that there was no money in poetry, and Ovid attempted to accede to his wishes, but even when he tried to write prose it came out in verse. When he came of age he gave up the struggle and relinquished all thought of a senatorial career, devoting all his genius to literature.

Rome was a kind of paradise for a young poet in those days; never, perhaps, before or since, has there been such a gathering of important literary figures at one time and place. This was the day of Vergil, Horace, Tibullus, Propertius, Livy, and many lesser writers. Augustus had early realized the importance of supporting his reforms with the intellectual and emotional appeal of the arts, for his program embraced much more than the stabilization of the government. He wished to call the Romans back to the old-fashioned ways of their ancestors, to impose upon this urban and urbane society all the old agrarian virtues of the early republic: a love of the land, veneration of the gods of Rome, reverence for the sanctity of marriage and the integrity of the family, thrift, honor, and dignity. At the same time he wished to make its citizens aware of Rome's great destiny as the mistress of the world.

His comprehensive program of urban renewal, the erecting and restoration of public buildings and temples, served to demonstrate the greatness of Rome and her gods. At the same time his patronage of the great writers of the day, sought out and subsidized through Maecenas, his cultural minister, reinforced his new programs through literature. Vergil's *Georgics* glorified the farmer's life, creating a cultural atmosphere sympathetic to Augustus' desire that the aristocrats of Rome should rehabilitate Italian agriculture by investing in land. His *Aeneid* and the *Odes* of Horace gave a new sanctity to the gods of Rome; they also gave a cosmic meaning to the role of Rome as ruler of the world, as did Livy's history. Horace and Livy also extolled the old Roman virtues. These were writers of such genius that their work could not fail to have an effect on the educated class. And Augustus (or Maecenas) was intelligent enough not to coerce their genius; this was not official government propaganda, but literature. The writers were even allowed to express opposition to the regime: Livy explicitly, and Vergil implicitly, regretted the passing of the republic.

The poet fails to conform.

Rome seemed a literary Olympus full of real gods to young Ovid; but he himself did not fit into their pattern. He may not have liked the vices of urban aristocratic society, but he loved its civilized gaiety and wit, and had temperamentally no sympathy with the new seriousness which the new regime was hoping to inspire in the frivolous hearts of the upper classes.

He did begin an epic about the wars of the gods and giants, but it was never finished. The lofty strains of epic verse he found uncongenial; his Muse was Thalia, not Calliope, and he found a genre suited to his talents in elegiac poetry, already developed to a high degree of sophistication by Tibullus and Propertius. Such a collection of elegies typically tells the story of a love affair, recounting incidents in its development or expressing the feelings of the lover; and Ovid's three books of *Amores* follow this pattern, telling of the poet's love for a girl he calls Corinna, and for other girls as well. Whether these women had any real existence is doubtful; Ovid himself later claimed that the love-affair was fictitious.

Certainly the tone of Ovid's love-elegies is quite different from that of his predecessors; the *Amores* are light-hearted whereas the verses of Tibullus are serious. The lover's pleasure in his love affairs springs as much from a consciousness of his own virtuosity in conducting them as from the girls themselves; he is a connoisseur of love, a tactician who can enjoy even his reverses as part of the pattern. The cardinal virtue of lovers is their sophistication, *urbanitas;* the deadliest sin, a lack of cultivation, *rusticitas.* In this Ovid goes against the literary trend of his time, which exalts antique rustic simplicity and decries modern decadence. Ovid obviously loved the urban social life of his day; the *Amores* are a series of vignettes of daily life among the aristocracy.

Ovid is most un-Augustan in other ways as well. He takes no interest in the stirring political and military events of the time: the victories over the Germans engage his attention only because the hair of captive German women provides blonde wigs for the beauties of the capital. He also lacks the reverence for the gods which the other poets show: the gods themselves are seen chiefly as amorists, and their love-affairs set a precedent for those of mankind; he cannot imagine that they will punish the perjuries of lovers.

The first book of the *Amores* is a narrative of the beginning and almost continuous progress of a love affair. The other two books continue in the same vein, but there are traces of a more serious tone: for example, we find (to our surprise) a passage in praise of Ovid's rustic home town, and an account of a pilgrimage made with his wife to a rural festival of Juno, in which he shows a real reverence for the religious ritual and its meaning.

There are also hints of other, more serious works to come. Corinna and her kind are not the only ladies who engage Ovid's interest; the Muses themselves vie for his affections. At the beginning of the first book Ovid tells us how Elegy stole his heart from Epic, and at the end he asserts that Elegy can make him immortal without help from her sisters. Book Two begins with another account of the victory of Elegy over Epic; but near the end he speaks with some pride of having written a tragedy, as well as a new kind of elegiac, the letters of famous heroines to their lovers, with some of the replies.

The tragedy was the *Medea*, a work now lost, but admired in antiquity. It is perhaps surprising that Ovid was capable of writing a successful tragedy, of treating ancient myth seriously. Indeed it is a safe guess that his Medea was not a tragic figure in the older sense, but a study in feminine psychology; for the other work he mentions, the epistles of heroines, *Heroides,* amply demonstrates his amazing understanding of the workings of the female mind. The Penelope, Briseis and Phaedra, the Dido, Ariadne, Medea, and other heroines of the *Heroides* are not in fact figures of heroic stature at all—they are fully human, with all the complex moods of real women. Occasionally Ovid cannot resist the temptation to be merely clever, and then his words ring false, but for the most part the work is serious enough; yet the myths, merely by being acted, as it were, in modern dress, do suffer a certain loss of dignity.

Ars Amatoria, an affront to the Emperor.

If Ovid's works thus far could be accused of ignoring Augustus' program of moral rearmament, the next one amounted almost to a direct attack. Ovid had already written, at some point, a short didactic poem on the use of cosmetics (and indeed the didactic tradition did not exclude poems on trivial subjects); he had already shown his understanding of the psychology of lovers. Now he published an elaborate didactic poem professing to teach nothing less than the Science of Seduction, *Ars Amatoria,* in three books, two addressed to male readers, one to women. Lavishly embellished with vignettes and illustrations from myth and legend, this work explains in detail the principles of the science, the techniques of the art, the rules of the game.

It is doubtful that Ovid himself realized how much such a poem could do to sabotage Augustus' reform program; there is no reason to doubt his sincerity when in his later apologies he points out that no one could have learned anything new from his instructions. Nevertheless, the *Ars Amatoria* undoubtedly did a disservice to the official policies just as Vergil's *Georgics* served them. It is surely unlikely that any young gallant set out to court his mistress with Ovid's book under his arm; it is equally unlikely that any farmer followed his plow with Vergil's poetry in one hand. The point is that just as the *Georgics* served to make agriculture and the country virtues respectable and admirable to the upper class, so the *Ars Amatoria* performed the same service for adultery. The effect of each work lay in the moral context it assumed, not in the actual instructions it gave.

In the same work, just as innocently, Ovid undermines the dignity of the Emperor. The poet can be very funny, and one of the sharpest weapons in his arsenal of wit is his use of anticlimax, or bathos. In one part of the *Ars Amatoria,* in which he instructs the young man where to find a suitable mistress, he suddenly launches into a panegyric of the young Gaius Caesar (Augustus' grandson and adopted son), setting out on a campaign against the Parthians. It is full of exaggerated flattery of the imperial family and is most unlike Ovid's usual tone. What is this piece of official propaganda doing in the *Ars Amatoria?* The question is soon answered: Gaius' triumphal procession, when he returns victorious, will be a perfect occasion for picking up girls. Mockery of the dignity of the imperial family is not confined to this passage: the very buildings with which Augustus has commemorated his family and dignified the capital are in this poem merely a setting for the lover's pursuit of beautiful girls. Ovid is pleased with Augustus' urban renewal program, but for quite the wrong reasons: now the cultivated life of the most civilized city in the world has an architectural background worthy of its elegance.

Love for Rome, its history and religious rituals, revealed in the *Fasti*.

In Book III of the *Amores* there are suggestions of more serious literary projects; and in the last poem Ovid bids farewell to Venus, Cupid, and his present Muse, promising himself that he will now turn to greater themes. He probably had in mind two such projects, the literary almanac called the *Fasti* and an epic, the *Metamorphoses*. The *Fasti* were a calendar with one book of elegiac verse devoted to each month, providing etymological, astronomical, religious, and historical information about the various months and days. In this poem Ovid explains the derivations of the names of the months, gives the dates of the risings and settings of the different constellations, describes the rites by which the numerous religious feasts were celebrated, and commemorates the anniversaries of important historical events. Here at last is the kind of poem which might have earned Ovid a place alongside the laureates of the new regime; for, although Ovid's wit is very much in evidence, the poem shows a real love for the rituals of religion and a real interest in the history of Rome, which make it complementary to the works of Vergil and Livy. It is an unlikely poem to have come from the pen of a man who has hitherto devoted his talents to the service of Venus and Cupid, a mocker of the gods, unaware of political history. It is true that the gods of the *Fasti* are not mysterious, awe-inspiring figures—the poet speaks to them in quite familiar terms—but they emerge as lovable beings, friends of mankind, as they do in no other ancient writer. Ovid is the only writer to suggest to us the love which the unsophisticated common people must have had for their divinities; he also shows great sympathy for the simple pleasures of the poor. Of his earlier work only his few lines in praise of Sulmo and his account of the Faliscan festival which he attended with his wife suggest such feelings in Ovid. The sophisticated man-about-town of the *Amores* and the *Ars Amatoria* seems quite a different person from the poet of the *Fasti*. One may ask which is the real Ovid, but the question is irrelevant; one of the characteristics of a true poet is his ability to see the world from many different points of view.

Literary artistry of his epic, the *Metamorphoses*.

Ovid speaks with many voices in his greatest work, his epic, the *Metamorphoses;* and in fact the skillful combination of diverse elements is one of the most striking features of the poem. The framework of the epic is itself extremely complex: the poet proposes to tell the stories of all the transformations undergone by the characters of myth and legend. With a sure touch that hides his consummate artistry he weaves these stories together in the most intricate patterns. The basic structure is chronological, running from the primeval chaos to the deification of Julius Caesar in 42 B.C.; but many of the stories occur as flashbacks, either introduced as background material or put into the mouths of characters in other stories. Because metamorphosis is a frequent event in pagan myth and legend, Ovid is able to include the whole sweep of Greek and Roman mythology in his work, so that it is a handbook as well as an epic. But it is far from being a pagan Bible: Ovid's stories, though they amuse and interest, do not inspire belief. By a curious paradox, the gods and heroes of the *Metamorphoses* are unconvincing as gods and heroes merely because they are so completely believable as human beings. To be taken seriously the myths of pagan religion must be seen through the mists of antiquity, the protagonists frozen in quaint archaic attitudes; but Ovid brings them to life. With his amazing talent for seeing the world through the eyes of anyone, man or woman, old or young, rich or poor, god or hero, even human or semihuman (like the centaurs), he shows us just what the feelings of the various characters must have been. And this psychological verisimilitude throws into sharp relief the primitive naiveté of the stories themselves: the characters come to life, and the myths die. Much of the charm of the work lies in this repeated *reductio ad absurdum*. Ovid's epic, like Vergil's, shows the whole history of the universe tending toward the glorification of Rome; but what is the meaning of Rome's destiny when the history itself is obviously a tissue of fairy tales?

Not only did the *Metamorphoses* strike a blow at Augustus' policy of religious revival; they may also have insulted the Emperor himself. In the epic all the gods except Diana are amorous (she shows a spinsterish naiveté), and none more so than Jupiter himself, for most of his own metamorphoses—bull, swan, shower of gold—were for the purpose of illicit love affairs. Reduced to the terms of human psychology, the King of Gods and Father of Men is merely a typical unfaithful husband, afraid of his nagging wife but tempted again and again. If Augustus remembered the passages in the *Fasti* in which Ovid had called him the Jupiter of the earth, what were his feelings as he watched the adulterous antics of Jupiter in the *Metamorphoses?*

"Carmen et error" bring banishment.

Augustus might well be sensitive on the subject of adultery; his attempted reforms had failed miserably. The first person to be punished under his new legislation was his only child, Julia, whom he had been forced to exile for her adulteries in A.D. 2. And now, in A.D 8, his granddaughter, the younger Julia, was found guilty of the same offense. This was the last straw for Augustus, and in his rage he banished Ovid also, to Tomis on the Black Sea.

It is obvious that a popular poet of Ovid's tastes was, and had been from the first, a threat to all that Augustus was trying to do; the reasons for Ovid's exile are no mystery. The immediate pretexts for the sentence are, however, shrouded in mystery. They were, according to Ovid, a poem and an error *(carmen et error)*. The *carmen* was the *Ars Amatoria,* presumably singled out (though it had been written some eight years earlier) as the only one of Ovid's works to which a definite charge—that of immorality—could be attached. What the *error* was will probably never be known; the closest Ovid comes to telling us is the statement that it was something he saw rather than something he did: he had unwittingly become the sharer of some guilty secret. Various suggestions have been made, that he was involved in the younger Julia's immoralities, that he had found out something to the discredit of Augustus himself, had been implicated in some conspiracy—but it is pointless to speculate. The real reason for his banishment must have been that he represented the only force truly dangerous to an autocratic regime, that of ridicule.

In *Tristia,* Ovid depicts the tragedy of exile.

Tomis (the modern Constanta, a seaport of Rumania on the Black Sea) was in every way as remote from the Rome loved by Ovid as any place could be. The climate was cold and the people barbarous, speaking Getic or Sarmatian, with little Greek and no Latin. Ovid was alone, for his wife—his third (he had had two earlier unsuccessful marriages)—remained in Rome to work for his recall. Yet his literary production continued without interruption. Even on the ship which carried him through winter storms to his place of exile he began a new series of elegies, the *Laments (Tristia)* complaining of the unjust severity of his sentence. He eventually completed five books of these elegies, of which the second is a lengthy appeal to the Emperor for some mitigation of his sentence.

His banishment had interrupted his work on the *Metamorphoses*, which he had completed except for the finishing touches, and the *Fasti*, of which only six books had been completed. In his first despair at hearing of his sentence he had burnt his own copy of the *Metamorphoses*, but luckily there were other copies in existence. He did some further work on the *Fasti*, revising the first six books, but apparently he never finished the last six, perhaps because away from Rome the inspiration for this very Roman poem was lacking.

Besides the *Tristia* Ovid wrote in his exile several minor works and one larger one, a collection of letters in elegiacs *(Epistulae ex Ponto)* to his wife and to various friends, as well as to Augustus' popular grand-nephew, Germanicus Caesar.

Ovid was far from happy in Tomis, but as it became more and more clear that he could never hope to be recalled he grew resigned to his fate, and even made a new life for himself there. He learned to speak the languages of his barbarian neighbors, and even composed in Getic a panegyric (now lost) on the imperial family; he made friends with the semi-barbarous inhabitants of the town, who showed their affection for him by passing decrees honoring him and exempting him from taxes. He died at Tomis in A.D. 17 or 18, without ever seeing Rome again.

Versification

Length of Syllables

The rhythms of Latin verse depend primarily on patterns of long and short syllables, not (as in English verse) on patterns of accented and unaccented syllables. The analysis of these patterns of long and short syllables is called *scansion,* or *scanning;* in scansion a long syllable is marked by a macron (‾), a short syllable by a breve (˘). A syllable may be long by nature or by position.

A syllable is long *by nature* if it contains a diphthong or a long vowel, e.g. claudit, aurae, poena, tōtās, fātīs, tēla.

A syllable is long *by position* if its vowel, though short, is followed by two or more consonants, or by a double consonant (x = cs, z = dz), e.g. iamque, sparsus, fulmen, possumus, axis.

All other syllables are short.

NOTES: 1. The consonants which make a syllable long by position need not be in the same word, e.g. sed timuit nē, nec maris.

2. If a short vowel is followed by a mute (b, c, d, g, p, t) and a liquid (l, r), its syllable is *common,* i.e., either short or long, e.g. pătris, săcrum.

3. H is not considered a consonant; hence fugăt hoc, ĕt habet.

4. Qu is taken as one consonant, the u not counting as a separate vowel.

5. In words like **maior, peior, eius,** the i stands for two i's, the first of which forms a diphthong with the preceding vowel, while the second i is a consonant; e.g. **maior** will be pronounced as if it were **mae-ior,** the first syllable being long because of the diphthong.

Elision

If a word ends in a vowel, or in a vowel followed by **m** (**am, em, im, um**), this syllable is usually omitted or slurred in pronunciation if the next word begins with a vowel or **h,** and is disregarded in the meter. The omission (called *elision*) may be indicated by an elision mark (‿) placed below the line, connecting the syllable to be omitted with the first syllable of the next word. In Ovid's verse there are relatively few elisions, and usually of short vowels, e.g. **agere‿alta, exstantem‿atque, fīxumque‿hastīle, iacere‿hōs.**

NOTES: 1. Occasionally the final vowel is not elided, and *hiatus* (lit. "gaping") occurs, e.g. **Ō utinam.**

2. Before words like **iubeō** where the i is a consonant, elision does not occur, e.g. **īnspīrāre iubet, utrōque iacentia.**

Metrical Feet

Only three kinds of feet occur in Ovid, the *dactyl,* the *spondee,* and the *trochee.*

A dactyl consists of a long syllable followed by two short syllables, ‿ ᴗ ᴗ .
A spondee consists of two long syllables, ‿ ‿ .
A trochee consists of a long syllable followed by a short syllable, ‿ ᴗ .

The first syllable of each verse foot receives a slight stress or *ictus* (lit. "beat"), indicated by an oblique stroke above the syllable; a vertical stroke may be used to separate one verse foot from another: **séd tǐmŭ|ǐt nē.**

The Hexameter

In the *Metamorphoses* Ovid uses the dactylic hexameter (also called *heroic verse*). The hexameter consists of six metrical feet. The first four are normally dactyls, but a spondee may be substituted for any of the four dactyls; the fifth foot is almost always a dactyl (on the very rare occasions when the fifth foot is a spondee, the line is called *spondaic*); the sixth foot is always a spondee or a trochee:

1	2	3	4	5	6
dactyl	dactyl	dactyl	dactyl	dactyl	spondee
´	´	´	´	´	´
‿ ᴗ ᴗ	‿ ᴗ ᴗ	‿ ᴗ ᴗ	‿ ᴗ ᴗ	‿ ᴗ ᴗ	‿ ‿
spondee	spondee	spondee	spondee		trochee
´	´	´	´		´
‿ ‿	‿ ‿	‿ ‿	‿ ‿		‿ ᴗ

Caesura (lit. "cutting") is the formal name for the slight pause that occurs about halfway through any hexameter line, i.e., in the third or the fourth foot. It comes at the end of a word, but within the verse foot, and is indicated by two vertical strokes (‖).

To scan a hexameter line:
1. Indicate any elision of a final vowel or final *m* syllable.
2. Mark off the fifth foot as a dactyl and the sixth as a spondee or trochee.
3. Mark long all syllables which are long by nature.
4. Mark long all syllables which are long by position.
5. Mark all other syllables short.
6. Separate the feet with vertical lines.
7. Mark the ictus of each foot.
8. Indicate with a caesura mark where the main pause is likely to come.

The opening lines of *The Flood* are divided into syllables and scanned as follows:

Iam que͜e rắt | ĭn tō|tās‖ spar|sū rus | ful mĭ nā | ter rās.

Sed tĭ mŭ|lit nē | for tĕ sā|cer‖tŏt ăb | ig nĭ bŭs | ae thēr

con cĭ pĕ|ret flam|mās ‖ lon|gŭs que͜ ar|dēs cĕ rĕt | ac sĭs.

The Elegiac Couplet

All the selections from Ovid except the *Metamorphoses* are written in elegiac couplets, Ovid's favorite meter. The elegiac couplet consists of a hexameter followed by a *pentameter*. The pentameter line divides into two halves, called *penthemims,* each penthemim consisting of 2½ metrical feet. In the first penthemim, the two complete feet may be either dactyls or spondees, and the half foot which follows them is always a long syllable. In the second penthemim the two complete feet are always dactyls, but the single syllable which follows them may be long or short.

dactyl	dactyl	long syllable ‖	dactyl	dactyl	long syllable
⌣ ⌣ ⌣	⌣ ⌣ ⌣	⌣	⌣ ⌣ ⌣	⌣ ⌣ ⌣	⌣
spondee	spondee				short syllable
⌣ —	⌣ —				⌣

The division between the two penthemims is marked by two vertical lines.

To scan a pentameter line:
1. Indicate any elisions.
2. Mark the last syllable long or short.
3. Mark the six syllables before the last as two dactyls.
4. Mark the syllable before them long.
5. Mark the rest of the syllables of the first penthemim long or short.
6. Separate the feet with vertical lines.
7. Mark the ictus of each foot or half foot.
8. Indicate the division between the two penthemims.

The opening lines of the *Ars Amatoria* are to be scanned as follows:

Sī quis ĭn|hōc ar|tĕm pŏ pŭ|lō || nōn| nō vĭt a|man dī

hōc lĕ găt|ĕt lēc|tō || car mĭ nĕ |dōc tŭs a|mĕt.

Ār tĕ cĭ|tae vē|lō quĕ ra|tēs || rē|mō quĕ mŏ|ven tŭr,

ar tĕ lĕ|vēs cur|rūs, || ar tĕ re|gen dŭs a|mor.

Adaptations of Forms to Meter

The Latin language tends in general to have long syllables in word endings.
For metrical reasons, Ovid likes to find possible alternatives:

1. For neuter nouns he commonly prefers the plural forms of the nominative
or accusative, so that the final syllable will be short, **silentia, aequora, rēgna,**
etc.

2. Similarly, for ease in versification he will prefer the unusual word to the
more common, as when he uses **hortāmine** for **hortātū** or **hortātiōne** (which
is metrically impossible), **cōnāmine** for **cōnātū.**

3. He likes the ending **-fer** in compound adjectives, as in **cādūcifer, opifer,
venēnifer.**

4. For the ending of the perfect active, third person plural, **-ēre** is preferred
to **-ērunt,** doubtless to acquire the final short syllable; hence **mīsēre** for **mīsē-
runt, effēcēre** for **effēcērunt.**

5. Similarly, to reduce the number of long syllables, **-iī** is preferred to **-īvī**
in the perfect indicative; hence **cupiī** for **cupīvī, cupiit** for **cupīvit, cupīstī** for
cupīvistī.

6. He often prefers the simple verb to the more specific compound; thus
pōnō for **dēpōnō, ferō** for **auferō.**

Rhetorical Figures

Ovid uses most of the devices of rhetoric which were analyzed and named
by Greek and Roman grammarians and literary critics. We still use many of
the technical terms which they coined for them. Among them are:

1. Alliteration, the effective use of words beginning with or containing the
same letter or sound:

> "Et, modo quā gracilēs grāmen carpsēre capellae
> Nunc ibi dēfōrmēs pōnunt sua corpora phōcae."

Metamorphoses, The Flood, 44–45

2. Anaphora, the repetition of a word or phrase in successive clauses or sentences:

"Sīc agna lupum, sīc cerva leōnem,
sīc aquilam pennā fugiunt trepidante columbae."

Metamorphoses, The Flood, 250–251

3. Anticlimax (bathos), a falling-off of the dignity or importance of ideas or expression in a passage:

"Nēve meī sceleris tam trīstia signa supersint,
pōne recompositās in statiōne comās!"

Amores, I. 7. 59–60

4. Antithesis, arrangement of words to emphasize a contrast:

"Fugat hoc, facit illud amōrem.
Quod facit, aurātum est et cuspide fulget acūtā;
quod fugat, obtūsum est et habet sub harundine plumbum."

Metamorphoses, The Flood, 214–216

5. Apostrophe, the figure in which the poet turns away from his narrative to address pointedly some person or thing, whether absent or present. Sometimes the effect is that the poet is so interested that he tries, as it were, to intervene, as in *Fasti, Arion* 19–20; at other times apostrophe is little more than a mannerism, as in *Metamorphoses, The Flood*, 183–5.

6. Enallage, the substitution of one word or form for another. For example, the poet may use with a verb the case appropriate to another verb of similar meaning: **quod** (for **quōcum**) **lūdere possīs**, *Ars Amatoria*, 39.

7. Hellenism, the use of Greek forms or syntax; with Greek proper names Ovid prefers the Greek case endings to the Latin equivalents: **Daphnēn** (acc.), **Daphnēs** (gen.).

8. Hendiadys, the joining of two nouns by a coordinating conjunction when one of them expresses a subordinate or modifying idea: **locum requiemque** (for **locum requiētis**) **petentēs**, *Metamorphoses, Philemon and Baucis*, 11; **cristīs praesignis et aurō** (for **cristīs praesignis aureīs**), *Metamorphoses, Cadmus*, 32.

9. Historic Infinitive, Historic Present, the use of the present indicative or infinitive to narrate past events, in order to add vividness or a sense of urgency: *Metamorphoses, The Flood*, 4–35.

10. Hyperbole, exaggeration for effect:

"tantōque est corpore quantō
... geminās quī sēparat Arctōs."

Metamorphoses, Cadmus, 44–45

11. Hysteron Proteron, a reversing of the natural order of ideas:

"genus mortāle sub undīs
perdere, et ex omnī nimbōs dēmittere caelō."

Metamorphoses, The Flood, 5–6

12. Litotes, understatement to produce emphasis by substituting for a positive statement its opposite with a negative: **nec inīquā mente ferendō,** "and by bearing cheerfully," *Metamorphoses, Philemon and Baucis,* 17.

13. Metonymy, the change of name when an attributive or other suggestive word is substituted for the name of the thing meant. Ovid particularly likes to use the name of a god for that which he symbolizes, as **Mārs** for **bellum** (*Fasti, Fabii,* 14), or an abstract noun for a concrete, as **custōdia** for **custōs** (*Metamorphoses, Philemon and Baucis,* 64).

14. Oxymoron, the joining of contradictory words: **gaudet malō, dīvesque miserque,** *Metamorphoses, Midas,* 7 and 28.

15. Parataxis, a coordinated arrangement of ideas where one is logically subordinate. Ovid frequently omits conjunctions, especially in short sentences, and the clauses may be left without subordination, e.g. **rīserit: adrīdē,** "if she laughs, you are to smile," *Ars Amatoria,* 335.

16. Periphrasis, a roundabout mode of expression. Ovid particularly likes to use a circumlocution for the actual name of hero or heroine; thus Cadmus will be **Agēnoridēs** or **Agēnore nātus,** *Metamorphoses, Cadmus,* 8 and 51, and Ariadne will be "the girl from Cnossos" (**Cnōsis, Cnōsias,** *Ars Amatoria,* 149, 178) or "the girl from Crete" (**Crēssa,** *Amores* I, 16).

17. Pleonasm, the use of unnecessary words. Ovid's store of ideas and phrases is so abundant that he sometimes finds it difficult to let well enough alone. In describing the great flood he has the effective phrase **Omnia pontus erant.** This should have been enough, but he wants to complete the hexameter and so adds **Deerant quoque lītora pontō,** *Metamorphoses, The Flood,* 37.

18. Polysyndeton, the use of a conjunction to add each member in a series:
"cumque satīs arbusta simul pecudēsque virōsque
tēctaque cumque suīs rapiunt penetrālia sacrīs."
Metamorphoses, The Flood 31–32.

19. Prolepsis, the application of a modifier to a noun in anticipation of the action of the verb: **vitiātās īnficit aurās,** "he infects the breezes (and makes them) corrupt," *Metamorphoses, Cadmus* 76.

20. Simile, an illustrative comparison. Ovid likes to use similes, and usually offers more than one to illustrate his point, as in 2 above, or *Metamorphoses, Arethusa,* 55–58.

21. Synchysis, an interlocked word order. An adjective will usually precede the noun it modifies, and in the pentameter one will be in each penthemim:
"quī *nova* nunc prīmum mīles in *arma* venīs."

When there are two pairs of nouns and adjectives, the adjectives will commonly be separated from their nouns and the word order will usually be adj. 1, adj. 2, noun 1, noun 2:

"quālibet hirsūtās fronde tegente comās
    adj. 1   adj. 2 noun 1   noun 2

Illōs longa domant inopī iēiūnia vīctū."
    adj. 1   adj. 2 noun 1 noun 2

22. Transferred Epithet, an adjective, the logical modifier of one noun, placed in syntactical agreement with another: **Rēx iussae succēdit aquae** (for **Rēx iussus succēdit aquae**), *Metamorphoses, Midas*, 43.

23. Zeugma, the use of a verb or an adjective with two different words, in a different sense with each:

"Ūna domus vīrēs et onus suscēperat urbis."

Fasti, Fabii, 3

Grammar

Some forms and syntactical constructions are more common in poetry than in prose; a few of these are reviewed here.

Verb Forms

1. The verb **sum, esse** has in the imperfect subjunctive besides the usual **essem, essēs,** etc.):

	Singular	Plural
1st person	forem	_____
2nd person	forēs	_____
3rd person	foret	forent

2. The future imperative, which is common in poetry, is formed as follows (using **amō, amāre** as a model):

Active

	Singular	Plural
2nd person	amātō, thou shalt love	amātōte, ye shall love
3rd person	amātō, he shall love	amantō, they shall love

Passive

	Singular	Plural
2nd person	amātor, thou shalt be loved	———
3rd person	amātor, he shall be loved	amantor, they shall be loved

Middle Voice

The passive forms are sometimes used, like the Greek middle voice, to indicate that the subject is both acting and acted upon:

> fertur, he takes himself, he goes
> cingitur, he girds himself
> recingor, I ungird myself

A verb used in the middle voice may take a direct object:

> Induitur faciem Diānae.   She puts on herself the appearance of Diana.

Independent Subjunctives

The subjunctive may be used as the verb of a principal clause. Such subjunctives indicate that the action of the verb is not seen as a real action.

1. Potential subjunctive, used when the action is seen merely as a possibility (negative **nōn**):

> videās, you would see
> nōn putārēs, you would not have thought

2. Deliberative subjunctive, used when the subject is trying to choose a course of action (negative **nōn**):

> Quid faciam?   What am I to do?
> Nōn venīret?   Was he not to come?

3. Optative subjunctive, used when the action is wished for (negative **nē**, occasionally **nōn**):

> Nē hoc videam!   May I not see this!
> Adesset pater!   Would that father were here!

4. Jussive subjunctive, used when the action is commanded (negative **nē**, occasionally **nōn**):

> Hoc faciat.   Let him do this.
> Nē abeant.   Let them not go away.

5. Hortatory subjunctive, used to urge others to join in some action (negative **nē**, occasionally **nōn**):

> Eāmus.   Let's go.

Clauses

1. Relative clause of characteristic. A relative clause with its verb in the subjunctive is used to define its antecedent as being of a certain character or kind, rather than merely to state a fact about it. Since such a clause may indicate purpose, result, cause, restriction, condition—in fact, almost any idea which may be conveyed by the subjunctive—no standard translation can be given, except the cumbersome "who (which) is (was) of such a sort as to . . ." Translations for relative clauses of characteristic will be suggested in the notes.

2. Result clauses. Because the subjunctive in result clauses is potential in its origin, the present or imperfect subjunctive in a result clause may be translated with *can* or *could*, even without any form of **possum** (the perfect subjunctive in a result clause indicates a real, not a potential, action).

3. **Dum** clauses.

    dum + present indicative: while
    dum + indicative: so long as (= as long as)
    dum + subjunctive: so long as (= provided that)
    dum + present, perfect, or future perfect indicative: until (action seen as real)
    dum + present or imperfect subjunctive: until (action seen as potential)

4. Disjunctive questions. A disjunctive question is one in which the two halves cannot both be true; the second half may be introduced by **an** or the enclitic **-ne:**

> Manēbis an abībis?
> Manēbis abībisne?   } Will you stay or go?

If the first half is omitted, and **an** alone introduces a question, it is implied that some alternative has been rejected, and so the question may indicate likelihood or surprise.

Case Uses

1. Predicate genitive. The genitive is often used with the verb *to be* when an infinitive is the subject:

Cuiusvīs hominis est errāre.	It is of any man (characteristic of any man) to make a mistake.
Sapientis est pauca loquī.	It is of a wise man (the part of a wise man) to say little.

2. Dative of agent. The dative is frequently used (instead of the ablative with **ab**) to express agency with the passive of the perfect tenses, as well as with the passive periphrastic, its chief use in prose.

3. Dative of reference. This dative is much more widely used in poetry than in prose. Its many uses are summarized in the cumbersome but descriptive old name for it, the *dative of advantage or disadvantage:* i.e., it tells to whose advantage or disadvantage the action of the sentence occurs. The sense often requires that it be translated with *of* or *from* instead of *to* or *for*.

4. Accusative of exclamation. Exclamations in Latin are normally in the accusative, e.g. **mē miserum!** woe is me!

5. Internal accusative. The neuter of an adjective or pronoun is often used as a limiting object even of an intransitive verb. Such an internal object is best translated as an adjective modifying a noun created from the meaning of the verb.

Multum potest.	He has much power.
Hoc errat.	He makes this mistake.
Dulce rīdet.	She has a sweet laugh.

6. Accusative of respect. This accusative, a kind of accusative of extent, names the part affected by the action of a perfect passive participle or the quality of an adjective:

Notus . . . tēctus cālīgine vultum.	Notus, his face covered (covered as to his face) by a dark cloud
nūda pedem	barefoot (bare as to foot)

7. Ablative of place where, ablative of place from which. These ablatives often occur without the usual prepositions.

MAPS

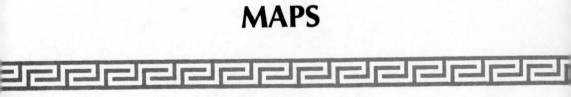

ITALY ~ SICILY

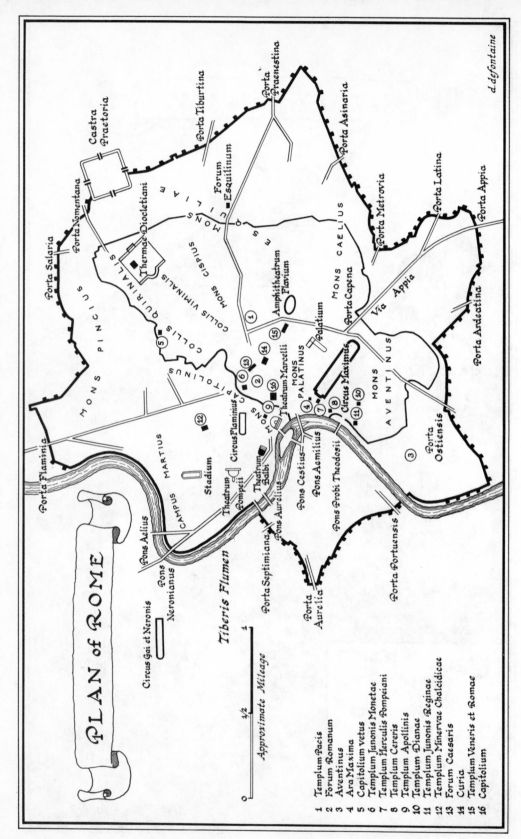

PLAN of ROME

d. de fontaine

Tiberis Flumen

Approximate Mileage

Circus Gai et Neronis

1/2

0   1/4   1/2   3/4   1

1   Templum Pacis
2   Forum Romanum
3   Aventinus
4   Ara Maxima
5   Capitolium vetus
6   Templum Junonis Monetae
7   Templum Herculis Pompeiani
8   Templum Cereris
9   Templum Apollinis
10 Templum Dianae
11 Templum Junonis Reginae
12 Templum Minervae Chalcidicae
13 Forum Caesaris
14 Curia
15 Templum Veneris et Romae
16 Capitolium

THE LEVANT

PONTUS EUXINUS

THRACIA

Troia

ASIA

MYSIA

PHRYGIA

LYDIA

Maeander Fl.

MINOR

LYCIA

BITHYNIA

Sakarya Fl.

Kizil Fl.

CAPPODOCIA

Cydnus

CILICIA

Tarsus

Euphrates Fl.

CYPRUS

Idalium

MARE

INTERNUM

PHOENICIA

Sidon

Tyros

0   100   200

Miles

AEGYPTUS

Nilus Fl.

d defontaine

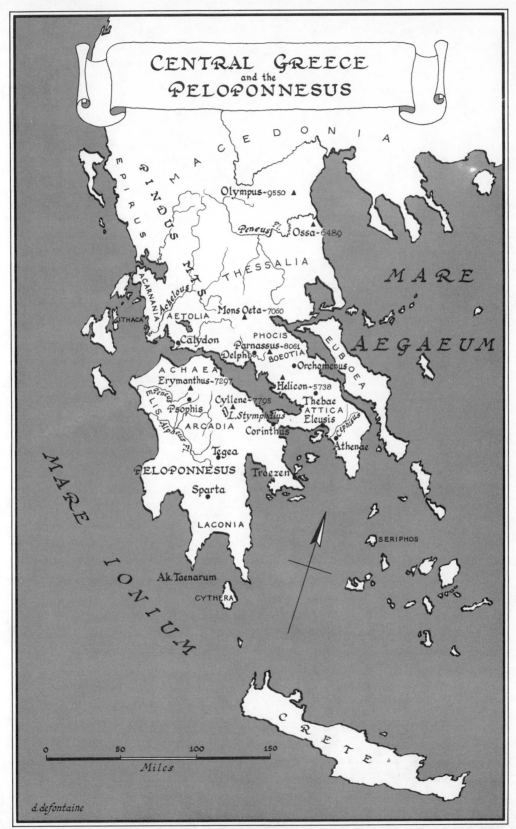

CENTRAL GREECE
and the
PELOPONNESUS

MACEDONIA

EPIRUS

PINDUS

Olympus~9550 ▲

Peneus Fl.

Ossa~6489 ▲

THESSALIA

MARE

ACARNANIA

Achelous Fl.

ITHACA

AETOLIA

Mons Oeta~7060 ▲

Calydon

PHOCIS

Parnassus~8061 ▲

Delphi

BOEOTIA

AEGAEUM

EUBOEA

Orchomenus

ACHAEA

Erymanthus~7297 ▲

Helicon~5738

Peneus

ELIS

Psophis

Cyllene~7795 ▲

L. Stymphalus

Thebae

ATTICA

Eleusis

Cephisus

Alpheus Fl.

ARCADIA

Corinthus

Athenae

Tegea

PELOPONNESUS

Troezen

Sparta

LACONIA

MARE

SERIPHOS

IONIUM

Ak. Taenarum

CYTHERA

CRETE

0   50   100   150

Miles

d. defontaine

Hairdressing scene. Villa of the Mysteries, Pompeii.
Alinari, Fototeca Unione

AMORES

1-5

addō, -ere, -didī, -ditus, put, place
vinc(u)lum, chain, bonds, handcuffs
mereō, -ēre, -uī, -itus, earn, deserve
catēna, chain, fetter
* dum, *w. indic.*, while
furor, -ōris, *m.* madness, frenzy
* abeō, -īre, -iī, -itum, go away
* domina, mistress
temerārius, rash, thoughtless
bracchium, arm
* fleō, -ēre, flēvī, flētus, cry, weep (for)
vēsānus, mad, insane
* laedō, -ere, laesī, laesus, injure
* tunc, then, accordingly, hence
* cārus, dear
violō (1), do violence to, outrage
* parēns, -entis, *m. and f.* parent

6-10

saevus, fierce, cruel
* sānctus, holy, sacred
verber, -eris, *n.* lash, blow
clipeus, shield
septemplex, -plicis, sevenfold
Āiāx, -ācis, *m.* Ajax
* sternō, -ere, strāvī, strātus, spread, lay low
dēprēnsus, seized, surprised
* arvum, field
grex, gregis, *m.* flock, herd
vindex, -dicis, *m.* champion, avenger
ultor, -ōris, *m.* avenger, punisher
Orestēs, -is and -ae, *m.* Orestes
arcānus, secret, mysterious
* poscō, -ere, poposcī, ask for, demand

11-15

dīgestus, arranged, carefully done
laniō (1), tear to pieces, mangle
* capillus, hair
dēdeceō, -ēre, -uī, disgrace, be unbecoming to

* coma, hair, foliage
* fōrmōsus, beautiful
Schoenēis, -idis, *f.* daughter of Schoeneus, Atalanta
Maenalius, of Maenalus, Arcadian
arcus, -ūs, *m.* bow
sollicitō (1), stir up, hunt
* fera, wild beast
* periūrus, perjured, faithless
* prōmissum, promise
* vēlum, sail
Thēseus, -i, *m.* Theseus

16-20

* praeceps, -cipitis, headlong
Crēssa, girl from Crete
* Notus, South Wind
vittātus, wearing a headband
Cassandra, daughter of Priam
* prōcumbō, -ere, -cubuī, -cubitum, fall forward
* templum, temple
castus, pure, chaste
* dēmēns, -entis, mad, insane
* pavidus, trembling, quaking
* metus, -ūs, *m.* fear

21-25

* tacitus, silent
convīcium, outcry, protest
* vultus, -ūs, *m.* face, expression
* ōs, ōris, *n.* mouth
silēns, -entis, quiet, silent
reus, defendant; reum agō, accuse
* umerus, shoulder
lacertus, (upper) arm
* ūtiliter, usefully, profitably
* careō, -ēre, -uī, itum, *w. abl.*, do without, forfeit
dispendium, expense, cost

1 meruēre = meruērunt. 2 dum . . . abit: because it will not be safe to do so when the fit comes back. Ovid is suggesting that he is dangerously insane, and the idea of an insane action will be represented throughout the poem. sī . . . adest: *if anyone present is my friend.* 3 in: *against.* 5-6 Tunc . . . deōs: such an outrage proves that I could dishonor my parents and be guilty of sacrilege (Ovid chooses for comparison the two crimes most abhorrent to a Roman). 5 Tunc: i.e., when I did that. potuī violāre: *I could have dishonored* (English idiom requires that the infinitive be translated as if perfect with the perfect of possum); so too in lines 11 and 24. 7 Quid?: *Well? Why not?* 7, 9 Āiāx, Orestēs: the point of connection is that both heroes committed outrages in fits of temporary insanity; both examples would be familiar from stage presentations. 9 vindex . . . patris: *he who took revenge on his mother for his father.* malus ultor: *a criminal avenger;* oxymoron. 10 ausus . . . deās: to drive away the Furies who haunted him after he had murdered his mother. ausus: sc. est; *dared.* arcānās: because he alone could see them.

11 Ergō . . . capillōs: we now learn of his own outrageous act (which is somewhat comic by comparison). Ergō: i.e., is their example any excuse for me? dīgestōs: *carefully arranged.* 13 sīc: girls in distress always seem more beautiful to Ovid. 13-18 Ovid dwells on the beauty of Corinna and assures us that her hair remained as attractive as ever, by comparing her to three heroines of mythology in times of distress: Atalanta while hunting in Arcadia, Ariadne

Remorse

Like Ajax and Orestes, I have been guilty of foul crime and sacrilege.

> Adde manūs in vincla meās (meruēre catēnās),
>   dum furor omnis abit, sī quis amīcus adest.
> Nam furor in dominam temerāria bracchia mōvit;
>   flet mea vēsānā laesa puella manū.
> Tunc egō vel cārōs potuī violāre parentēs,   5
>   saeva vel in sānctōs verbera ferre deōs.
> Quid? Nōn et clipeī dominus septemplicis Āiāx
>   strāvit dēprēnsōs lāta per arva gregēs,
> et vindex in mātre patris, malus ultor, Orestēs
>   ausus in arcānās poscere tēla deās?   10

Yet, despite my action, she was as lovely as Atalanta, Ariadne or Cassandra.

> Ergō ego dīgestōs potuī laniāre capillōs?
>   (Nec dominam mōtae dēdecuēre comae:
> sīc fōrmōsa fuit; tālem Schoenēida dīcam
>   Maenaliās arcū sollicitāsse ferās;
> tālis periūrī prōmissaque vēlaque Thēsei   15
>   flēvit praecipitēs Crēssa tulisse Notōs:
> sīc, nisi vittātīs quod erat Cassandra capillīs,
>   prōcubuit templō, casta Minerva, tuō.)

Though she was silent, her eyes and tears accused me.

> Quis mihi nōn "dēmēns!", quis nōn mihi "barbare!" dīxit?
>   Ipsa nihil. Pavidō est lingua retenta metū.   20
> Sed tacitī fēcēre tamen convīcia vultūs:
>   ēgit mē lacrimīs, ōre silente, reum.

My hands, as agents of crime, should at least be bound.

> Ante meōs umerīs vellem cecidisse lacertōs;
>   ūtilius potuī parte carēre meī.
> In mea vēsānās habuī dispendia vīrēs   25

when deserted by Theseus, and Cassandra (except that her hair was ribboned) about to be dragged from the temple of Minerva. **13-14 tālem Schoenēida dīcam sollicitāsse:** compressed from **tālem fuisse Schoenēida dīcam cum sollicitāret;** similarly w. **tālis flēvit Crēssa. Schoenēida:** Greek acc. sing. of **Schoenēis. 16 tulisse Notōs:** depending on **flēvit;** *wept that the south winds had carried.* **17 nisi quod:** *except that.* **vittātīs capillīs:** abl. of description; *she was of fillet-bound hair = she had her hair bound with a fillet (the formal headband of a priestess).* **18 Minerva:** voc. case; Ovid is fond of this rhetorical device (apostrophe) whereby a person, absent or distant, is addressed as if present.

19 Quis: i.e., Which of my readers? **20 Ipsa nihil:** sc. **dīxit. est lingua retenta:** *her tongue was held = she was tongue-tied.* **21 tacitī . . . vultūs:** *her looks, though silent, made protests = cried out in protest.*

23 Ante: adv.; implied is *Before I had done this.* **umerīs:** abl. of separation w. **cecidisse;** *had fallen off my shoulders.* **vellem:** potential subjv.; *I would have wanted.* **24 meī:** partitive gen. of the pron. **ego. 25 In mea dispendia:** *To my own loss.* **27 Quid:** sc. **est. mihi:** dat. of

3

* scelus, -leris, n. crime
ministra, (female) servant, abettor
* dēbitus, due, deserved
sacrilegus, sacrilegious, wicked
* subeō, -īre, -iī, -itus, undergo, submit to
an, or
pulsō (1), beat, strike
Quirīs, -ītis, m. Roman citizen
plēctō, -ere, beat, punish

31-35

Tȳdīdēs, -ae, m. son of Tydeus, Diomedes
* monumentum, reminder, memorial
percellō, -ere, -culī, -culsus, strike
* minus, less
* nocēns, -entis, guilty
* profiteor, -ērī, -fessus sum, claim, profess
magnificus, magnificent, splendid
* victor, -ōris, m. conqueror
mōlior, -īrī, -ītus sum, toil for, work at
* triumphus, triumph

36-40

* cingō, -ere, cīnxī, cīnctus, surround, encircle
* laurus, -ī, f. laurel
* vōtum, vow, prayer
* Iuppiter, Iovis, m. Jupiter

currus, -ūs, m. chariot
comitor (dep. 1), accompany, attend
* turba, crowd
iō, exclamation of joy
effūsus, poured out, loosened, disheveled
* trīstis, -e, sad
* captīva, captive girl
* sinō, -ere, sīvī, situs, allow, permit
candidus, white, radiant, beautiful
gena, cheek

41-45

* frōns, frontis, f. brow, forehead
ferreus, made of iron, cruel
ingenuus, freeborn, frank, ingenuous
* unguis, -is, m. fingernail
notō (1), mark, brand
astō, -āre, -stitī, stand nearby
āmēns, -entis, insane, dumbfounded
* albus, pale, white
Parius, of Paros
* quālis, -e, what kind of, such as
* iugum, yoke, mountain peak
exanimis, -e, lifeless, terrified
artus, -ūs, m. joint, limb
membrum, limb
tremēns, -entis, trembling

possession; *What have I (to do) with you?* ministrae: referring to his hands; ministrae and sacrilegae manūs are both in the voc. Ovid professes to disown the hands that have done the sacrilegious deed, perpetrated "crimes" and "murder" in disarranging her hair. 29 pulsāssem = pulsāvissem: past contrary-to-fact condition; *if I had struck.* 30 plēcterer: present contrary-to-fact conclusion; *I would be beaten* (the legal penalty for striking a Roman citizen). iūs: *legal right.*

31-32 Pessima . . . ego: in Homer (*Iliad* V. 329-351) Diomedes wounded Aphrodite; now Ovid, too, has wounded a goddess. 32 alter: *the second.* 33 Et . . . nocēns: sc. *erat*; *And he was less guilty.* Mihi: dat. of agent w. laesa. quam: sc. illa or domina as antecedent. 34 in hoste: *in dealing with an enemy.*

35 Ī: imper. of eō; Ovid is addressing himself. mōlīre: present imper. 36 cinge . . . Iovī: as a triumphing general would do. 37 quaeque turba = et turba quae. comitantum = comitantium (the present active participle often becomes a consonant-stem when used as a noun). 38-39 clāmet, eat: jussive subjvs. 38 Iō: the shout of triumph raised during the parade. virō: dat. of agent w. victa. 40 sinerent: verb of present contrary-to-fact condition; the conclusion is expressed in candida, *all fair, if her scratched cheeks permitted it.* This is the first specific reference to any injury done apart from the mussing of Corinna's hair.

41 At nunc sustinuī: *But did I actually have the nerve?* 42 ferreus notāre: the combination of ferreus and notāre suggests to Ovid branding, which was used only on slaves. 43 albō: note the distinction, albus, *white, pale;* candidus, *white, fair.* 44 caeduntur . . . iugīs: *as the rocks quarried from the mountain ridges of Paros,* which was famous for the whiteness of its marble. In the next six lines Ovid offers four more similes suggested by the effect of his action, but all are soft and gentle in their quality. 48 summave . . . Notō: *or when the crest of a wave is ruffled by the warm South Wind.* 49 flūxēre = flūxērunt. ōra: pl. for sing., as often w. parts of the body. 50 abiectā: *fallen.*

Lady's coiffure, with an elaborate arrangement of curls rising in the form of a halo. Period of the Flavian Emperors (A.D. 70-96). National Museum, Naples.

Anderson, Fototeca Unione

> et valuī poenam fortis in ipse meam.
> Quid mihi vōbīscum, caedis scelerumque ministrae?
>   Dēbita, sacrilegae, vincla subīte, manūs.
> An, sī pulsāssem minimum dē plēbe Quirītem,
>   plēcterer, in dominam iūs mihi maius erit?   30

I had no justification when I lifted my hand against my sweetheart.

> Pessima Tȳdīdēs scelerum monumenta relīquit:
>   ille deam prīmus perculit; alter ego.
> Et minus ille nocēns. Mihi quam profitēbar amāre
>   laesa est: Tȳdīdēs saevus in hoste fuit.

Now let me celebrate a proud triumph over a helpless girl.

> Ī nunc, magnificōs victor mōlīre triumphōs,   35
>   cinge comam laurō vōtaque redde Iovī,
> quaeque tuōs currūs comitantum turba sequētur,
>   clāmet, "Iō, fortī victa puella virō est!"
> Ante eat effūsō trīstis captīva capillō,
>   sī sinerent laesae, candida tōta, genae.   40

She stood pale as marble and wept.

> At nunc sustinuī raptīs ā fronte capillīs
>   ferreus ingenuās ungue notāre genās?
> Astitit illa āmēns albō et sine sanguine vultū,
>   caeduntur Pariīs quālia saxa iugīs.
> Exanimēs artūs et membra trementia vīdī,   45

5

pōpuleus, of the poplar tree
ventilō (1), wave, blow through
° aura, air, breeze
lēnis, -e, soft, gentle
Zephyrus, West Wind, zephyr
gracilis, -e, slender, thin
vibrō (1), shake, agitate
harundō, -dinis, f. reed
tepidus, warm
stringō, -ere, strīnxī, strictus, touch, graze
° unda, wave
suspēnsus, hung up, poised, repressed
° fluō, -ere, flūxī, flūxum, flow
quāliter, in what way, just as
nix, nivis, f. snow
mānō (1), flow, drip

° ter, three times
° supplex, -licis, suppliant
formīdō (1), fear, dread
° dubitō (1), doubt, hesitate
° minuō, -ere, -uī, -ūtus, lessen
vindicta, revenge, punishment

° prōtinus, at once
quamlibet, however, as much as you like
° īnfirmus, weak
° adiuvō, -āre, -iūvī, -iūtus, help
nēve, and not
° supersum, -esse, -fuī, be left, remain
recompositus, rearranged
° statiō, -ōnis, f. standing, position

51 Tunc prīmum: when he noticed the effect on Corinna. **52 sanguis erat lacrimae:** *my blood was the tears;* a highly rhetorical exaggeration. **55 tū nē dubitā:** *for your part, do not hesitate;* from this point on the poet addresses Corinna. **57 nec parce:** *and do not spare;* parcō takes the dat. **58 adiuvat īra:** *anger aids.* **59 Nēve signa supersint:** *And so that the traces may not be left.* **60 pōne . . . comās:** only now, at the end of the poem, does Ovid make clear the true nature of his crime; *comb your hair again and rearrange it.*

medicō (1), heal, treat, drug
° capillus, (a single) hair
tingō, -ere, tīnxī, tīnctus, dip, color, dye
° coma, hair
spatiōsus, ample, great, long
° contingō, -ere, -tigī, -tāctus, touch, reach to
° pateō, -ēre, -uī, spread out, extend
usque, all the way
tenuis, -e, thin, fine
° ōrnō (1), adorn, set off

vēlum, cloth, covering, veil
° colōrātus, colored
° quālis, -e, of what sort, such as

Sēres, -um, m. pl. people of Asia, Chinese
° gracilis, -e, thin, slight, slender
° dēdūcō, -ere, -dūxī, -ductus, draw down, spin out
arānea, spider
fīlum, thread
dēsertus, forsaken, abandoned, left alone
trabs, trabis, f. beam, timber
nectō, -ere, nexuī, nexus, weave
āter, ātra, ātrum, black, dark
° aureus, golden
° quamvīs, although
° misceō, -ēre, miscuī, mixtus, mix, mingle, blend
° color, -ōris, m. color

The poet alternately addresses Corinna and his reader: thus, 1-14 to Corinna; 15-34 to the reader; 35-50 to Corinna; 51-54 to the reader; and 55-56 to Corinna.

1 Dīcēbam: Ovid, like most of us, cannot refrain from saying "I told you so." **2 possīs:** subjv. in rel. clause of characteristic; *for you to be able to dye.* **3 passa forēs = passa essēs:** subjv. in past contrary-to-fact condition; *if you had let it alone.* **illīs:** abl. of comparison; the antecedent is **capillōs. 4 īmum . . . latus:** *to the end of your side as far as it (your side) extends = all the way down your back.*

ut cum pōpuleās ventilat aura comās,
ut lēnī Zephyrō gracilis vibrātur harundō,
summave cum tepidō stringitur unda Notō.
Suspēnsaeque diū lacrimae flūxēre per ōra,
quāliter abiectā dē nive mānat aqua.   *50*

Now I realize my guilt; punish me as I deserve.

Tunc ego mē prīmum coepī sentīre nocentem;
sanguis erat lacrimae, quās dabat illa, meus.
Ter tamen ante pedēs voluī prōcumbere supplex;
ter formīdātās reppulit illa manūs.
At tū nē dubitā (minuet vindicta dolōrem)   *55*
prōtinus in vultūs unguibus īre meōs,
nec nostrīs oculīs nec nostrīs parce capillīs:
quamlibet īnfirmās adiuvat īra manūs.

Rearrange your hair so as to remove all traces of my crime.

Nēve meī sceleris tam trīstia signa supersint,
pōne recompositās in statiōne comās.   *60*

AMORES 1,7

Corinna Bleaches and Loses Her Hair

In spite of my warnings you continued to dye your beautiful hair until
now you have lost it.

Dīcēbam, 'Medicāre tuōs dēsiste capillōs.'
Tingere quam possīs, iam tibi nūlla coma est.
At sī passa forēs, quid erat spatiōsius illīs?
Contigerant īmum, quā patet usque, latus.
Quid, quod erant tenuēs et quōs ōrnāre timērēs,   *5*
vēla colōrātī quālia Sērēs habent,
vel pede quod gracilī dēdūcit arānea fīlum,
cum leve dēsertā sub trabe nectit opus?
Nec tamen āter erat neque erat tamen aureus ille
sed, quamvīs neuter, mixtus uterque color,   *10*

5-14 Ovid continues reproachfully to recall the other attractive qualities of Corinna's hair.
5 **Quid, quod:** *What of the fact that, Moreover.* **timērēs:** subjv. in rel. clause of characteristic; *the kind you would be afraid to dress.* 6 **vēla . . . habent:** *like the clothes the dark Chinese have.* **Sērēs:** Greek nom. pl. (hence the short final **e**). 7 **pede:** belongs inside the rel. clause; **fīlum,** outside. 9 **ille:** modifies **color.** 11 **quālem:** sc. **tālis** as correlative; *such a color*

7

clīvōsus, hilly
madidus, moist, wet
vallēs, -is, f. valley
Īda, mountain near Troy
arduus, high, tall
° dēripiō, -ere, -ripuī, -reptus, tear off,
    snatch away
cortex, -ticis, m. bark
cedrus, -ī, f. cedar tree
° addō, -ere, -didī, -ditus, add, put also
° docilis, -e, easily trained, manageable
flexus, -ūs, m. bending, shaping
° aptus, suitable, right, adapted
° acus, -ūs, f. needle, hairpin, curling iron
° abrumpō, -ere, -rūpī, -ruptus, break off,
    tear away
° vāllum, wall, rampart, palisade
pecten, -tinis, m. comb

16-20

ōrnātrīx, -trīcis, f. hair dresser
° tūtus, safe, uninjured
bracchium, arm
saucius, wounded, injured
dīgestus, arranged
māne, in the morning
purpureus, purple
° iaceō, -ēre, -uī, lie
sēmisupīnus, reclining halfway
torus, couch

21-25

neglēctus, neglected, not yet groomed

decēns, attractive
Thrācius, Thracian
Bacchē, -ae, f. Bacchante, woman votary
    of Bacchus
temere, rashly, by chance
viridis, -e, green
grāmen, -minis, n. grass
lassus, weary
lānūgō, -ginis, f. down, fleece
īnstar, n. indeclin., likeness
heu, exclam. of sorrow, alas!
vexō (1), trouble, ill treat, frizzle
° praebeō, -ēre, -uī, -itus, offer, submit
° ferrum, iron, curling iron
° patienter, patiently

26-30

tortus, twisted, tortured
nexilis, -e, connected, bound, winding
° orbis, -is, m. circle, ring
sinus, -ūs, m. curl, ringlet
° scelus, -leris, n. crime
° ūrō, -ere, ussī, ustus, burn
° crīnis, -is, m. hair
° sponte, unaided, of one's self
° deceō, -ēre, -uī, be graceful, be becoming
° ferreus, made of iron, unfeeling, cruel
° hinc, hence, from here
° removeō, -ēre, -mōvī, -mōtus, remove, keep
    away
ērudiō, -īre, -iī, -ītus, train, teach
° admōtus, applied

---

as the cedar tree has. Her hair had apparently been reddish-brown, a favorite color with Roman ladies, but Corinna wanted it to be blond. 13 Adde quod: Add the fact that, Moreover. 14 erant: sc. capillī as subject.

15 vāllum: a metaphor for a comb, with its palisade of teeth. 16 tūtō: this is explained in the next couplet; if the hairdresser hurt a Roman lady by pulling her hair the lady might punish her by jabbing her arm with a pin. Corinna's hair was so free of tangles that her hairdresser never hurt her. 18 bracchia . . . acū: made arms wounded with a snatched-up pin = snatched up a pin and wounded her arms. 19 nōndum . . . capillīs: in the morning when her hair had not yet been arranged. 21 neglēcta: i.e., as to her hair. Bacchē: a Bacchante, frenzied follower of Bacchus. 22 temere: carelessly, just as she was.

23 tamen et: yet also. 24 mala quanta: what punishment. vexātae: assaulted. tulēre = tulērunt. 25 Quam: modifies patienter. praebuerant: the pluperfect emphasizes the fact that the action is finished; How patiently, in days past, it submitted. ferrō et ignī: Ovid uses the phrase, appropriately enough, for the heated curling-iron, but it is a standard cliché, like our "fire and sword," for devastation. 26 ut . . . sinus: freely, so that there would be a cluster of ringlets. 27 Scelus, scelus: the repetition indicates the fervor of the protest. 28 Sponte decent: It is pretty just as it is. capitī parce tuō: a Roman idiom for spare your own life; Ovid applies it with its literal meaning, be merciful to your head. ferrea: word play again; woman of iron has both its usual metaphorical meaning, hard-hearted woman, and the more literal woman with the (curling) iron. A sentence which in another context would mean Don't kill yourself with a sword here means Don't use a curling-iron on your head. 29 hinc: as though Ovid stands near to protect the long-suffering hair. est: the singular implies there is not one (hair). dēbeat: subjv. in rel. clause of characteristic; that deserves to be burnt. 30 ērudit . . . acūs: i.e., any one hair can teach the curling-irons how to curl, since her hair is naturally curly.

> quālem clīvōsae madidīs in vallibus Īdae
> ardua dērepto cortice cedrus habet.

It never caused the hairdresser any trouble; even in its natural state it was attractive.

> Adde quod et docilēs et centum flexibus aptī
> et tibi nūllīus causa dolōris erant.
> Nōn acus abrūpit, nōn vāllum pectinis illōs;   *15*
> ōrnātrīx tūtō corpore semper erat;
> ante meōs saepe est oculōs ōrnāta nec umquam
> bracchia dērepta saucia fēcit acū.
> Saepe etiam nōndum dīgestīs māne capillīs
> purpureō iacuit sēmisupīna torō;   *20*
> tum quoque erat neglēcta decēns, ut Thrācia Bacchē,
> cum témere in viridī grāmine lassa iacet.

Despite my constant protests it was put to the torture, hair which Apollo, Bacchus and Venus would be proud to own.

> Cum gracilēs essent tamen et lānūginis īnstar,
> heu! mala vexātae quanta tulēre comae!
> Quam sē praebuerant ferrō patienter et ignī,   *25*
> ut fieret tortō nexilis orbe sinus!
> Clāmābam, 'Scelus est istōs, scelus, ūrere crīnēs.
> Sponte decent: capitī, ferrea, parce tuō.
> Vim procul hinc removē: nōn est quī dēbeat ūrī;
> ērudit admōtās ipse capillus acūs.'   *30*

Apollo Belvedere. Marble copy of a lost bronze original. Vatican Museum, Rome.

Satyr and Bacchante. Pompeian wall painting. House of the Dioscuri. National Museum, Naples.

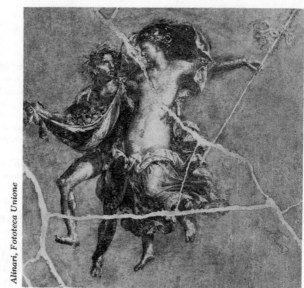

Alinari, Fototeca Unione

Alinari, Fototeca Unione

9

31-35

° fōrmōsus, beautiful
° pereō, -īre, -iī, -itum, perish, be lost
Apollō, -linis, m. Apollo
īnsum, inesse, īnfuī, w. dat., be in, be on
° cōnferō, -ferre, contulī, collātus, bring together, compare
° quondam, once, formerly
Diōnē, -ēs, f. Dione, another name for Venus
° pingō, -ere, pīnxī, pictus, paint, depict
ūmēns, -entis, wet, moist
° dispōnō, -ere, -posuī, -positus, arrange
queror, -ī, questus sum, complain, lament

36-40

speculum, mirror
maestus, sad, sorrowful
ineptus, silly, foolish
cōnsuētus, usual, ordinary
ocellus, eye
° immemor, -oris, w. gen., unmindful, forgetful
cantō (1), sing, chant, enchant, charm
° laedō, -ere, laesī, laesus, harm, injure
paelex, -icis f. concubine, rival
herba, grass, herb
anus, -ūs, f. old woman
Haemonius, Thessalian
perfidus, treacherous
lavō, -āre, lāvī, lavātus (lautus, lōtus), wash, bathe

41-45

° morbus, disease
° ōmen, ōminis, n. omen, portent

° minuō, -ere, -uī, -ūtus, lessen, reduce
° dēnsus, thick, dense
invidus, envious, jealous
° culpa, blame, fault
dispendium, loss
venēnum, poison

46-50

triumphātus, triumphed over, conquered
° mūnus, -neris, n. service, gift
rubeō, -ēre, be red, blush with shame
° emō, -ere, ēmī, ēmptus, buy, purchase
merx, mercis, f. merchandise, goods
probō (1), approve, commend
nescioquis, -quae, -quod (-quid), I know not who, someone, something, some
Sygambra, woman of the Sygambri, a German tribe
° meminī, -isse, remember

51-56

° ōs, ōris, n. mouth, face
° prōtegō, -ere, -tēxī, -tēctus, cover, shield, protect
ingenuus, frank, candid, tender
rubor, -ōris, m. blush, modesty, shame
° gena, cheek
gremium, bosom, lap
ei, exclam. of sorrow, ah! alas!
° dignus, w. abl., worthy of, deserving
colligō, -ere, -lēgī, -lēctus, gather, compose
° vultus, -ūs, m. face, expression
reparābilis, -e, able to be remedied
damnum, loss
postmodo, shortly, presently
nātīvus, native, natural

31 Fōrmōsae periēre (= periērunt) **comae:** *The lovely hair has been lost;* the hair loss brings us back to line 2; everything else up to this point has been a description of the natural beauty of the hair. But not satisfied that he has made his meaning clear, Ovid now provides three rather extravagant comparisons, reaching a climax in the comparison to Aphrodite. **vellet:** subjv. in rel. clause of characteristic; *the kind Apollo would want.* **33 Illīs:** the antecedent is **comae. contulerim:** potential subjv.; *I would have compared.* **quās:** sc. **comās** as antecedent. **34 pingitur:** Ovid refers to a much-copied painting of Aphrodite by Apelles (IVth century B.C.) in which the goddess was represented as rising from the sea and wringing sea water from her hair. **35 Quid . . . capillōs:** *Why do you complain that your hair has been lost because it was badly treated?* **36 pōnis** = **dēpōnis. inepta:** voc.; *foolish girl.* **37 Nōn bene cōnsuētīs ocellīs:** *With eyes not well-accustomed to the sight.* **38 tuī:** objective gen. w. **immemor;** to look good to herself she must forget what she used to look like.

40 Haemoniā: Thessaly was traditionally the habitat of witches, sorcerers, and brewers of poisons. **41 procul . . . abestō:** a formula habitually used by the Romans if anything ill-omened was mentioned, like death or, as in this case, disease; **abestō** is fut. imper. 3rd person sing. **42 minuit lingua:** i.e., by casting a spell; to the modern reader there is here a strange mixture of possible causes: the drugs (**Haemonia aqua,** applied by a treacherous slave, and **herbae,** added to the food by a jealous rival) and disease would be natural, but

Fōrmōsae periēre comae, quās vellet Apollō,
    quās vellet capitī Bacchus inesse suō.
Illīs contulerim, quās quondam nūda Diōnē
    pingitur ūmentī sustinuisse manū.

Why lament when you have only yourself to blame?

Quid male dispositōs quereris periisse capillōs?   *35*
    Quid speculum maestā pōnis, inepta, manū?
Nōn bene cōnsuētīs ā tē spectāris ocellīs;
    ut placeās, dēbēs immemor esse tuī.
Nōn tē cantātae laesērunt paelicis herbae,
    nōn anus Haemoniā perfida lāvit aquā,   *40*
nec tibi vīs morbī nocuit (procul ōmen abestō!),
    nec minuit dēnsās invida lingua comās.
Facta manū culpāque tuā dispendia sentīs;
    ipsa dabās capitī mixta venēna tuō.

Now to your mortification you must buy blond German hair and be admired for it.

Nunc tibi captīvōs mittet Germānia crīnēs;   *45*
    culta triumphātae mūnere gentis eris.
Ō quam saepe comās aliquō mīrante rubēbis
    et dīcēs, 'Ēmptā nunc ego merce probor.
Nescioquam prō mē laudat nunc iste Sygambram.
    Fāma tamen meminī cum fuit ista mea.'   *50*

Take courage; your hair will grow out again.

Mē miserum! Lacrimās male continet ōraque dextrā
    prōtegit ingenuās picta rubōre genās.
Sustinet antīquōs gremiō spectatque capillōs,
    ei mihi! nōn illō mūnera digna locō.
Collige cum vultū mentem. Reparābile damnum est.   *55*
    Postmodo nātīvā cōnspiciēre comā.

                                AMORES 1.14

---

the enchanting of the herbs and the casting of a spell by someone with the evil eye are to us supernatural. **44 dabās:** imperfect for a repeated action; *used to give.* **mixta venēna:** *the poisonous mixtures,* i.e., the dye, or bleach, which Corinna used.

45 Germānia: chosen because the hair would be blond, a fashionable color. **47 quam saepe:** *how often.* **comās:** direct object of **mīrante. aliquō mīrante:** abl. abs. **49 Nescioquam Sygambram:** *I know not what Sygambrian = Some unknown barbarian woman.* **prō:** *instead of.* **50 Fāma:** belongs inside of the **cum**-clause.

51 Mē miserum. acc. of exclamation. **male** = vix or nōn. **52 genās:** acc. of respect w. **picta;** lit. *having been colored as to her tender cheeks.* **53 antīquōs:** *former.* **54 ei mihi** = mē miserum. **locō:** abl. of specification w. digna; *worthy of.* **55 Collige . . . mentem:** lit. *Compose mind along with expression,* i.e., *Be easy in your mind and look cheerful.* **56 cōnspiciēre** = cōnspiciēris.

. . . qui sustinet hamos,
novit quae multo pisce natentur aquae.

Bronze statuette from a Pompeian garden. National Museum, Naples.

ARS AMATORIA

° **ars, artis,** *f.* art, science, skill
° **nōscō, -ere, nōvī, nōtus,** get to know; **nōvī,** I know
° **legō, -ere, lēgī, lēctus,** read
  carmen, -minis, *n.* poem
° **doceō, -ēre, -uī, doctus,** teach, inform
  citus, swift, quick, lively
° **vēlum,** sail, veil, curtain, screen
° **ratis, -is,** *f.* raft, boat, ship
° **levis, -e,** light
° **currus, -ūs,** *m.* chariot
  Automedōn, -ontis, *m.* Automedon, charioteer of Achilles
  lentus, pliant
° **aptus,** suitable, fitted, favorable
  habēnae, -ārum, *f. pl.* reins

6-10

  Tīphys, -yos, *m.* Tiphys, helmsman of the Argo
  Haemonius, Haemonian, Thessalian
  puppis, -is, *f.* stern of a ship; *by metonymy,* ship
° **magister, -trī,** *m.* master, pilot
  Venus, -neris, *f.* Venus, goddess of love
  artifex, -ficis, *m.* artist, craftsman
° **tener, -era, -erum,** tender, delicate
° **praeficiō, -ere, -fēcī, -fectus,** put in charge of
° **ūsus, -ūs,** *m.* training, experience
° **vātēs, -is,** *m.* poet, bard
° **pāreō, -ēre, -uī, -itum,** *w. dat.,* obey
  perītus, skillful, experienced
  canō, -ere, cecinī, cantus, sing
° **coeptum,** beginning, undertaking

11-15

° **prīncipium,** beginning, first place

  prīmum, for the first time
  placitus, pleasing
  exōrō (1), prevail upon, win over
  dūrō (1), last, endure
° **modus,** measure, limit
° **signō** (1), mark, designate
  ārea, space, area

16-20

  admissus, racing, hurrying
  mēta, turning point, goal
° **premō, -ere, pressī, pressus,** press, keep close to
  rota, wheel
  dum, *w. indic.* while, as long as
  lōra, -ōrum, *n. pl.* thongs, reins
° **passim,** everywhere
° **solvō, -ere, solvī, solūtus,** free, loosen
° **ēligō, -ere, ēlēgī, ēlēctus,** pick out
  placeō, -ēre, -uī, -itum, *w. dat.,* please
° **tenuis, -e,** thin, slight
  dēlābor, -ī, -lāpsus sum, glide down
° **aura,** air

21-25

  vēnātor, -ōris, *m.* hunter
  cervus, stag, deer
  rēte, rētis, *n.* net
  tendō, -ere, tetendī, tentus, stretch, spread
  frendēns, -entis, gnashing
° **vallēs, -is,** *f.* valley
  aper, aprī, *m.* boar
  auceps, -cupis, *m.* fowler, bird hunter
  frutex, -ticis, *m.* bush, shrub
  hāmus, hook
° **piscis, -is,** *m.* fish
° **natō** (1), swim
° **māteria,** material

---

1 Sī quis: *If anyone.* **2 legat:** jussive subjv., *let him read.* **lēctō carmine:** abl. abs., *by having read the poem.* **3 Arte:** note the emphatic position and the repetition. Ovid is stressing the know-how. **4 regendus:** sc. **est;** pass. periphrastic, *must be guided.*

5-6 Automedōn, Tīphys: the leading experts in their fields. **6 Haemoniā puppe:** the Argo. **8 dīcar:** *I shall be called.* **9 Ūsus . . . hoc:** *Experience inspires this work.* **10 Coeptīs:** dat. w. **ades** (imper.); *Be present for* (= *Favor*) *my undertaking.* **māter Amōris:** Venus.

11 quod: sc. **id** as antecedent; **quod** is used instead of **quam** to maintain the scientific tone of this didactic poem. **velīs:** subjv. in rel. clause of characteristic; *the kind of thing you would wish to love* (= *an object of love*). **labōrā:** *make an effort.* **12 nova mīles in arma:** *as soldier for a new war;* Ovid is fond of this metaphor. **13 exōrāre:** in apposition with **labor;** in the next line the construction is changed by the use of a purpose (**ut**) clause. **14 longō tempore:** ablative of measure; *lasting by a long time = long-lasting.* **15 modus:** sc. **erit;** in outlining his syllabus Ovid now uses the metaphor of the race-track. **16 haec erit mēta premenda:** *this is the turn that we must keep close to.* **admissā rotā:** *with the wheel let go = at full speed.*

17 Dum licet . . . solūtīs: i.e., while you are young and fancy-free. **18 cui dīcās:** rel. clause of characteristic; (*someone*) *to whom you may say.* **20 oculīs:** dat. of agent w. **quaerenda est** and also dat. w. **aptus;** *congenial to your eyes.*

Ars Amatoria

Ovid, well qualified by training and experience, offers a course on the art and science of love: how and where to find girls; how to win their fancy; how to make love lasting.

Sī quis in hōc artem populō nōn nōvit amandī,
   hoc legat et lēctō carmine doctus amet.
Arte citae vēlōque ratēs rēmōque reguntur,
   arte levēs currūs: arte regendus Amor.
Curribus Automedōn lentīsque erat aptus habēnīs,   5
   Tīphys in Haemoniā puppe magister erat:
mē Venus artificem tenerō praefēcit Amōrī;
   Tīphys et Automedōn dīcar Amōris ego.
Ūsus opus movet hoc; vātī pārēte perītō;
   vēra canam. Coeptīs, māter Amōris, ades.   10
Prīncipiō, quod amāre velīs, reperīre labōrā,
   quī nova nunc prīmum mīles in arma venīs.
Proximus huic labor est placitam exōrāre puellam;
   tertius, ut longō tempore dūret amor.
Hic modus; haec nostrō signābitur ārea currū;   15
   haec erit admissā mēta premenda rotā.

Like hunter or fisherman, you must know where to go.

Dum licet et lōrīs passim potes īre solūtīs,
   ēlige cui dīcās "Tū mihi sōla placēs."
Haec tibi nōn tenuēs veniet dēlāpsa per aurās;
   quaerenda est oculīs apta puella tuīs.   20
Scit bene vēnātor, cervīs ubi rētia tendat,
   scit bene, quā frendēns valle morētur aper;
aucupibus nōtī fruticēs; quī sustinet hāmōs,
   nōvit quae multō pisce natentur aquae.
Tū quoque, māteriam longō quī quaeris amōrī,   25

21 ubi tendat: *where he is to stretch;* deliberative subjv. in an indir. question. **22 quā:** modifies valle; *in what valley.* **23 fruticēs:** sc. **sunt. quī sustinet hāmōs:** = **piscātor,** i.e., *a fisherman.* **24 multō pisce:** collective sing. for **multīs piscibus;** so too (1. 26) **frequēns puella** = **frequentēs puellae. 25 amōrī:** dat. of purpose w. **māteriam. 26 ante . . . locō:**

Cupids in a chariot race. The charioteer on the right is a victor. Details from fresco of a large dining room. House of the Vettii, Pompeii.

26-30

* frequēns, -entis, frequent, in throngs
* discō, -ere, didicī, learn
  ventō dare vēla, set sail, put out to sea
  terō, -ere, trīvī, trītus, wear away, tread
* niger, -gra, -grum, black, dusky
  Indus, Indian
  Phrygius, Phrygian, Trojan
  Grāius, Greek

31-35

* tot, so many; tot . . . quot, as many . . . as
* fōrmōsus, beautiful, shapely
* quisquis, quidquid, whoever, whatever
* orbis, -is, m. circle, world
  Gargara, -ōrum, n. pl. Gargara, district near Troy
  seges, -getis, f. field of grain
  Mēthymna, town on the island of Lesbos
  racēmus, bunch of grapes
* aequor, -oris, n. sea
* frōns, -ondis, f. foliage, branch
* tegō, -ere, tēxī, tēctus, hide, conceal
* avis, -is, f. bird

36-40

  Aenēās, -ae, m. Aeneas, son of Anchises and Venus, and legendary ancestor of Romans
  cōnsistō, -ere, -stitī, -stitum, stop, settle
* praecipuē, chiefly
  curvus, curved
  vēnor (dep. 1), hunt
* theātrum, theater
* vōtum, vow, wish
* fertilis, -e, fertile, productive

* illīc, there
* lūdō, -ere, lūsī, lūsus, play with, beguile
  semel, once, at some time
* tangō, -ere, tetigī, tāctus, touch

41-45

  formīca, ant
* agmen, -minis, n. line, column of march
  grānifer, -era, -erum, carrying grain
* solitus, customary, usual
* vehō, -ere, vexī, vectus, carry
* ōs, ōris, n. mouth, face
  apis, -is, f. bee
  saltus, -ūs, m. glade
  olēns, -entis, fragrant
* nancīscor, -ī, nactus sum, come upon, find
  pāscuum, pasture
* flōs, flōris, m. flower
  thymum, thyme
* volō (1), fly
* ruō, -ere, ruī, rutum, rush, hurry
  celeber, -bris, -bre, crowded, popular
  cultus, fashionable, smartly dressed
* lūdī, -ōrum, m. pl. public games, plays

46-50

* iūdicium, judgment, decision
* moror (dep. 1), delay, make difficult
* castus, pure, virtuous, modest
* damnum, loss, harm
  pudor, -ōris, m. modesty, decency
* sollicitus, disturbed, troubled
* iuvō, -āre, iūvī, iūtus, help, delight
  viduus, unmarried, widowed
  Sabīnus, Sabine

in prose order, ante disce quō locō frequēns puella sit. puella: collective sing., as one might say to a big-game hunter, "where the elephant is to be found."

27 quaerentem: used as a noun; the seeker. 28 tibi: dat. of agent w. terenda via est; lit. a road is to be trodden by you. 29 Andromedān: Greek acc. ending. portārit: shortened form of portāverit; concessive use of the jussive subjv., let Perseus have carried = though Perseus carried (so too rapta sit). nigrīs ab Indīs: from the dusky Indians is intended as from Ethiopia. 30 Phrygiō virō: Paris; dat. of agent w. rapta sit. Grāia puella: Helen.

31 tot, tam fōrmōsās: leading into the clause of result ut dīcās, that you can say. 32 Haec: She (Rome). 33-35 quot . . . quot: correlatives w. tot puellās; your Rome has as many girls as . . . 33 habet: w. both Gargara and Methymna. 34 teguntur: w. both piscēs and avēs. 35 habet: w. both caelum and Rōma. 36 suī: w. Aenēae, of her Aeneas; Aeneas, the founder of the Roman people, was the son of Venus; his mother would favor Rome.

37 vēnāre: imper. mood. theātrīs: abl. of place where without prep. 38 vōtō tuō: dat. w. fertiliōra; for your wish. 39-40 amēs, possīs, tangās, velīs: subjvs. in rel. clauses of characteristic; something to love, etc. 39 lūdere: to flirt with.

41-43 Ut, ut: introducing the comparison of the industrious ant and the busy bee to the smartly dressed woman. 43 suōs: their own = congenial to them. 45 ruit: chosen to suggest eagerness.

46 Cōpia . . . est: i.e., When there are so many it is often difficult to choose. 47 Spectātum: supine, to express purpose; They come to view.

ante frequēns quō sit disce puella locō.

You need not range far afield as Perseus and Paris did, for Rome will supply pretty girls to your heart's content.

Nōn ego quaerentem ventō dare vēla iubēbō,
    nec tibi ut inveniās longa terenda via est.
Andromedān Perseus nigrīs portārit ab Indīs,
    raptaque sit Phrygiō Grāia puella virō;   *30*
tot tibi tamque dabit fōrmōsās Rōma puellās
    "Haec habet," ut dīcās, "quidquid in orbe fuit."
Gargara quot segetēs, quot habet Mēthymna racēmōs,
    aequore quot piscēs, fronde teguntur avēs,
quot caelum stellās, tot habet tua Rōma puellās: *35*
    māter in Aenēae cōnstitit urbe suī.

The theater, where attractive women go to see and be seen, offers you interesting opportunities.

Sed tū praecipuē curvīs vēnāre theātrīs;
    haec loca sunt vōtō fertiliōra tuō.
Illīc inveniēs quod amēs, quod lūdere possīs,
    quodque semel tangās, quodque tenēre velīs.   *40*
Ut redit itque frequēns longum formīca per agmen,
    grāniferō solitum cum vehit ōre cibum,
aut ut apēs saltūsque suōs et olentia nactae
    pāscua per flōrēs et thyma summa volant,
sīc ruit ad celebrēs cultissima fēmina lūdōs.   *45*
    Cōpia iūdicium saepe morāta meum est.
Spectātum veniunt, veniunt spectentur ut ipsae;
    ille locus castī damna pudōris habet.

Romulus himself set the precedent, for at his theatricals he allowed his citizens to take the law into their own hands and the Sabine girls into their arms.

Prīmus sollicitōs fēcistī, Rōmule, lūdōs,
    cum iūvit viduōs rapta Sabīna virōs.   *50*

An Etruscan flute player. Detail from the fresco of the Tomb of the Leopards. Fifth century, B.C. Tarquinia, Italy.

Alinari, Fototeca Unione

17

* tunc, then
* marmoreus, of marble
* pendeō, -ēre, pependī, hang down
* liquidus, clear, bright
  pulpita, -ōrum, *n. pl.* platform, stage
  tingō, -ere, tīnxī, tīnctus, stain, dye
  crocus, saffron
  nemorōsus, well wooded, woody
* Palātium, Palatine Hill
* simpliciter, simply
* scēna, stage, scene
* gradus, -ūs, *m.* step
* sedeō, -ēre, sēdī, sessum, sit
  caespes, -pitis, *m.* sod

56-60

  quīlibet, quae-, quod-, any at all
  hirsūtus, shaggy, rough, bristly
* coma, hair
* respiciō, -ere, -spexī, -spectus, look back at
* notō (1), mark, note
* quisque, quae-, quod- (quid-), each
* tacitus, silent
* pectus, -toris, *n.* breast, heart
  rudis, -e, rough, untrained, awkward
* praebeō, -ēre, -uī, -itus, provide
* modus, measure, beat, manner, limit
  tībīcen, -cinis, *m.* flute player
* Tuscus, Tuscan, Etruscan
  lūdius, player, actor
  aequō (1), equal, level, smooth
* ter, three times
* pulsō (1), strike, beat
* humus, -ī, *f.* ground, earth

61-65

* plausus, -ūs, *m.* applause
* careō, -ēre, -uī, -itum, *w. abl.,* be without, lack

* prōtinus, at once
  exsiliō, -īre, -siluī, leap out
* fateor, -ērī, fassus sum, confess, reveal
* iniciō, -ere, -iēcī, -iectus, put . . . on
* fugiō, -ere, fūgī, fugitus, flee (from)
  aquila, eagle
  timidus, fearful, timid
* turba, crowd, flock
* columba, dove

66-70

  agna, ewe lamb
  novellus; *dimin. of* novus, new, young
* lupus, wolf
  color, -ōris, *m.* color
* faciēs, -ēī, *f.* face, appearance
  laniō (1), mar, tear
* crīnis, -is, *m.* hair

71-75

  maestus, sad, dejected
  sileō, -ēre, -uī, be silent
* frūstrā, in vain
  queror, -ī, questus sum, complain
  stupeō, -ēre, -uī, be bewildered
  geniālis, -e, nuptial, for marriage
  decet, -ēre, -uit, be becoming to
  repugnō (1), fight back, resist
  nimium, too much
* negō (1), deny, refuse

76-80

* tollō, -ere, sustulī, sublātus, lift up, remove
  sinus, -ūs, *m.* curve, bosom, embrace
* lacrima, tear
* corrumpō, -ere, -rūpī, -ruptus, ruin, spoil
  ocellus; *dimin. of* oculus, pretty eye
* commodum, advantage

---

49 Rōmule: with this apostrophe of Romulus the poet begins to set the scene so that the reader will be an immediate witness; hence the use of the present tense after l. 57. **50 viduōs:** *when they lacked wives.* **Sabīna:** where prose would use the plural. **51-55 Tunc . . . factīs:** Ovid is contrasting the simple setting of Romulus' day with the elaborate theater of the Augustan era. **51 vēla:** awnings to shade spectators from the hot sun. **52 crocō:** the expensive bright-yellow essence of saffron, which was used to give the stage a pleasant odor. **53 Palātia:** n. pl.; the Palatine Hill, forested in those days, was the site of the infant city which Romulus founded. His games were held in the valley of Consus (later the site of the Circus Maximus), just southwest of the Palatine. **54 positae:** sc. **sunt. 56 quālibet fronde:** i.e., not the floral garlands of Ovid's day.

57 sibi quisque: *every man for himself.* **quisque:** loosely in apposition with the subject contained in **notant; quisque** is then retained as the subject of **velit. 58 velit:** subjv. in rel. clause of characteristic; *whom he would like.* **multa:** internal acc. **multa movent:** *they make many plans.* **59 tībīcine Tuscō:** the Romans were too primitive to have their own. **60 aequātam:** i.e., leveled off for the occasion. **ter:** i.e., in the tripudium, a very ancient Roman religious dance. **61 plausūs . . . carēbant:** in Ovid's day artificial applause was provided by hired claques. **62 petīta:** *eagerly sought.*

64 iniciuntque: -que should go in prose on the first word of the clause. **65-66 Ut fugiunt, utque fugit:** Ovid is usually generous with similes, preferring to give more than one.

18

Tunc neque marmoreō pendēbant vēla theātrō,
　nec fuerant' liquidō pulpita tīncta crocō.
Illīc quās tulerant nemorōsa Palātia frondēs
　simpliciter positae; scēna sine arte fuit.
In gradibus sēdit populus dē caespite factīs,　　　　　　55
　quālibet hirsūtās fronde tegente comās.
Respiciunt oculīsque notant sibi quisque puellam
　quam velit, et tacitō pectore multa movent;
dumque rudem praebente modum tībīcine Tuscō
　lūdius aequātam ter pede pulsat humum,　　　　　　60
in mediō plausū (plausūs tunc arte carēbant)
　rēx populō praedae signa petīta dedit.
Prōtinus exsiliunt animum clāmōre fatentēs,
　virginibus cupidās iniciuntque manūs.
Ut fugiunt aquilās, timidissima turba, columbae　　　　　65
　utque fugit vīsōs agna novella lupōs,
sīc illae timuēre virōs sine lēge ruentēs;
　cōnstitit in nūllā quī fuit ante color.
Nam timor ūnus erat, faciēs nōn ūna timōris:
　pars laniat crīnēs, pars sine mente sedet;　　　　　　70
altera maesta silet, frūstrā vocat altera mātrem;
　haec queritur, stupet haec; haec manet, illa fugit.
Dūcuntur raptae, geniālis praeda, puellae,
　et potuit multās ipse decēre timor.
Sī qua repugnārat nimium nimiumque negārat,　　　　　75
　sublātam cupidō vir tulit ipse sinū,
atque ita, "Quid tenerōs lacrimīs corrumpis ocellōs?
　Quod mātrī pater est, hoc tibi," dīxit, "erō."
Rōmule, mīlitibus scīstī dare commoda sōlus;
　haec mihi sī dederis commoda, mīles erō.　　　　　　80

67 timuēre = **timuērunt. sine lēge:** *helter-skelter.* **68 cōnstitit . . . color:** i.e., the pale ones blushed and the rosy-cheeked ones turned pale.

69 nōn ūna = **multa** (litotes), but used to contrast with **ūnus. 73 geniālis praeda:** *as marriage booty;* in apposition w. **puellae. 75 Sī qua:** *If any* = *Whoever.* **repugnārat, negārat:** shortened forms of **repugnāverat, negāverat. 77 Quid** = **Cūr.**

79 Rōmule: Ovid ends the episode as he began, by addressing Romulus, but this time with even more enthusiasm. **scīstī:** shortened form of **scīvistī;** *you knew how to.* **commoda:** in

Ergo erit illa dies . . . Reconstruction of a scene in a triumphal parade. Museum of Roman Civilization, Rome.

Felbermeyer, Fototeca Unione

° scīlicet, to be sure, obviously
sollemnis, -e, customary, festive, solemn
° mōs, mōris, m. habit, custom
īnsidiōsus, treacherous, full of traps
° nōbilis, -e, noble, thoroughbred
° certāmen, -minis, n. contest, race
° capāx, -ācis, capacious
opus est, w. abl., there is need of
° digitus, finger
arcānus, secret, private

nūtus, -ūs, m. nod
nota, sign, signal
° prohibeō, -ēre, -uī, -itus, hinder, prevent
° iungō, -ere, iūnxī, iūnctus, join, bring
close
° latus, -teris, n. side
usque, as far as
° cōgō, -ere, coēgī, coāctus, force
līnea, line

socius, friendly, sociable
° sermō, -ōnis, m. conversation
orīgō, -ginis, f. source, beginning
° pūblicus, common, general, commonplace
sonus, sound, noise
studiōsus, eager, enthusiastic
requīrō, -ere, -quīsīvī, -quīsītus, ask carefully

° faveō, -ēre, fāvī, fautum, w. dat., support,
favor
pompa, procession, parade
caelestia, -ium, n. pl. statues of the gods
eburnus, of ivory

plaudō, -ere, plausī, plausum, applaud
° fīō, fierī, factus sum, happen, occur
gremium, bosom, lap
° pulvis, -veris, m. dust
° forte, by chance
° dēcidō, -ere, -cidī, fall down
excutiō, -ere, -cussī, -cussus, shake off,
brush away
° etsī, even if
° officium, service, duty, courtesy

pallium, cloak
dēmissus, lowered, dropped, let fall
° iaceō, -ēre, -uī, lie, rest
° colligō, -ere, -lēgī, -lēctus, gather up
immundus, dirty, soiled
sēdulus, careful, busy
° efferō, -ferre, extulī, ēlātus, lift up
° pretium, price, reward
contingō, -ere, -tigī, -tāctus, befall, come
as good fortune to
crūs, crūris, n. leg
quīcumque, quae-, quod-, whoever, whatever

the military sense, *bonuses*. **81 Scīlicet:** indicating that Ovid makes this remark tongue in cheek. **82 fōrmōsīs īnsidiōsa:** *full of traps for pretty girls.*

83 nōbilium: *highly bred* when used of animals. **fugiat:** jussive subjv., *And let not the competition escape you = Don't miss . . .* **84 populī:** objective gen. w. **capāx;** *capable of holding a large crowd.* **85 Nīl** = nihil; a stronger word for **nōn. loquāris:** subjv. in rel. clause of characteristic, *for communicating secrets.* Ovid means that you do not need to wave or make signs from a distance. **87 Proximus ā:** *Right next to.* **sedētō:** fut. active imper., *you shall sit = simply sit.* **88 laterī:** sc. **puellae,** *the girl's.* **quā usque:** *as far as = wherever.* **89 Et bene (potes):** *And well you can = And with good reason.* **quod . . . iungī:** *because, whether she likes it or not, the line forces you to sit close together.* **līnea:** *the line (marked on the bench between seats);* spectators were not allowed to take up more than one place, so that they were forced to sit touching each other.

91 quaerātur: cf. for mood **fugiat** (1. 83). **92 pūblica verba:** i.e., words that anyone may hear, words of common courtesy. **93 facitō:** fut. imper. (ut) **requīrās;** *take care to inquire.* **studiōse:** voc. case, *you racing fan;* i.e., if you are an expert on horses, be sure to conceal your knowledge. **94 nec mora:** sc. **sit;** *and let there be no delay = at once.* **95-96** These lines refer to the opening ceremonies, when a procession enters, composed of the giver of the games, images of the gods, priests, officials, and the racing chariots. Each spectator applauds the god whose favor he desires.

98 digitīs: dat. of agent w. pass periphrastic **excutiendus erit;** *your fingers will have to brush it off.* **99 nūllum:** i.e., imaginary dust. **100 sit:** jussive subjv. **103 officiī pretium:** in apposition w. 1. 104; *as a reward for your courtesy.* **105-106 Respice . . . nē premat:** *Watch out lest whoever is sitting behind you* (**post vōs quīcumque sedēbit**) *may bump . . .*

Scīlicet ex illō sollemnia mōre theātra
nunc quoque fōrmōsīs īnsidiōsa manent.

The chariot races in the Circus Maximus, where spectators must sit
crowded together, are also useful.

Nec tē nōbilium fugiat certāmen equōrum;
multa capāx populī commoda Circus habet.
Nīl opus est digitīs per quōs arcāna loquāris,   85
nec tibi per nūtūs accipienda nota est.
Proximus ā dominā, nūllō prohibente, sedētō,
iunge tuum laterī, quā potes usque, latus.
Et bene, quod cōgit, sī nōlit, līnea iungī,
quod tibi tangenda est lēge puella locī.   90

Strike up a casual conversation and back the horse that she is interested
in.

Hīc tibi quaerātur sociī sermōnis orīgō,
et moveant prīmōs pūblica verba sonōs.
Cuius equī veniant facitō, studiōse, requīrās,
nec mora, quisquis erit cui favet illa, favē.

Applaud the statue of Venus when it enters; brush dirt off her lap, even
if there is none, and perform other little courtesies.

At cum pompa frequēns caelestibus ībit eburnīs,   95
tū Venerī dominae plaude favente manū;
utque fit, in gremium pulvis sī forte puellae
dēciderit, digitīs excutiendus erit;
etsī nūllus erit pulvis, tamen excute nūllum;
quaelibet officiō causa sit apta tuō.   100
Pallia sī terrā nimium dēmissa iacēbunt,
collige et immundā sēdulus effer humō;
prōtinus, officiī pretium, patiente puellā,
contingent oculīs crūra videnda tuīs.
Respice praetereā, post vōs quīcumque sedēbit,   105

. . . quattuor in niveis aureus ibis equis. In this partial reconstruction of a triumph twelve lictors go in front of the imperator.

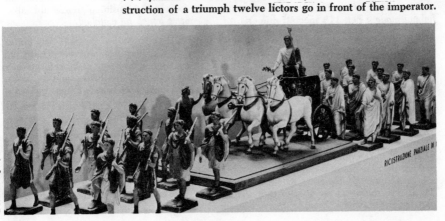

* oppōnō, -ere, -posuī, -positus, put against
* mollis, -e, soft, gentle
* genū, -ūs, n. knee
  pulvīnus, cushion
* compōnō, -ere, -posuī, -positus, arrange
  prōsum, prōdesse, prōfuī, benefit, be helpful to
  tabella, tablet, writing pad
* cavus, hollow
  scamnum, footstool

aditus, -ūs, m. method of approach, introduction
* sparsus, strewn, scattered
* trīstis, -e, sad, unhappy
* harēna, sand, arena
* forum, market place, forum
* poscō, -ere, poposcī, ask for, demand
  libellus, small book, program

pignus, -noris, n. pledge, bet
* uter, utra, utrum, which of two
  saucius, wounded
  ingemō, -ere, -gemuī, groan, sigh (at)
  volātilis, -e, flying, winged
  mūnus, -neris, n. gladiatorial show, contest

niveus, snow white
* aureus, golden

* onerātus, burdened, loaded
* collum, neck
  catēna, chain
* tūtus, safe, protected
  prius, before, earlier
* laetus, happy, joyful
  iuvenis, -is, m. youth, young man
  mixtus, intermingled
  diffundō, -ere, -fūdī, -fūsus, pour out
* aliquis, aliqua, aliquid, someone, something

-ve, *enclitic,* or
* nesciō, -īre, -iī, -ītus, not know
* nōtus, known, familiar
* referō, -ferre, rettulī, relātus, relate, speak of
  Euphrātēs, -is, m. Euphrates, river in Mesopotamia
  praecīnctus, surrounded
  harundō, -dinis, f. reed, cane
  frōns, frontis, f. brow
  dēpendeō, -ēre, hang down
  caerulus, sky-colored, dark
  Tigris, -ridis, m. Tigris, the second great river in Mesopotamia

---

107 Parva . . . animōs: a general maxim. **fuit:** for variety Ovid changes tenses; i.e., past experience shows that it is useful. **109 tenuī tabellā:** Roman gentlemen sometimes carried writing tablets, for sending messages or for literary composition.

111-112 Circusque, sparsaque: -que, -que, *both . . . and . . .* **112 sparsa harēna:** sand was spread over the combat area to absorb the blood; hence, it is called **trīstis. 113 Illā:** emphatic by position. **puer Veneris:** Cupid with his arrows. **114 vulnus habet:** the next four lines explain how the male spectator (**quī spectāvit vulnera**) comes to be wounded. **115 tangit manum:** i.e., shaking hands on a bet. **poscit libellum:** *asks to see her program* (he has thoughtfully forgotten to have one of his own). **116 positō pignore:** abl. abs., *having made a bet.* **118 spectātī mūneris:** *of the contest which he watched.*

119 pulcherrime: voc. case. **rērum:** a defining gen., so that the phrase means *most glorious in your exploits.* Ovid addresses the absent Gaius Caesar, who had been sent out to head the campaign on the eastern frontier of the Empire. Ovid imagines the scene at his return when a triumph would be celebrated for victories over Armenians, Parthians, and Persians. **120 aureus . . . equīs:** a general in triumph wore a toga embroidered in gold and rode in a chariot drawn by four white horses. **121 ante:** adv., *in front.* **colla:** acc. of respect w. **onerātī;** *their necks loaded with chains.* **124 animōs:** *high spirits.*

125 aliqua: a girl among the spectators. **rēgum:** captive kings. **126 loca, montēs, aquae:** paintings of battles and statues of the divinities of places which had been conquered would be carried in the procession. **127 nec . . . rogābit:** *and not only if she will ask anything = and not only the questions she asks.* **128 nesciērīs:** subjv. in rel. clause of characteristic; *such things as you don't know.* **ut bene nōta:** *as though thoroughly familiar.* **129-130 Euphrātēs, Tigris:** i.e., statues of the gods of these rivers. **129 frontem:** acc. of respect with perf. pass. participle; lit. *encircled with respect to brow = its brow wreathed.* **131 hōs:** some of the

A river god (the Nile) on the
Capitoline Hill, Rome.

Fototeca Unione

    nē premat oppositō mollia terga genū.
Parva levēs capiunt animōs: fuit ūtile multīs
    pulvīnum facilī composuisse manū;
prōfuit et tenuī ventōs mōvisse tabellā
    et cava sub tenerum scamna dedisse pedem.   *110*

This advice will apply also to the gladiatorial contests in the Forum.

    Hōs aditūs Circusque novō praebēbit amōrī
    sparsaque sollicitō trīstis harēna forō.
Illā saepe puer Veneris pugnāvit harēnā
    et, quī spectāvit vulnera, vulnus habet;
dum loquitur tangitque manum poscitque libellum   *115*
    et quaerit, positō pignore, vincat uter,
saucius ingemuit tēlumque volātile sēnsit
    et pars spectātī mūneris ipse fuit.

When Gaius Caesar returns from his campaigns in the East and cele-
brates his victories with a triumphal parade, you will be able to impress
the girls by your knowledge.

    Ergō erit illa diēs, quā tū, pulcherrime rērum,
    quattuor in niveīs aureus ībis equīs.   *120*
Ībunt ante ducēs onerātī colla catēnīs,
    nē possint tūtī, quā prius, esse fugā.
Spectābunt laetī iuvenēs mixtaeque puellae,
    diffundetque animōs omnibus ista diēs.
Atque aliqua ex illīs cum rēgum nōmina quaeret,   *125*
    quae loca, quī montēs quaeve ferantur aquae,
omnia respondē, nec tantum sī qua rogābit;
    et quae nescierīs, ut bene nōta refer:
hic est Euphrātēs, praecīnctus harundine frontem;
    cui coma dēpendet caerula, Tigris erit;   *130*

Armenius, Armenian
Danaēius, of Danaë
Persis, -idis, *f.* Persia
Achaemenius, of Achaemenes, ancestor of the Persian kings
° **vērē**, truthfully
° **sī minus**, if not
° **fōrma**, beauty, appearance
neglēctus, unconcerned, casual
Mīnōis, -idis, *f.* daughter of Minos, Ariadne

136-140

° **auferō**, -ferre, abstulī, ablātus, carry away
tempora, -um, *n. pl.* temples (of the head)
cōmptus, dressed (of the hair)
acus, -ūs, *f.* needle, curling iron
cultus, groomed
Adōnis, -idis, *m.* Adonis, hunter loved by Venus
munditiēs, -ēī, *f.* cleanliness
fuscō (1), darken, tan
conveniēns, -entis, fitting
lābēs, -is, *f.* stain, spot

141-145

dēfōrmō (1), disfigure, mar
° **rigidus**, stiff, bristly
° **tōnsūra**, clipping
° **capillus**, hair
scītus, experienced, skillful
° **barba**, beard
resecō, -āre, -secuī, -sectus, cut back, trim
ēmineō, -ēre, -uī, stand out, protrude
sordēs, -is, *f.* dirt
° **unguis**, -is, *m.* fingernail

nāris, -is, *f.* nostril
° **pilus**, hair
odōrātus, odorous, smelling
° **anhēlitus**, -ūs, *m.* breath

146-150

° **laedō**, -ere, laesī, laesus, hurt, annoy, injure
grex, gregis, *m.* flock, herd
° **ecce**, lo! behold!
Līber, -erī, *m.* Liber, name of Bacchus
° **adiuvō**, -āre, -iūvī, -iūtus, help
caleō, -ēre, -uī, be hot, glow
Cnōsis, -idis, *f.* the girl from Cnossos, Ariadne
° **ignōtus**, unknown, strange
° **āmēns**, -entis, frantic, frenzied
° **brevis**, -e, brief, small
aequoreus, of the sea
Dīa, old name for Naxos
feriō, -īre, strike, pound

151-155

° **somnus**, sleep
tunica, tunic
vēlō (1), veil, cover, dress
recīnctus, ungirdled, loose
croceus, yellow, golden, blonde
inreligātus, not bound up, unbraided
° **crūdēlis**, -e, cruel
surdus, deaf
° **indignus**, undeserving, undeserved
imber, -bris, *m.* rain, shower
rigō (1), water, wet
° **gena**, cheek
° **fleo**, -ēre, flēvī, flētus, weep

---

prisoners. **facitō**: fut. imper.; *you shall make;* i.e., *call them Armenians* (*whether they are or not*). **131-132 haec, ista**: statues or paintings. **Danaēia**: *of Danae;* Perses, grandson of Danaë, was the legendary ancestor of the Persians. **133 ille**: *so and so.* **erunt ... dīcās**: *there will be what names you may say* = *there will be names for you to give.* **134 sī ... tamen**: *but if not, plausible ones* (*names*) *anyway.*

135 Mīnōida. Greek acc. sing. ending. **136 tempora**: for construction compare **frontem** in l. 129. **137-138 Hippolytum, Adōnis**: both hunters, the healthy outdoor type. **137 Phaedrā**: Greek nom. sing.; hence, the long **ā**. **138 cūra deae**: *the favorite of a goddess.* **139 placeant**: first of a series of verbs (ending with **laedat** in l. 146) in jussive subjv. because they give instructions. **corpora**: subject of **placeant** and **fuscentur**. **Campō**: the Campus Martius is used to represent outdoor exercise in general. **140 conveniēns**: the toga of this period was very voluminous and most elaborately draped; if it was not cut to exactly the right shape and size it was difficult to keep it in place. **141 rigidōs**: if your hair is stiff, have it carefully cut. **143 nihil**: *not at all.* **145 trīstis**: *offensive;* the social consequences of this breach of etiquette are formidable even today. **146 virque ... gregis**: Roman poets delicately refer to the odor of underarm perspiration by mentioning the he-goat (**caper**), a smelly animal. **vir**: *husband.*

147 Ecce ... vocat: this phrase leads Ovid into a digression, because Ovid is the poet of lovers, and lovers are aided by the wine god. **148 flammae**: dat. w. **favet**. **150 quā**: adv., *where.* **Dīa**: Naxos. **151 utque ... somnō**: *just as she was when waking from sleep.* **152 pedem**: acc. of respect w. **nūda**, lit. *bare as to foot;* similarly **comās** is acc. of respect w. **inreligāta**. **153 Thēsea**: Greek acc. sing., object of **clāmābat**; *she kept calling* (*the name of*) *cruel Theseus.* **154 imbre**: of tears.

hōs facitō Armeniōs, haec est Danaēia Persis;
    urbs in Achaemeniīs vallibus ista fuit;
ille vel ille ducēs, et erunt quae nōmina dīcās,
    sī poteris, vērē, sī minus, apta tamen.

Be casual but careful about your personal appearance.

Fōrma virōs neglēcta decet; Mīnōida Thēseus   *135*
    abstulit, ā nūllā tempora cōmptus acū.
Hippolytum Phaedrā, nec erat bene cultus, amāvit;
    cūra deae silvīs aptus Adōnis erat.
Munditiē placeant, fuscentur corpora Campō;
    sit bene conveniēns et sine lābe toga.   *140*
Nec mala dēfōrmet rigidōs tōnsūra capillōs:
    sit coma, sit scītā barba resecta manū.
Et nihil ēmineant et sint sine sordibus unguēs,
    inque cavā nūllus stet tibi nāre pilus.
Nec male odōrātī sit trīstis anhēlitus ōris,   *145*
    nec laedat nārēs virque paterque gregis.

Ariadne had been deserted by Theseus on the island of Naxos, but
Bacchus fell in love with her and exalted her to be a constellation.

Ecce, suum vātem Līber vocat; hic quoque amantēs
    adiuvat, et flammae quā calet ipse favet.
Cnōsis in ignōtīs āmēns errābat harēnīs,
    quā brevis aequoreīs Dīa ferītur aquīs;   *150*
utque erat ē somnō, tunicā vēlāta recīncta,
    nūda pedem, croceās inreligāta comās,
Thēsea crūdēlem surdās clāmābat ad undās,
    indignō tenerās imbre rigante genās.
Clāmābat flēbatque simul, sed utrumque decēbat;   *155*

Ariadne gives Theseus the
thread. Detail from a marble
sarcophagus, second-third century, A.D.

The Metropolitan Museum of Art,
Gift by subscription, 1890

25

* turpis, -e, shameful, ugly
* iterum, again
  tundō, -ere, tutudī, tūnsus, beat, smite
* palma, palm
  perfidus, treacherous
* sonō, -āre, -uī, -itum, sound, ring out
  cymbalum, cymbal
  attonitus, thunderstruck, inspired, frenzied
  tympanum, drum, tambourine
* pellō, -ere, pepulī, pulsus, drive, beat, pound

161-1o5

* excidō, -ere, -cidī, fall out, faint, swoon
* metus, -ūs, m. fear
* rumpō, -ere, rūpī, ruptus, break, cut short
  novissimus, newest, last
  exanimis, -e, lifeless, unconscious
  Mimallonis, -idis, f. a Bacchante
* sparsus, spread, flowing
  Satyrus, a Satyr
  praevius, going ahead, preceding
  ēbrius, drunken
* senex, senis, m. old, old man
  pandus, curved, rounded
  asellus, donkey

166-170

* vix, hardly, with difficulty
  prēndō, -ere, prēndī, prēnsus, grasp, catch
* contineō, -ēre, -uī, -tentus, contain, hold firmly
  iuba, mane
  Baccha, a Bacchante

quadrupēs, -pedis, m. quadruped
ferula, staff, stick
urgeō, -ēre, ursī, urge on
aurītus, long-eared
* dēlābor, -ī, -lāpsus sum, slip off
* surgō, -ere, surrēxī, surrēctum, rise, get up

171-175

ūva, grape, bunch of grapes
tigris, -is, m. and f. tiger, tigress
* adiungō, -ere, -iūnxī, -iūnctus, join to, harness
* lōra, -ōrum, n. pl. reins
* retineō, -ēre, -tinuī, -tentus, hold back
  horreō, -ēre, -uī, shudder
  sterilis, -e, barren, bare
  agitō (1), toss, sway
  arista, ear of grain

176-180

madidus, wet
canna, reed, cane
* palūs, -ūdis, f. marsh
  tremō, -ere, -uī, tremble, quiver
  ēn, see! behold!
* cūra, worry, care, object of concern, love
* fidēlis, -e, loyal, faithful
* inquam, def. I say; inquit, he says, he said
  Cnōsias, -adis, f. girl from Cnossos
* uxor, -ōris, f. wife
  sīdus, -deris, n. star
* dubius, doubtful, uncertain
  Crēssa corōna, Cretan crown, the Northern Crown

---

156 nōn turpior: litotes for *even more beautiful.* Ovid is always careful to remark on beauty in distress. **158 "Quid mihi fīet?" ait:** The repeated question suggests that her situation is hopeless. But with the very next word begins, as it were, the answer to Ariadne's question. **159 Sonuērunt,** etc.: there follows a description of a Bacchic rout, the thiasus (v. I.P.N. Bacchus). **160 manū:** collective sing., the hands are those of the Bacchantes, ecstatic women who accompany Bacchus. **161 Excidit:** her swoon is brief, as l. 172 will indicate. **metū:** abl. of cause.

163-165 Ecce: repeated to list each group as it appears, the Maenads with their disheveled hair, the lightfooted Satyrs, and old Silenus, constant attendant of Bacchus, on his sway-backed donkey. **163 Mimallonides:** said to be a Macedonian word for Bacchantes; Ovid has a penchant for words which reveal his learning. **165 Ēbrius ... senex:** Silenus. **166 ante:** adv. **170 Clāmārunt = Clāmāvērunt.** "Surge, age, surge": *"Get up, come on, get up."* **171 quem summum:** *the top of which.* **172 tigribus:** the tigers yoked to the chariot are symbolic of Bacchus as the god taming wild life. **lōra dabat:** *was slackening the reins (so that the tigers would go more quickly).*

173 color ... vōx: the poet compresses to stress the dramatic effect of the god's presence; hence, **Thēseus** for *all thought of Theseus.* **puellae:** dat. of reference; *from the girl.* **175 agitat:** verb of the rel. clause. **176 ut levis,** etc.: Ovid is rarely satisfied with only one simile. **177 cūra:** *love,* in apposition with the subject of **adsum. 178 pōne = dēpōne. 179 Mūnus:** in apposition w. **caelum;** *as a gift.* **180 dubiam:** *unsteady,* a frequent epithet for ships. **Crēssa Corōna:** *as the Cretan Crown,* the constellation known also as the Crown of Ariadne or Corona Borealis.

Ariadne in Naxos (waking from
sleep). Oil painting by G. F.
Watts (1817-1904). Metropolitan Museum of Art, N.Y.C.

nōn facta est lacrimīs turpior illa suīs.
Iamque iterum tundēns mollissima pectora palmīs,
   "Perfidus ille abiit. Quid mihi fīet?" ait.
"Quid mihi fīet?" ait. Sonuērunt cymbala tōtō
   lītore et attonitā tympana pulsa manū.   *160*
Excidit illa metū rūpitque novissima verba;
   nūllus in exanimī corpore sanguis erat.
Ecce, Mimallonides, sparsīs in terga capillīs!
   Ecce, levēs Satyrī, praevia turba deī!
Ēbrius, ecce, senex! Pandō Sīlēnus asellō   *165*
   vix sedet et prēnsās continet ante iubās.
Dum sequitur Bacchās, Bacchae fugiuntque petuntque,
   quadrupedem ferulā dum malus urget eques,
in caput aurītō cecidit dēlāpsus asellō;
   clāmārunt Satyrī, "Surge age, surge, pater."   *170*
Iam deus in currū, quem summum tēxerat ūvīs,
   tigribus adiūnctīs aurea lōra dabat.
Et color et Thēseus et vōx abiēre puellae,
   terque fugam petiit terque retenta metū est.
Horruit, ut sterilēs agitat quās ventus aristae,   *175*
   ut levis in madidā canna palūde tremit.
Cui deus, "Ēn, adsum tibi cūra fidēlior," inquit,
   "pōne metum, Bacchī, Cnōsias, uxor eris.
Mūnus habē caelum: caelō spectābere sīdus;
   saepe regēs dubiam Crēssa Corōna ratem."   *180*

27

dēsiliō, -īre, -uī, -sultum, jump down
* impōnō, -ere, -posuī, -positus, place on
* cēdō, -ere, cessī, cessum, yield, give way
implicō, -āre, -uī, -itus, enfold
* sinus, -ūs, m. fold, hollow, embrace
* valeō, -ēre, -uī, -itum, have strength
Hymenaeus, Hymen, god of marriage
Euhius, a name of the god Bacchus
euhoe: shout of joy in the festival of Bacchus

coeō, -īre, -iī, -itum, come together, unite
* sacer, -cra, -crum, sacred, holy
nūpta, bride
torus, couch, bed
amāns, amantis, m. lover
imitor (dep. 1), imitate, pretend
* fidēs, -eī, f. credit, belief
* nūllus, -a, -um, (gen. -īus), none, no; nūllus nōn, everyone

* vērē, truly, genuinely
simulātor, -ōris, m. pretender
* incipiō, -ere, -cēpī, -ceptus, begin
* fingō, -ere, finxī, fictus, pretend
quō, wherefore, accordingly
* magis, more, rather
* modo, just now, recently
* falsus, false, pretended
blanditiae, -ārum, f. pl. flattery, blandishments
* fūrtim, stealthily, secretly
* dēprēndō, -ere, -prēndī, -prēnsus, take by surprise, capture

pendēns, -entis, hanging
subedō, -ere, -ēdī, eat away from below
piget, -ēre, -uit, impers. irk, weary, be boring to
teres, -retis, slender, shapely
exiguus, narrow, small
* dēlectō (1), delight
praecōnium, proclaiming, praise, advertisement
* grātus, welcome, pleasing

* Phrygius, Phrygian, Trojan
* Iūnō, -ōnis, f. Juno
Pallas, -adis, f. Pallas, Athene
* pudet, -ēre, -uit, impers. shame
* ostendō, -ere, -tendī, -tentus, show, reveal
* pinna, feather
recondō, -ere, -didī, -ditus, hide away, conceal
* opēs, opum, f. pl. wealth, attractions
rapidus, rushing, swift
* cursus, -ūs, m. running, speed

dēpexus, combed down
* iuba, mane
plausus, applauded, patted
* timidē, timidly
* trahō, -ere, trāxī, trāctus, draw, attract
prōmissum = pollicitum, a promise
* testis, -is, m. witness
periūrium, perjury
* rīdeō, -ēre, rīsī, rīsus, laugh at
Aeolius, of Aeolus, god of the winds
inritus, invalid, null and void
Notus, South Wind

183 implicitam: sc. eam; w. abstulit; *he embraced and carried her off*. 184 ut: *how*. posse: subj. of est. 185 Pars = Aliī: hence verbs in pl. Hymenaee: voc. case; this invocation of Hymen was a part of Roman weddings. clāmant: *invoke*. Euhion: Greek acc. sing.

187 Est . . . amāns: pass. periphrastic; *You must act the lover*. imitanda: sc. sunt. vulnera: i.e., of Cupid's arrows. 188 haec tibi quaerātur . . . fidēs: *let this belief in you be your aim = in this try to be convincing*. tibi: w. fidēs. 189 crēdī: subject of est; *being believed is* . . . amanda: *deserving to be loved = lovable*. 190 pessima = turpissima: *very ugly*. sit: jussive subjv. expressing concession; *let her be = though she be*. 192 quod: *that which*; sc. id as antecedent (and as subjective complement with fuit). 193 facilēs: *approachable, agreeable* (the usual meaning of facilis when applied to persons).

195 animum dēprēndere nunc sit: lit. *there may now be a trapping (of) the mind = it may now be possible to steal away her affection*. 196 subēstur: present pass. indic. 3rd sing. of subedō; edō and its compounds are irregular in the present indic. and subjv. 197 pigeat: jussive subjv. 200 virginibus cūrae: double dative; virginibus is also used w. the adjective grāta; cūrae and grāta are connected by -que.

201-202 Nam . . . pudet: the everlasting resentment of Juno and Athena at the judgment of Paris shows that girls are vain of their beauty. 201 Pallada: Greek acc. sing. 202 iūdicium nōn tenuisse: *not to have taken the prize*. 203 Laudātās: emphatic by position; *when they have been praised*. avis Iūnōnia: the peacock. 204 spectēs: subjv. in fut. less vivid condition; *if you should look on*. 209 ex altō: sc. caelō. amantum = amantium. 210 inrita: sc. periūria. 211 Styga: Greek acc. sing. falsum: internal acc.; *to take a false oath*.

Dīxit et ē currū, nē tigrēs illa timēret,
    dēsilit (impositō cessit harēna pede)
implicitamque sinū, neque enim pugnāre valēbat,
    abstulit: ut facile est omnia posse deō!
Pars "Hymenaee" canunt, pars clāmant Euhion, "euhoe!"   *185*
    Sīc coeunt sacrō nūpta deusque torō.

Compliment and flatter.

Est tibi agendus amāns, imitandaque vulnera verbīs;
    haec tibi quaerātur quālibet arte fidēs.
Nec crēdī labor est: sibi quaeque vidētur amanda.
    Pessima sit, nūllī nōn sua fōrma placet.   *190*
Saepe tamen vērē coepit simulātor amāre.
    Saepe, quod incipiēns fīnxerat esse, fuit.
Quō magis, Ō, facilēs imitantibus este, puellae:
    fīet amor vērus, quī modo falsus erat.
Blanditiīs animum fūrtim dēprēndere nunc sit,   *195*
    ut pendēns liquidā rīpa subēstur aquā.
Nec faciem nec tē pigeat laudāre capillōs
    et teretēs digitōs exiguumque pedem.
Dēlectant etiam castās praecōnia fōrmae;
    virginibus cūrae grātaque fōrma sua est.   *200*
Nam cūr in Phrygiīs Iūnōnem et Pallada silvīs
    nunc quoque iūdicium nōn tenuisse pudet?
Laudātās ostendit avis Iūnōnia pinnās;
    sī tacitus spectēs, illa recondit opēs.
Quadrupedēs inter rapidī certāmina cursūs   *205*
    dēpexaeque iubae plausaque colla iuvant.

Follow the example of Jupiter, who swore the most solemn oaths in order to deceive Juno and will therefore be lenient toward broken promises and vows.

Nec timidē prōmitte: trahunt prōmissa puellās;
    pollicitō testēs quōslibet adde deōs.
Iuppiter ex altō periūria rīdet amantum
    et iubet Aeoliōs inrita ferre Notōs.   *210*

Triumph of Bacchus and Ariadne. Fresco by Carracci on the ceiling of the Farnese Palace, Rome. Notice the corona over Ariadne's head and Silenus (right) on the donkey.

Alinari, Fototeca Unione

29

Styx, Stygis, f. Styx, river in Hades
iūrō (1), swear, vow, offer an oath
° soleō, -ēre, solitus sum, be accustomed
° exemplum, example, pattern, precedent
expedit, it is useful
tūs, tūris, n. incense
merus, pure, undiluted; merum (vīnum),
   pure wine
focus, hearth, altar

216-220

° remaneō, -ēre, -mānsī, remain, endure
vāstus, enormous, vast
pervagus, roving about
geminī, twin
° āvolō (1), fly away
° āla, wing

221-225

° hospes, -pitis, m. guest, stranger
effugium, escape
praestruō, -ere, -strūxī, strūctus, block up
Mīnōs, -ōis, m. Minos, king of Crete
° claudō, -ere, clausī, clausus, close, im-
   prison
concipiō, -ere, -cēpī, -ceptus, take up, conceive
° crīmen, -minis, n. charge, crime
sēmibōs, -bovis, half-ox
sēmivir, -ī, half-man
bōs, bovis, m. and f. ox, cow
exsilium, exile
° iūstus, just, fair, righteous

226-230

cinis, -neris, m. ashes
° paternus, paternal, ancestral

° quoniam, since
° fātum, fate
° agitō (1), pursue, chase
° inīquus, unjust, unkind
° reditus, -ūs, m. return
vīlis, -e, cheap, worthless
volō, velle, voluī, wish, be willing

231-235

° plūs, plūris, more
licet, -ēre, -uit (licitum est), be allowed;
   as conj., licet, licēbat, although
° ēgressus, -ūs, m. departure
simul ut = simul ac, as soon as
ingeniōsus, clever, inventive
possideō, -ēre, -sēdī, -sessus, possess, own

236-240

° tellūs, -ūris, f. earth, land
° pateō, -ēre, -uī, be open, be available
° unda, wave, water
restō, -āre, -stitī, remain, be left
venia, forgiveness, pardon
sīdereus, starry
affectō (1), aspire, aim
sēdēs, -is, f. seat, dwelling

241-245

Stygius, Stygian, of Styx
trānsnō (1), swim across
novō (1), renew, change
° ingenium, talent, ingenuity
āerius, of the air
carpō, -ere, carpsī, carptus, pick, choose,
   pursue
rēmigium, oarage, rowing
volucris, -is, f. bird
ōrdō, -dinis, m. order, arrangement

213-214 The gods serve a useful purpose and therefore we should believe in their existence, and the traditional ceremonies should be maintained. 213 Expedit: the subject is esse deōs. putēmus: hortatory subjv.; let us think. 214 dentur: jussive subjv.

215-298. The difficulty of keeping Cupid, with his wings, from escaping leads Ovid into a digression, the story of the escape of Daedalus and Icarus from the Labyrinth (later retold in META. VIII 183-235).

215 tibī: for you. mē vāte: abl. abs., with me as your poet. 217 Magna: object of dīcere. quās . . . per artēs: indir. question in apposition w. magna; important matters, by what skills . . . 218 puer: in apposition w. Amor. 219 Et, et: Not only . . . but also . . . āvolet: subjv. in rel. clause of characteristic; with which to fly away. 220 imposuisse: perf. infin. for completed action; to limit completely.

221 Hospitis: Daedalus. effugiō: dat. w. compound verb praestrūxerat; had put every obstacle (omnia, internal acc.) in the way of the escape. 223 conceptum: modifies virum and bovem. mātris: Pasiphaë, who had given birth to a monster, the Minotaur. 224 sēmi-bovemque . . . bovem: this line was one of three chosen by Ovid's friends as his worst and by Ovid as his best. 225 Sit: jussive subjv.; Let there be. iūstissime: Minos was famous for his justice. 227 patriā: Athens; he had been exiled for killing his nephew, who surpassed him in skill. 228 posse: direct object of dā; give me the ability = make it possible for me. morī: sc. in patriā. 229 puerō: his young son Icarus. 231-232 licēbat (ut) dīceret: it was permitted that he might say = granted that he might say = though he said.

Per Styga Iūnōnī falsum iūrāre solēbat
　　Iuppiter: exemplō nunc favet ipse suō.
Expedit esse deōs et, ut expedit, esse putēmus;
　　dentur in antīquōs tūra merumque focōs.

Ovid begins a new topic: how to retain the girl's affection.

Nōn satis est vēnisse tibī mē vāte puellam;　　　　　　　215
　　arte meā capta est, arte tenenda meā est.
Magna parō, quās possit Amor remanēre per artēs,
　　dīcere, tam vāstō pervagus orbe puer.
Et levis est et habet geminās, quibus āvolet, ālās;
　　difficile est illīs imposuisse modum.　　　　　　　　220

The story of Daedalus and Icarus.

Hospitis effugiō praestrūxerat omnia Mīnōs;
　　audācem pinnīs repperit ille viam.
Daedalus, ut clausit conceptum crīmine mātris
　　sēmibovemque virum sēmivirumque bovem,
"Sit modus exsiliō," dīxit, "iūstissime Mīnōs;　　　　　225
　　accipiat cinerēs terra paterna meōs,
et, quoniam in patriā fātīs agitātus inīquīs
　　vīvere nōn potuī, dā mihi posse morī.
Dā reditum puerō, senis est sī grātia vīlis;
　　sī nōn vīs puerō parcere, parce senī."　　　　　　　230
Dīxerat haec, sed et haec et multō plūra licēbat
　　dīceret, ēgressūs nōn dabat ille virō.
Quod simul ut sēnsit, "Nunc nunc, Ō Daedale," dīxit,
　　"māteriem, quā sīs ingeniōsus, habēs.
Possidet et terrās et possidet aequora Mīnōs;　　　　　235
　　nec tellūs nostrae nec patet unda fugae.
Restat iter caelī; caelō temptābimus īre.
　　Dā veniam coeptō, Iuppiter alte, meō.
Nōn ego sīdereās affectō tangere sēdēs.
　　Quā fugiam dominum, nūlla nisi ista via est.　　　　240
Per Styga dētur iter, Stygiās trānsnābimus undās.
　　Sunt mihi nātūrae iūra novanda meae."
Ingenium mala saepe movent. Quis crēderet umquam
　　āeriās hominem carpere posse viās?
Rēmigium volucrum, dispōnit in ōrdine pinnās　　　　　245

233 dīxit: Daedalus is speaking to himself. 234 sīs: subjv. in rel. clause of characteristic; *matter with which you may be ingenious = an opportunity to be ingenious.* 238 Dā veniam: Daedalus apologizes for intruding into the domain of Jupiter. 240 fugiam: subjv. in rel. clause of characteristic; *by which I may flee my master.* 241 Styga: Greek acc. sing. dētur: jussive subjv. equivalent to a conditional clause; *let a route be given = if a route is given.* 242 mihi: dat. of agent w. pass. periphrastic sunt novanda; *I must change the natural laws to which I am subject.*

243 Ingenium . . . movent: compare the proverb "Necessity is the mother of invention." crēderet: potential subjv.; *would have believed.* 245 Rēmigium: in apposition w. pinnās; lit. *The oarage of birds.* 246 leve: modifies opus; *the light material.* per vincula = vinculīs.

31

līnum, flax, thread
vinculum, bond, fastening
nectō, -ere, nexuī, nexus, weave, connect
īmus, lowest, bottom
° cēra, wax
  adstringō, -ere, -strīnxī, -strictus, bind, tighten
° solvō, -ere, solvī, solūtus, loosen, melt
° fīniō, -īre, -īvī, -ītus, finish
  trāctō (1), handle, touch, treat
  renīdeō, -ēre, be cheerful, smile
  nescius, unaware, not knowing
° umerus, shoulder

  carīna, keel, ship
° effugiō, -ere, -fūgī, escape (from)
  (ops), opis, f. help, means
  āer, āeris, (Greek acc. āera), m. air
° inventum, invention, discovery
  Tegeaeus, of Tegea
  Boōtēs, -ae, m. Boötes, the Plowman

  ēnsiger, -era, -erum, sword-bearing
  Ōriōn, -ōnis, m. Orion, the Hunter
° aspiciō, -ere, -spexī, -spectus, look at, view
  sector (dep. 1), keep following
  praevius, leading the way
° sīve ... sīve, if ... or if
  aetherius, of the upper air
° vīcīnus, near, neighboring

impatiēns, -entis, unable to endure
calor, -ōris, m. heat

humilis, -e, low
° propior, -ius, nearer, too close
  fretum, strait, sea
° iactō (1), toss, ply, flap
° mōbilis, -e, movable, pliant
° aequoreus, of the sea
  madēscō, -ere, become wet
° nātus, son
  quā, where, whichever way
  secundus, following, successful
  aptō (1), fit, adjust
° mōnstrō (1), point out, show (how)

  ērudiō, -īre, -iī, -ītus, train, teach
° īnfirmus, weak, young
  accommodō = aptō
  lībrō (1), poise, balance
  ōsculum, kiss
° patrius, of a father, paternal
° contineō, -ēre, -uī, -tentus, hold back, check

° hinc, from here
  bīnī, -ae, -a, two at a time, two, both
° sustineō, -ēre, -uī, -tentus, hold up, support, sustain
  usque, constantly, all the way

Theseus fighting the Minotaur. Attic black-figured amphora, sixth century, B.C.

The Metropolitan Museum of Art, Fletcher Fund, 1956

et leve per līnī vincula nectit opus,
    īmaque pars cērīs adstringitur igne solūtīs,
    fīnītusque novae iam labor artis erat.
Trāctābat cēramque puer pinnāsque renīdēns   *250*
    nescius haec umerīs arma parāta suīs.
Cui pater, "Hīs," inquit, "patria est adeunda carīnīs,
    hāc nōbīs Mīnōs effugiendus ope.
Āera nōn potuit Mīnōs, alia omnia clausit;
    quem licet, inventīs āera rumpe meīs.
Sed tibi nōn virgō Tegeaea comesque Boōtae,   *255*
    ēnsiger Ōrīōn, aspiciendus erit.
Mē pinnīs sectāre datīs; ego praevius ībō.
    Sit tua cūra sequī, mē duce tūtus eris.
Nam, sīve aetheriās vīcīnō sōle per aurās
    ībimus, impatiēns cēra calōris erit;   *260*
sīve humilēs propiōre fretō iactābimus ālās,
    mōbilis aequoreīs pinna madēscet aquīs.
Inter utrumque volā; ventōs quoque, nāte, timētō,
    quāque ferent aurae, vēla secunda datō."
Dum monet, aptat opus puerō mōnstratque movērī,   *265*
    ērudit īnfirmās ut sua māter avēs.
Inde sibī factās umerīs accommodat ālās
    inque novum timidē corpora lībrat iter,
iamque volātūrus parvō dedit ōscula nātō,
    nec patriae lacrimās continuēre genae.   *270*
Monte minor collis, campīs erat altior aequīs;
    hinc data sunt miserae corpora bīna fugae.
Et movet ipse suās et nātī respicit ālās
    Daedalus et cursūs sustinet usque suōs.
Iamque novum dēlectat iter, positōque timōre   *275*

---

249 -que, -que: *both . . . and.* 250 haec arma parāta (esse): indir. statement depending on nescius. arma: in the naval sense, *rigging, equipment.* 251 carīnīs: = nāvibus (metonymy), metaphor for *wings.* 252 nōbīs: dat. of agent. 253 potuit: sc. claudere. 254 quem: antecedent is āera; sc. nōbīs rumpere.

255 tibi: dat. of agent w. aspiciendus erit. virgō Tegeaea: Callisto, placed in the heavens by Jupiter as the Great Bear. Boōtae: gen. of Boōtēs. 256 ēnsiger: three of the stars of Orion seem to be arranged in the shape of a sword. 257 sectāre: present imper. 258 Sit: jussive subjv.; the subject is sequī. 260 calōris: objective gen. w. impatiēns; *unable to endure the heat.*

263-264 timētō, datō: fut. imper.; *you shall . . .* 264 quāque = et quā, *and where.* vēla secunda datō: *you are to sail with the favoring wind.*

266 ērudit . . . avēs: *as their mother teaches the nestlings.* 267 sibī: dat. of agent w. factās. 269 volātūrus: fut. act. participle; *about to fly.* 270 continuēre = continuērunt. 272 miserae: anticipating what happens to Icarus. 274 cursūs . . . suōs: *all the while holds his course.*

275 positō: for dēpositō. 278 dextra relīquit: *the right hand has let fall* (*in amazement*).

tremulus, trembling, pliant
captō (1), catch, try to catch
harundō, -dinis, f. reed, rod
laevus, -a, -um, left
Clarius, of Clarus, an Ionian town with
  an oracle of Apollo
umbrōsus, shaded
cīnctus, girded, surrounded
piscōsus, full of fish
vadum, shallow water
* incautus, incautious
* nimium, too, too much
temerārius, rash, impulsive
* iter agō, set a course
* dēserō, -ere, -seruī, -sertus, desert
vinclum = vinculum
labō (1), totter, give way
liquēscō, -ere, licuī, melt
bracchium, arm
* dēspiciō, -ere, -spexī, -spectus, look down
pavidus, quaking, trembling
oborior, -īrī, -ortus sum, w. dat., rise before
tābeō, -ēre, -uī, melt away
quatiō, -ere, —, quassus, shake, flap
lacertus, (upper) arm
trepidō (1), tremble, be alarmed
viridis, -e, green
* īnfēlīx, -īcis, unhappy
axis, -is, m. axis, pole (of sky), part
* os, ossis, n. bone
compescō, -ere, -pescuī, restrain, check
volucer, -cris, -cre, flying, winged

* dētineō, -ēre, -tinuī, -tentus, hold back,
  detain
dōs, dōtis, f. dowry, gift
bonum, advantage, blessing
fragilis, -e, fragile, frail
carpō, -ere, carpsī, carptus, pluck, weaken
viola, violet
hiō (1), gape, open, be open
līlium, lily
flōreō, -ēre, -uī, blossom, flower
rigeō, -ēre, be stiff
spīna, thorn, prickle
cānus, white, gray
rūga, wrinkle, crease
arō (1), plough, furrow, wrinkle
* ingenuus, native, noble, liberal
ēdiscō, -ere, ēdidicī, learn thoroughly
fācundus, eloquent, fluent
Ulixēs, -is, m. Ulysses
* torqueō, -ēre, torsī, tortus, torment, twist
* quotiēns, how many times
* properō (1), hasten
Calypsō, -ūs, f. Calypso
* aliter, otherwise, differently
exigō, -ere, -ēgī, -āctus, drive out, demand,
  ask about
Odrysius, Odrysian, Thracian
cruentus, bloody, cruel
virga, rod, stick
spissus, thick, close
* pingō, -ere, pīnxī, pictus, paint, depict
Simoīs, -entis, m. river near Troy

---

279 Samos, etc.: these islands (all nom. sing. f.) are in the Aegean Sea. **280 Clariō** . . . **deō**: dat. of agent w. **amāta**; *loved by Apollo of Claros.* **281 dextra**: *right = on the right.*

285 deō: the Sun. **288 oculīs**: dat. w. **oborta. 290 quō sustineātur**: rel. clause of characteristic; *anything by which he may be supported = anything to support him.*

296 tellūs: he was buried by Hercules. **aequora**: the southeastern part of the Aegean Sea was called *Mare Icarium.* **297-298 Nōn . . . parō**: with this couplet Ovid returns from his digression, having shown that it will require genius of a very high order if he is to hold down permanently the winged Cupid. **298 dētinuisse**: for tense, see note on **imposuisse**, 1. 220.

299 mīrēre = mīrēris: subjv. in clause of purpose; *and so that you may not be surprised that you have been jilted.* **301 quantumque . . . annōs**: *as much as is added to the years = the older you grow;* for an antecedent for **quantum**, sc. **tantō** w. **minor**, (*so much*) *the less it becomes.* **302 spatiō . . . suō**: *it* (i.e., *handsome appearance*) *is eaten away by its own time span.* **304 āmissā rosā**: abl. abs., *when the rose has withered.* **305 tibi**: *for you.* **306 arent**: subjv. in rel. clause of characteristic; *to furrow.* **308 sit**: jussive subjv.; *and let it be no light concern.* **linguās duās**: Latin and Greek. A knowledge of Greek literature was regarded as essential.

310 tamen: i.e., although he was not good-looking. **deās**: Circe and Calypso; v. *Odyssey*, IX 29-32. **311 illum . . . Calypsō**: *Calypso grieved that he was in a hurry to leave;* verbs of grieving take acc. and infinitive. **312 rēmigiō**: specific for the more general **nāvigandō. 313 Haec**: Calypso. **rogābat**: *kept asking for,* because her guest was a born story teller.

Īcarus audācī fortius arte volat.
Hōs aliquis, tremulā dum captat harundine piscēs,
    vīdit, et inceptum dextra relīquit opus.
Iam Samos ā laevā—fuerant Naxosque relictae
    et Paros et Clariō Dēlos amāta deō—   *280*
dextra Lebinthos erat silvīsque umbrōsa Calymnē
    cīnctaque piscōsīs Astypalaea vadīs,
cum puer incautīs nimium temerārius annīs
    altius ēgit iter dēseruitque patrem.
Vincla labant et cēra deō propiōre liquēscit,   *285*
    nec tenuēs ventōs bracchia mōta tenent.
Territus ā summō dēspexit in aequora caelō;
    nox oculīs pavidō vēnit oborta metū.
Tābuerant cērae; nūdōs quatit ille lacertōs,
    et trepidat nec, quō sustineātur, habet.   *290*
Dēcidit atque cadēns, "Pater, Ō pater, auferor!" inquit.
    Clausērunt viridēs ōra loquentis aquae.
At pater īnfēlīx, nec iam pater, "Īcare!" clāmat,
    "Īcare!" clāmat, "ubi es, quōque sub axe volās?
Īcare!" clāmābat. Pinnās aspexit in undīs.   *295*
    Ossa tegit tellūs, aequora nōmen habent.
Nōn potuit Mīnōs hominis compēscere pinnās,
    ipse deum volucrem dētinuisse parō.

Handsome appearance is not enough; cultivate an attractive personality
and the gifts of the mind.

Ut dominam teneās nec tē mīrēre relictum,
    ingeniī dōtēs corporis adde bonīs.   *300*
Fōrma bonum fragile est, quantumque accēdit ad annōs,
    fit minor et spatiō carpitur ipsa suō.
Nec violae semper nec hiantia līlia flōrent,
    et riget āmissā spīna relicta rosā.
Et tibi iam venient cānī, fōrmōse, capillī,   *305*
    iam venient rūgae, quae tibi corpus arent.
Nec levis ingenuās pectus coluisse per artēs
    cūra sit et linguās ēdidicisse duās.

The experience of Ulysses shows that a good mind is even more attractive than good looks.

Nōn fōrmōsus erat, sed erat fācundus Ulixēs,
    et tamen aequoreās torsit amōre deās.   *310*
Ō quotiēns illum doluit properāre Calypsō
    rēmigiōque aptās esse negāvit aquās!
Haec Trōiae cāsūs iterumque iterumque rogābat;
    ille referre aliter saepe solēbat idem.
Lītore cōnstiterant; illīc quoque pulchra Calypsō   *315*
    exigit Odrysiī fāta cruenta ducis.
Ille levī virgā (virgam nam forte tenēbat),
    quod rogat, in spissō lītore pingit opus.
"Haec," inquit, "Trōia est" (mūrōs in lītore fēcit),
    "hic tibi sit Simoīs. Haec mea castra putā.   *320*

35

Dolōn, -ōnis, *m.* Dolon
* spargō, -ere, sparsī, sparsus, scatter, spread
Haemonius, Haemonian, Thessalian
vigil, -ilis, *m.* watchman, sentinel
* optō (1), want, wish for
Sīthonius, Sithonian, Thracian
tentōrium, tent
Rhēsus, Thracian king, ally of the Trojans
hāc, this way
revehō, -ere, -vexī, -vectus, carry back
Pergama, -ōrum, *n. pl.* Pergamum, Troy

* fīdus, trustworthy, reliable
* eō, īre, iī, itum, go
* perdō, -ere, -didī, -ditus, destroy, lose
fallāx, -ācis, deceitful, treacherous
cōnfīdō, -ere, -fīsus sum, *semidep. w. dat.*,
    trust in, rely on

repugnō (1), oppose, disagree
* modo, only, just
arguō, -ere, -uī, -ūtus, accuse, criticize
probō (1), approve, prove
adrīdeō, -ēre, -rīsī, -rīsus, laugh at
* meminī, -isse, remember; *imper.* mementō

* vultus, -ūs, *m.* face, expression
* seu = sīve, or if, if, whether
lūdō, -ere, lūsī, lūsus, play
numerus, number, dice
eburnus, of ivory
iactum, throw of the dice
tālī, -ōrum, *m. pl.* dice
damnōsus, injurious, harmful
canis, -is, *m.* dog, the worst throw of dice

Women playing with "tali." Painting on marble
from Herculaneum. National Museum, Naples.

Alinari, Fototeca Unione

Campus erat" (campumque facit) "quem caede Dolōnis
    sparsimus, Haemoniōs dum vigil optat equōs.
Illīc Sīthoniī fuerant tentōria Rhēsī;
    hāc ego sum captīs nocte revectus equīs . ."
Plūraque pingēbat, subitus cum Pergama flūctus   325
    abstulit et Rhēsī cum duce castra suō.
Tum dea, "Quās," inquit, "fīdās tibi crēdis itūrō
    perdiderint undae nōmina quanta, vidēs?"
Ergō age, fallācī timidē cōnfīde figūrae,
    quisquis es, aut aliquid corpore plūris habē.   330

Humor her in every way possible and gain favor by many little
services.

Cēde repugnantī; cēdendō victor abībis.
    Fac modo, quās partēs illa iubēbit, agās.
Arguet; arguitō. Quidquid probat illa, probātō.
    Quod dīcet, dīcās; quod negat illa, negēs.
Rīserit: adrīdē. Sī flēbit, flēre mementō.   335
    Impōnat lēgēs vultibus illa tuīs.
Seu lūdet numerōsque manū iactābit eburnōs,
    tū male iactātō, tū male iacta datō.
Seu iaciēs tālōs, victam nē poena sequātur,
    damnōsī facitō stent tibi saepe canēs.   340

315 Lītore cōnstiterant: here, and throughout the incident, Ovid exercises strict economy of words and gives only bare essentials. 316 Odrysiī ducis: Rhesus, a Thracian king who had come to help the Trojans. Note that Ulysses discreetly minimizes the part that Diomedes took in the exploit. 321 Dolōnis: a Trojan scout (vigil) sent out by Hector to spy on the Greeks; from him Diomedes and Ulysses learned the Trojan password before putting him to death. 322 Haemoniōs: *Thessalian;* the home of Achilles, whose horses Hector had promised to Dolon if his spying proved successful, was in Thessaly.

324 captīs equīs: the horses of Rhesus. For the story of Rhesus and Dolon see *Iliad* X. 327-328 Quās . . . vidēs: rearrange as Vidēs quanta nōmina undae perdiderint, quās tibi itūrō fīdās crēdis? The poet artfully allows his Calypso to confuse the word order, and thus suggests the disorder in the sand drawings and the danger from the sea. The reader is meant to conclude that Calypso was not eager to have Ulysses leave.

329 Ergō age: *Come then.* With these words Ovid returns to his theme. timidē cōnfīde: *be cautious about relying on.* 330 corpore: abl. of comparison. plūris: gen. of value. aliquid corpore plūris habē: *have something better than mere appearance.*

331 repugnantī: sc. puellae. 332 Fac: w. ut implied before agās; *See that you play.* 333 arguitō: fut. imper.; *you shall criticize, you are to criticize (but taking care to be on the girl's side).* Several other future imperatives follow: probātō, mementō, iactātō, datō, facitō. 334 dīcās, negēs: subjvs. in place of imperatives.

337 lūdet: in a game in which dice (numerī) control the moves, if you cannot always make a bad throw, then make a mistake in your move (male iacta datō). 339 tālōs: dice oblong in shape; four sides were numbered, but two opposite sides were rounded off and left unnumbered. victam (puellam) nē poena sequātur: *so that she does not suffer by losing.* 340 stent: with ut implied. canēs: the "dog throw" was worst (damnōsī) when each of the four dice showed the same number. 341 latrōciniī: a "war" game resembling checkers or chess, for which Ovid uses calculus, mīles and hostis when referring to the pieces or "men." 342 fac (ut) pereat ab: *see to it that (your soldier) loses to.*

37

341-345

latrōcinium, robbery
* imāgō, -ginis, f. likeness, form
calculus, pebble, piece, "man"
* pereō, -īre, -iī, -itum, perish, be lost
vitreus, of glass
distendō, -ere, -tendī, -tentus, spread out, stretch
umbrāculum, parasol, umbrella
virga, branch, rib
* turba, confusion, crowd
* dubitō (1), doubt, hesitate
teres, -etis, shapely, well-shaped
scamnum, stool
lectus, couch

346-350

solea, sandal, shoe
dēmō, -ere, dēmpsī, dēmptus, take off
* quamvīs, although
horreō, -ēre, -uī, shudder, shiver
algeō, -ēre, alsī, feel cold
calfaciō, -ere, -fēcī, -factus, make warm
* sinus, -ūs, m. fold, bosom, breast

speculum, mirror

351-355

repetō, -ere, -īvī, -ītus, claim, go back to
epulae, -ārum, f. pl. feast, banquet, dinner party
perfungor, -ī, -fūnctus sum, w. abl., perform, complete
* ōdī, ōdisse, hate
* iners, -ertis, inactive, lazy, idle
* rota, wheel, carriage
viam carpere, make one's way
sitiēns, -entis, dry, thirsty
canīcula, small dog; Canīcula, the Dog Star
tardō (1), delay, slow down

356-358

candidus, shining, white
nix, nivis, f. snow
mīlitia, military service, warfare
segnis, -e, slow, sluggish, lazy
tueor, -ērī, tūtus (tuitus) sum, guard, watch

343 Ipse tenē: first in a list of services commonly done by slaves. **345 scamnum:** a footstool, so that it will be less awkward to reach the dining couch. **346 tenerō pedī:** dat. w. the two compound verbs. **348 algentis:** w. **dominae. sinū:** w. **tuō** implied. **349 tibi turpe:** *beneath you,* since this too was a service performed by **ancilla.**

Sīve latrōciniī sub imāgine calculus ībit,
    fac pereat vitreō mīles ab hoste tuus.
Ipse tenē distenta suīs umbrācula virgīs,
    ipse fac in turbā, quā venit illa, locum.
Nec dubitā teretī scamnum prōdūcere lectō,   *345*
    et tenerō soleam dēme vel adde pedī.
Saepe etiam dominae, quamvīs horrēbis et ipse,
    algentis manus est calfacienda sinū.
Nec tibi turpe putā (quamvīs sit turpe, placēbit)
    ingenuā speculum sustinuisse manū.   *350*
Nocte domum repetēns epulīs perfūncta redībit;
    tunc quoque prō servō, sī vocat illa, venī.
Rūre erit et dīcet veniās. Amor ōdit inertēs.
    Sī rota dēfuerit, tū pede carpe viam.
Nec grave tē tempus sitiēnsque Canīcula tardet   *355*
    nec via per iactās candida facta nivēs.
Mīlitiae speciēs amor est: discēdite, segnēs;
    nōn sunt haec timidīs signa tuenda virīs.
ARS AMATORIA I, II (Selections)

---

351 epulīs perfūncta: *at the end of a dinner party.* **perfūncta:** in agreement w. **puella** implied. **352 prō servō:** *in place of a slave.* **353 dīcet** (ut) **veniās:** *she will say that you are to come.* **355 grave tempus:** *bad weather.* **sitiēns Canīcula:** by metonymy for *the hot weather of the dog days.* **358 timidīs virīs:** dat. of agent w. pass. periphrastic **sunt tuenda;** *are to be guarded by cowards.*

FASTI

1-5

* nōscō, -ere, nōvī, nōtus, get to know; nōvī, I know
* nesciō, -īre, -iī, -ītus, be ignorant of

Ariōn, -onis, *m.* Arion

tellūs, -ūris, *f.* earth, land

* carmen, -minis, *n.* poem, song
* agna, lamb
* lupus, wolf

avidus, eager, greedy

restō, -āre, -stitī, halt, stop

* canis, -is, *m. and f.* dog

lepus, -poris, *m.* hare

umbra, shade, shadow

* iaceō, -ēre, -uī, lie down

6-10

cerva, hind, deer

lea, lioness

līs, lītis, *f.* quarrel, dispute

* loquāx, -ācis, talkative, chattering

Pallas, -adis, *f.* Pallas, Athena

āles, ālitis, *m. and f.* bird

cornīx, -īcis, *f.* crow

accipiter, -tris, *m.* hawk

* columba, dove

Cynthius, of Cynthus, Cynthian

* ferō, ferre, tulī, lātus, bear, carry, relate, report

vōcālis, -e, vocal, melodious, tuneful

* tamquam, as if, as though

obstipēscō, -ere, -stipuī, become astounded

* modus, way, measure, music

11-15

Ariōnius, of Arion

Siculus, Sicilian

impleō, -ēre, -ēvī, -ētus, fill

lyricus, lyrical, of the lyre

Ausonis, -idis, Ausonian, Italian

* ōra, coast, shore
* sonus, sound
* repetō, -ere, -iī, -ītus, seek again, revisit
* puppis, -is, *f.* stern, ship
* quaerō, -ere, quaesīvī, quaesītus, search for, gain
* opēs, opum, *f. pl.* wealth

forsitan, perhaps

* īnfēlīx, -īcis, unhappy, unfortunate

16-20

* tūtus, safe

aequor, -oris, *n.* sea

gubernātor, -ōris, *m.* pilot, helmsman

dēstringō, -ere, -strīnxī, -strictus, draw, unsheathe

ēnsis, -is, *m.* sword

* cēterus, the other, the rest of

cōnscius, guilty, accomplice

* turba, band, crowd
* dubius, doubtful, unsteady, wavering
* regō, -ere, rēxī, rēctus, guide, control, steer

nāvita, -ae, *m.* sailor

* digitus, finger

Lyre reconstructed with diatonic scale of two octaves. Museum of Roman Civilization, Rome.

Museo della Civilta Romana, Fototeca Unione

Arion and the Dolphin

All the world knows about Arion and the spell that his music could cast
on birds and beasts.

> Quod mare nōn nōvit, quae nescit Arīona tellūs?
> Carmine currentēs ille tenēbat aquās.
> Saepe sequēns agnam lupus est hāc vōce retentus,
> saepe avidum fugiēns restitit agna lupum;
> saepe canēs leporēsque umbrā iacuēre sub ūnā,   5
> et stetit in saxō proxima cerva leae;
> et sine līte loquāx cum Palladis ālite cornīx
> sēdit, et accipitrī iūncta columba fuit.
> Cynthia saepe tuīs fertur, vōcālis Arīōn,
> tamquam frāternīs obstipuisse modīs.   10
> Nōmen Arīonium Siculās implēverat urbēs,
> captaque erat lyricīs Ausonis ōra sonīs.

With the wealth that he had amassed on a musical tour of Sicily and
Italy he was sailing home to Greece when the captain and crew plotted
to murder him for his gold.

> Inde, domum repetēns, puppem cōnscendit Arīōn,
> atque ita quaesītās arte ferēbat opēs.
> Forsitan, īnfēlīx, ventōs undāsque timēbās,   15
> at tibi nāve tuā tūtius aequor erat.
> Namque gubernātor dēstrictō cōnstitit ēnse,
> cēteraque armātā cōnscia turba manū.
> Quid tibi cum gladiō? Dubiam rege, nāvita, puppem!
> Nōn haec sunt digitīs arma tenenda tuīs.   20

The story of Arion is based on Herodotus, *History*, I. 23-24.

1 **Arīona:** Greek acc. sing. 2 **tenēbat** = **dētinēbat**, *used to hold back.* 4 **lupum:** object of
fugiēns. 5 **iacuēre** = **iacuērunt. ūnā:** *the same.* 6 **leae:** dat. w. **proxima.** 7 **Palladis ālite:**
the owl; chattering crow and silent owl were traditional enemies. 9 **Cynthia:** name for
Diana, from Mt. Cynthus in Delos, where she was born. **fertur:** *is said.* 10 **frāternīs:** i.e., of
Apollo, her brother. **modīs:** *melodies.* 11-12 **Nōmen . . . sonīs:** briefly suggesting that he had
made a musical tour of Sicily and southern Italy. 12 **capta:** *taken*, i.e., *enchanted.*

13 **domum:** to Corinth. 14 **ita quaesītās arte opēs:** *the riches he had earned thus by his
skill.* 15 **īnfēlīx:** apostrophe. Ovid is addressing Arion, as he had already done in l. 9; in
l. 19 he addresses the helmsman, and in l. 24, Apollo. 16 **nāve:** abl. of comparison; *safer
than your ship.* 18 **cōnscia:** i.e., they were in on the plot. 19 **tibi:** dat. of possession; *What
(business) have you with a sword?* 20 **Nōn haec arma:** a word-play on the two meanings
of **arma**, which can also mean the fittings of a ship.

* metus, -ūs, *m.* fear
vacuus, *w. abl.,* empty of, free from
* dēprecor (*dep.* 1), pray to avert
referō, -ferre, rettulī, relātus, take back, relate, recite
lyra, lyre
* venia, pardon, permission
corōna, crown, wreath
crīnis, -is, *m.* hair
decet, -ēre, -uit, suit, be becoming to
induō, -ere, -duī, -dūtus, put on
Tyrius, Tyrian
tīnctus, dyed, treated
mūrex, -ricis, *m.* purple fish, purple
palla, robe

26-30

ictus, struck
pollex, -licis, *m.* thumb
chorda, string, chord
flēbilis, -e, pitiful, sad
* numerus, number, measure, rhythm
velutī, as though
cānēns, -entis, white

* trāiciō, -ere, -iēcī, -iectus, put across, pierce
pinna (penna), feather
tempora, -um, *n. pl.* temples (of the head)
olor, -ōris, *m.* swan
* prōtinus, at once
ōrnātus, attired
dēsiliō, -īre, -siluī, -sultum, leap down
spargō, -ere, sparsī, sparsus, scatter, spatter
* impellō, -ere, -pulī, -pulsus, drive against
caerulus, dark blue, dark

31-36

delphīn, -īnis, *m.* dolphin
recurvus, curving
* memorō (1), relate, tell
* onus, oneris, *n.* burden, load
* suppōnō, -ere, -posuī, -positus, put . . . beneath
cithara, lyre
* pretium, price, value, reward
* vehō, -ere, vexī, vectus, carry, convey
aequoreus, of the sea
mulceō, -ēre, mulsī, mulsus, soothe, calm
* pius, pious, dutiful, virtuous
astrum, star

21 Mortem nōn dēprecor: *I am not pleading for life.* **22 liceat:** jussive subjv.; *let it be permitted = allow me.* **pauca referre:** *to sing and play a little.* **23 rīdent moram:** i.e., they are amused at his delaying tactics. **23-24 corōnam . . . tuōs:** i.e., laurel. **24 possit:** subjv. in rel. clause of characteristic; *the kind of wreath which could grace.* **25 bis tīnctam:** the double-dyed purple cloth was the most expensive kind. **26 suōs:** *its own = familiar, true.* **28 pinnā:** *feather, arrow* by metonymy. **tempora:** acc. of respect w. **trāiectus;** *having been pierced as to temples = wounded in the temples.* **olor:** according to legend, the song of a dying swan was peculiarly moving.

Vēiēns, -entis, of Veii
* ter, three times
* cadō, -ere, cecidī, cāsum, fall
* vīrēs, -ium, *f. pl.* power, strength

* onus, oneris, *n.* burden
* suscipiō, -ere, -cēpī, -ceptus, undertake
gentīlis, -is, *m.* man of the *gens* (clan)
profiteor, -ērī, -fessus sum, offer, volunteer
* generōsus, noble

Īd. Febr. = Īdūs Februāriae, the Ides of February, the thirteenth.

1 Vēientibus armīs: *by the arms of Veii,* i.e., *in fighting against the men of Veii;* Veii was an Etruscan town a few miles north of Rome. The story of the Fabii is also told in Livy (*Ab Urbe Condita,* II. 48-50). **2 ter centum ter duo** = 306. **3 vīrēs . . . suscēperat:** zeugma; *had sustained the strength and had taken up the burden.* **onus:** Rome was on the verge of war with the Aequi and the Volsci, and the Sabines and the other Etruscan towns were

The minstrel asked to perform one last time. Having done so, he leapt into the sea.

> Ille metū vacuus, "Mortem nōn dēprecor," inquit,
>   "sed liceat sūmptā pauca referre lyrā."
> Dant veniam rīdentque moram. Capit ille corōnam
>   quae possit crīnēs, Phoebe, decēre tuōs;
> induerat Tyriō bis tīnctam mūrice pallam;   25
>   reddidit icta suōs pollice chorda sonōs,
> flēbilibus numerīs velutī cānentia dūrā
>   trāiectus pinnā tempora cantat olor.
> Prōtinus in mediās ōrnātus dēsilit undās;
>   spargitur impulsā caerula puppis aquā.   30

A dolphin, charmed by his music, carried Arion safely to shore. As a reward Jupiter made the dolphin a constellation.

> Inde—fidē maius—tergō delphīna recurvō
>   sē memorant onerī supposuisse novō.
> Ille sedēns citharamque tenet, pretiumque vehendī,
>   cantat et aequoreās carmine mulcet aquās.
> Dī pia facta vident. Astrīs delphīna recēpit   35
>   Iuppiter et stellās iussit habēre novem.
>   FASTI II. 83–

31 **fidē maius:** *greater than belief* = *too strange to believe.* **delphīna:** Greek acc. sing.
32 **onerī novō:** *the strange burden* (*Arion and his lyre*); indir. object of **supposuisse.**
33 **pretiumque: pretium** is in apposition w. the next line, while **-que** joins **cantat** w. **tenet.**
35 **Dī = Deī. Astrīs:** indir. obj. of **recēpit,** *among the stars* (*as the constellation Delphīnus*).
36 **novem:** to match the number of Muses, indicating the musical tastes of dolphins.

The Fabii Go to War

ĪD. FEBR.

February 13th is the anniversary of the slaughter of the Fabian tribe.

> Haec fuit illa diēs, in quā Vēientibus armīs
>   ter centum Fabiī ter cecidēre duo.
> Ūna domus vīrēs et onus suscēperat Urbis,
>   sūmunt gentīlēs arma professa manūs.
> Ēgreditur castrīs mīles generōsus ab īsdem,   5

hostile. The year was 477 B.C. 4 **gentīlēs:** subject of **sūmunt;** *the men of the clan.* **professa manūs:** *that promise deeds of valor.* 5 **mīles:** collective sing.; *soldiery.* 6 **ē quīs = ē quibus;**

6-10

* fīō, fierī, factus sum, become, be made
quīlibet, quae-, quid-, any at all
* aptus, fit, suitable
Carmentis, -is, f. Roman goddess
Iānus, Italian god
* quisquis, quidquid, whoever, whatever
ōmen, ōminis, n. omen
* referō, -ferre, rettulī, relātus, relate, tell
vacō (1), w. abl., be free from
* culpa, guilt, blame

11-15

Cremera, -ae, m. stream near Veii, tributary of the Tiber
* tangō, -ere, tetigī, tāctus, touch, reach
rapāx, -ācis, greedy, rushing
turbidus, wild, stormy
hībernus, wintry
* fluō, -ere, flūxī, flūxum, flow, run
dēstrictus, drawn, unsheathed
ēnsis, -is, m. sword
Tyrrhēnus, Tyrrhenian, Etruscan
validus, strong, brave
* Mārs, Mārtis, m. god of war, war, battle
* aliter quam, otherwise than
Libycus, Libyan, African
leō, -ōnis, m. lion

16-20

invādō, -ere, -vāsī, -vāsus, go against, attack
sparsus, spread, scattered
arvum, field
grex, gregis, m. flock, herd
* inhonestus, dishonorable
Tuscus, Tuscan, Etruscan
rubeō, -ēre, -uī, be red
* iterum, again
* apertē, openly
* tēctus, hidden, concealed

21-25

* claudō, -ere, clausī, clausus, close, shut in

* ultimus, farthest
montānus, of the mountain
occulō, -ere, -uī, -tus, hide
fera, wild beast
armentum, herd
rārus, scattered, here and there
* cēterus, the rest of
virgultum, thicket
* abditus, hidden
* turba, crowd
* lateō, -ēre, -uī, be hidden, escape notice
velut, just as, as though
torrēns, -entis, m. torrent
unda, wave
pluviālis, -e, rainy, of rain
* auctus, increased, swollen

26-30

nix, nivis, f. snow
Zephyrus, West Wind
tepēns, -entis, warm, melting
sata, -ōrum, n. pl. crops
* soleō, -ēre, solitus sum, be accustomed
margō, -ginis, m. and f. margin, edge
* finiō, -īre, -iī, -ītus, end, confine
* vallēs, -is, f. valley
discursus, -ūs, m. running about, foray
* impleō, -ēre, -plēvī, -plētus, fill up
spernō, -ere, sprēvī, sprētus, despise, scorn
metus, -ūs, m. fear

31-35

quō, whither, (to) where
ruō, -ere, ruī, rutum, rush (blindly)
simplex, -plicis, simple, straightforward
nōbilitās, -ātis, f. nobility, nobleness
perfidus, treacherous, perfidious
* caveō, -ēre, cāvī, cautus, be on guard against
fraus, fraudis, f. treachery, trickery
* pereō, -īre, -iī, -itum, perish, be lost
prōsiliō, -īre, -uī, leap forth
* latus, -teris, n. side, region

with quīlibet, *any one of whom.* The antecedent is mīles; quīs is plural to agree with the suggested plural of the collective noun.

7 portae: gen. w. Iānō. The **porta Carmentis** or **Carmentālis,** in the early fortifications of Rome, was the gate on the Tiber side, near the only bridge across the river. **Iānō:** abl. of means with via; *The nearest way (the shortest route) is by the right-hand arch* . . . For an explanation of **Janus** = *arch* v.I.P.N., **Janus. 8 hanc:** the antecedent is **via. ōmen habet:** the route was unlucky because of the disaster which overtook the Fabii, as indicated in the next two lines. Livy (II, 49) calls the route **īnfēlīx:** [Fabiī], **īnfēlīce viā, dextrō Iānō portae Carmentālis** (*through the right-hand arch of the Carmental gate*) **profectī. 9 Illā:** supply viā; *By that route.* **11 tetigēre** = tetigērunt. **12 ille:** the antecedent is **Cremeram;** names of rivers are usually masculine, regardless of their declension. **13 locō:** abl. of place where without a preposition; *in a suitable place.* **14 Tyrrhēnum:** *Etruscan.* **Mārte** = **bellō** (by ē quīs dux fierī quīlibet aptus erat.

The Fabii march out and establish a camp on the Cremera, from which
they raid the territory of Veii.

Carmentis portae dextrō est via proxima Iānō;
　īre per hanc nōlī, quisquis es: ōmen habet!
Illā fāma refert Fabiōs exīsse trecentōs;
　porta vacat culpā, sed tamen ōmen habet.　　　　　　　　　*10*
Ut celerī passū Cremeram tetigēre rapācem,
　(turbidus hībernīs ille fluēbat aquīs)
castra locō pōnunt. Dēstrictīs ēnsibus ipsī
　Tyrrhēnum validō Mārte per agmen eunt
nōn aliter quam cum Libycā dē gente leōnēs　　　　　　　　*15*
　invādunt sparsōs lāta per arva gregēs.
Diffugiunt hostēs inhonestaque vulnera tergō
　accipiunt. Tuscō sanguine terra rubet.
Sīc iterum, sīc saepe cadunt.

The enemy prepare an ambush, and the Fabii are destroyed.

　　　　　　　Ubi vincere apertē
nōn datur, īnsidiās armaque tēcta parant.　　　　　　　　*20*
Campus erat, campī claudēbant ultima collēs
　silvaque montānās occulere apta ferās;
in mediō paucōs armentaque rāra relinquunt,
　cētera virgultīs abdita turba latet.
Ecce, velut torrēns undīs pluviālibus auctus　　　　　　　　*25*
　aut nive, quae Zephyrō victa tepente fluit,
per sata perque viās fertur nec, ut ante solēbat,
　rīpārum clausās margine fīnit aquās,
sīc Fabiī vallem lātīs discursibus implent,
　quodque vident, spernunt nec metus alter inest.　　　　　　*30*
Quō ruitis, generōsa domus? Male crēditis hostī!
　Simplex nōbilitās, perfida tēla cavē!
Fraude perit virtūs; in apertōs undique campōs
　prōsiliunt hostēs et latus omne tenent.
Quid faciant paucī contrā tot mīlia fortēs?　　　　　　　　*35*

metonymy); **validō Mārte**, *valiantly*. **15 Libycā dē gente:** favored by poets as particularly
ferocious lions.

20 datur: subject is **vincere** (**hostibus** is implied); *When the enemy cannot conquer . . .*
21 campī: gen. w. **ultima. ultima:** adj. used as a noun and object of **claudēbant;** *edges,
boundaries.* **26 victa:** *thawed, melted.* **28 fīnit:** *confines.* **30 metus alter:** *the other fear =
fear of the other group.*

31 Male crēditis: *You do wrong to trust.* **34 omne:** *every.* **35 faciant:** deliberative subjv.;
What are they to do? **36 restet:** subjv. in rel. clause of characteristic. With negatives, or

36-40

* restō, -āre, -stitī, remain, be left
* sīcut, just as
  aper, aprī, *m.* wild boar
  lātrātus, -ūs, *m.* barking
  fulmineus, like lightning
  dissipō (1), scatter
* canis, -is, *m. and f.* dog
  inultus, unavenged
  alternus, alternate, in turn

41-45

* perdō, -ere, -didī, -ditus, lose, destroy
  Herculeus, of Hercules

* supersum, -esse, -fuī, be left, survive
  sēmen, -minis, *n.* seed, offspring
* cōnsulō, -ere, -suluī, -sultus, plan, take counsel
  impūbēs, -is, beardless
* adhūc, hitherto, as yet

46-48

  Fabius, *adj.* Fabian
* scīlicet, of course, indeed
* ōlim, once, at some time
* nāscor, -ī, nātus sum, be born
  cūnctor (*dep.* 1), delay, hesitate
* restituō, -ere, -stituī, -stitūtus, restore

(as here) implied negatives, the subjv. is stronger than the indic.; *which can remain* rather than *which remains.* 37 silvīs: abl. of separation with longē; *far from.* 40 manū: in military terminology manus can mean *a sword-thrust;* hence, alternā manū means *with blows exchanged.*

43 ut . . . gentis: purpose clause, w. cōnsuluisse. Herculeae: for the claim of the Fabii to descent from Hercules, v. I.P.N., Fabii. 44 deōs cōnsuluisse: indir. statement, depending on crēdibile est. 47 Maxime: voc. Quintus Fabius Maximus Cunctator was the hero of the Hannibalic War as *the shield of Rome.* 48 cui: dat. of agent with restituenda. rēs cūnctandō restituenda: meant to recall a famous line in the *Annales* of the old Roman poet Ennius,

1-5

* trahō, -ere, trāxī, trāctus, draw, derive
* mēnsis, -is, *m.* month
  ultimus, last
* rēgnum, kingdom, reign
* iniūstus, unjust
* ēvertō, -ere, ēvertī, ēversus, overthrow, cause to fall

6-10

  turpis, -e, shameful, base
* ars, artis, *f.* skill, trick
* minimus, smallest, youngest
  prōlēs, -is, *f.* offspring, child
  manifestus, clear, evident, obvious
  sileō, -ēre, -uī, be silent
* nūdō (1), bare, expose
  inermis, -e, unarmed

Heading. Ante diem sextum Kalendās Mārtiās. Rēgifugium. Nefāstus: *The sixth day before the Kalends of March,* i.e., 24 February. Expulsion of the Kings. Unlucky. On a diēs nefāstus no legal or legislative business could be done. The story is based on Livy I. 54.

1 rēgis fuga: the expulsion of Tarquin the Proud, last king of Rome. illā: antecedent is fuga. 2 ab extrēmō mēnse: *from the end of the month.* nōmina = nōmen, i.e., rēgifugium. 4 iniūstus: he had succeeded to the throne by the murder of the previous king, his father-in-law, Servius Tullius. ad: *for.* 5 aliās, aliās: *some, other.* 6 Gabiōs: a powerful enemy of early Rome, 12 miles to the east (many Italian towns had plural names).

7 minimus: sc. nātū; *the youngest.* prōlēs manifesta: i.e., a chip off the old block. 9 Nūdārant = Nūdāverant: subject is hostēs. inermem: used as a noun; *an unarmed man.* 10 cupiant: potential subjv.; *would like.* 11 terga: pl. for sing., as often with parts of the

quidve, quod in miserō tempore restet, habent?
Sīcut aper, longē silvīs lātrātibus āctus,
  fulmineō celerēs dissipat ōre canēs,
mox tamen ipse perit, sīc nōn moriuntur inultī
  vulneraque alternā dantque feruntque manū.   *40*
Ūna diēs Fabiōs ad bellum mīserat omnēs,
  ad bellum missōs perdidit ūna diēs.

One boy survives to become the ancestor of Q. Fabius Maximus.

Ut tamen Herculeae superessent sēmina gentis,
  crēdibile est ipsōs cōnsuluisse deōs;
nam puer impūbēs et adhūc nōn ūtilis armīs   *45*
  ūnus dē Fabiā gente relictus erat,
scīlicet ut possēs ōlim tū, Maxime, nāscī
  cui rēs cūnctandō restituenda foret.
                                           FASTI II. 195–

Ūnus homō nōbīs cūnctandō restituit rem, *One man by delaying restored the common-*
wealth for us. restituenda foret, *was to be restored.* foret = esset; subjv. in rel. clause of
characteristic.

![Greek key border pattern]

How Gabii Was Taken

VI KAL. MĀRT. RĒGIF. N.

Tarquin, last of Rome's kings, captured the town of Gabii by trickery.

Nunc mihi dīcenda est rēgis fuga. Trāxit ab illā
  sextus ab extrēmō nōmina mēnse diēs.
Ultima Tarquinius Rōmānae gentis habēbat
  rēgna, vir iniūstus, fortis ad arma tamen.
Cēperat hic aliās, aliās ēverterat urbēs   5
  et Gabiōs turpī fēcerat arte suōs.

Tarquin's youngest son pretended that he had been cruelly beaten by
his father and expelled from Rome.

Namque trium minimus, prōlēs manifesta Superbī,
  in mediōs hostēs nocte silente venit.
Nūdārant gladiōs: "Occīdite," dīxit, "inermem!
  Hoc cupiant frātrēs Tarquiniusque pater,   *10*

49

crūdēlis, -e, cruel
lacerō (1), lacerate, mangle, disfigure
verber, -eris, n. lash
° patior, -ī, passus sum, bear, endure
iuvenis, -is, m. youth, young man
recondō, -ere, -didī, -ditus, put back
° dēdūcō, -ere, -dūxī, -ductus, draw down
° vestis, -is, f. clothing
notō (1), mark, brand
° fleō, -ēre, flēvī, flētus, weep
tueor, -ērī, tūtus sum, protect, care for
° precor (dep. 1), pray, plead

16-20

callidus, -a, -um, crafty, wily, shrewd
ignārus, ignorant, unaware
adnuō, -ere, -nuī, -nūtum, nod assent
° potēns, -entis, powerful
genitor, -ōris, m. father
appellō (1), appeal to
° perdō, -ere, -didī, -ditus, destroy, ruin, lose
° hortus, garden
odōrātus, fragrant
subsum, -esse, -fuī, be nearby

° cultus, cultivated, tended
° herba, grass, herb
secō, -āre, secuī, sectus, cut, divide
° humus, -ī, f. ground, soil
° rīvus, stream
lēne = lēniter, gently
sonō, -āre, sonuī, sonitum, sound, murmur

21-26

° illīc, there
mandātum, message, instruction
latēns, -entis, hidden, secret
° nātus, son
virga, rod, stick
līlium, lily
metō, -ere, messuī, messus, reap, cut off
dēcutiō, -ere, -cussī, -cussus, strike down, cut off
° agnōscō, -ere, agnōvī, agnitus, recognize, understand
° aiō, def. say
Gabīnus, of Gabii
° moenia, -ium, n. pl. walls, fortifications
° nūdus, bare, defenseless

body. **12 Dīcere . . . posset:** purpose clause. **verbera . . . erat:** through connivance with his father; the beating had been carried out in public to make the deception more convincing.

15 Flent quoque: the beating must have been very severe. **ut . . . bella:** indir. command; *that he should support the wars with them,* i.e., *that he support them in the war.* **bella:** against King Tarquin. **17 potēns:** sc. **factus;** *having become powerful.* **18 perdendī . . . iter:** indir. question depending on the idea of asking implied in **appellat;** *what way he would show him of destroying Gabii.* **20 humum:** acc. of respect w. **sectus;** *having been cut as to the ground = where the ground was channeled.*

1-5

elementum, rudiment, beginning
° moenia, -ium, n. pl. walls, town
angustus, narrow, restricted

° turba, crowd, mob
° tunc, then
nimis, too, too much
° rēgia, (sc. domus), royal palace
° nātus, son

1 velīs: subjv. in fut. less vivid condition; *if you should wish to recall.* Mars is speaking to Ovid. **4 crēdita . . . suae:** *but believed at that time to be too large for its population.* **5 nostrī nātī:** *of my son,* i.e., Romulus. **6 aspice . . . domum:** *behold his house of reeds and thatch;* a primitive hut on the Palatine was long preserved as the house of Romulus.

qui mea crūdēlī lacerāvit verbere terga."
(Dīcere ut hoc posset, verbera passus erat.)

The men of Gabii readily believed the story and he soon rose to power
among them.

Lūna fuit; spectant iuvenem gladiōsque recondunt
    tergaque dēductā veste notāta vident.
Flent quoque et, ut sēcum tueātur bella, precantur;   15
    callidus ignārīs adnuit ille virīs.

The son then sent to his father for further instructions.

Iamque potēns missō genitōrem appellat amīcō,
    perdendī Gabiōs quod sibi mōnstret iter.
Hortus odōrātīs suberat cultissimus herbīs
    sectus humum rīvō lēne sonantis aquae.   20
Illīc Tarquinius mandāta latentia nātī
    accipit et virgā līlia summa metit.

The son did as ordered and Gabii was rendered defenseless. Gabii was
surrendered without a struggle.

Nūntius ut rediit dēcussaque līlia dīxit,
    fīlius, "Agnōscō iussa parentis," ait.
Nec mora, prīncipibus caesīs ex urbe Gabīnā,   25
    trāduntur ducibus moenia nūda suīs.
                                        FASTI II. 685–

23 ut: *when.* **dēcussa:** sc. **esse;** *that the lilies had been lopped off.* **25 Nec mora:** sc. **est;** *Nor is there delay = At once.* **26 ducibus.** abl. of separation w. **nūda;** *stripped of their leaders.*

The Sabine Women Intervene for Peace

The god Mars explains to Ovid why Roman matrons celebrate their
festival (Mātrōnālia) on the first day of his month (March 1).

"When Rome was first founded, her citizens could not find wives.
Wealthy neighbors refused to allow their daughters to marry Romans."

"Parva fuit, sī prīma velīs elementa referre,
    Rōma, sed in parvā spēs tamen Urbis erat.
Moenia iam stābant populīs angusta futūrīs,
    crēdita sed turbae tunc nimis ampla suae.
Quae fuerit nostrī, sī quaeris, rēgia nātī,   5

51

* aspiciō, -ere, aspexī, aspectus, look at, view
canna, reed, cane
strāmen, -minis, n. straw, thatch
stipula, stalk, stubble
placidus, calm, peaceful
* mūnus, -neris, n. service, gift
* somnus, sleep
* astrum, star
torus, couch, bed
* coniūnx, -iugis, m. and f. husband, wife
* socer, -erī, m. father-in-law

11-15

* spernō, -ere, sprēvī, sprētus, scorn, despise
* gener, -erī, m. son-in-law
inops, -opis, destitute, needy
* vīcīnia, neighborhood
* dīves, -vitis, rich
sanguis, sanguinis, m. blood, family, race
auctor, -ōris, m. author, founder
stabulum, stable, stall
* ovis, -is, f. sheep
* pāscō, -ere, pāvī, pāstus, feed, graze
iūgerum, land measure (about ⅔ of an acre)

* incultus, uncultivated
* solum, ground, land
* coeō, -īre, -iī, -itum, meet, assemble, mate
volucris, -is, f. bird
fera, wild beast

16-20

prōcreō (1), beget, produce
anguis, -is, m. and f. snake
* cōnūbium, marriage
* nūbō, -ere, nūpsī, nūptum, w. dat., marry
indolēscō, -ere, -doluī, feel pained
* patrius, of the father
* prex, precis, f. prayer, entreaty

21-25

* fēstum, feast, festival
Cōnsus, ancient Italian god
cēterī, -ae, -a, the other, the rest
sacrum, holy thing, rite
* canō, -ere, cecinī, cantus, sing, prophesy
intumēscō, -ere, -tumuī, begin to swell, become angry
Curēs, -ium, m. pl. Cures, a Sabine town
attingō, -ere, -tigī, -tāctus, touch, affect
ferē, nearly, generally

8 vēnit in astra: after his death Romulus was deified under the name Quirinus. 9 locō: abl. of comparison, *too big for the place;* Rome's fame had begun to spread. Rōmānus: collective sing. for Rōmānī. 10 illī: collective sing., dat. of possession. 11 vīcīnia dīves: *the rich neighboroood = the rich neighbors.* 12 male = nōn. crēdēbar: sc. esse; *I was not believed to be the author of their birth (as father of the twins, Romulus and Remus).*

13 nocēbat: the infinitives are the subject; *it hurt* (i.e., *damaged their reputation*) *that they had dwelt,* etc. 15 Cum pare quaeque suō: *Each with its own mate.* pare: 3rd declension adjectives having only one form in the nom. sing. often have an abl. sing. ending in -e. 16 prōcreet: subjv. in rel. clause of characteristic; *of whom to beget offspring.* 17 cōnūbia: *the right of intermarriage;* a technical term in Roman law, meaning that a marriage between citizens of different states would be recognized as legal by both states. 18 vellet: subjv. in rel. clause of characteristic; *who would be willing.*

19 patriam: *of your father,* i.e., a martial or warlike spirit. tibi, Rōmule: the rhetorical apostrophe is used here perhaps because Rōmulō is awkward metrically. 20 Quod: sc. id as antecedent; *What you seek,* i.e., wives. 21-22 Cōnsus . . . canēs: Ovid presumably intended to treat the festivals of Consus (19 August and 15 December) in Books VIII and XII of the *Fasti,* and would tell the story of the Sabine girls (already told in lines 49-78 of *Ars Amatoria*) under one of those headings. 23 Intumuēre (= Intumuērunt) . . . īdem: *Cures and those whom the same resentment touched* (= *The men of Cures and others who felt the same resentment*) *were furious.* Cures was the chief town of the Sabines. 24 tum prīmum: *that was the first time,* but not the last, Ovid implies; he has in mind the civil war between Caesar and Pompey, Caesar's son-in-law. intulit socer: for metrical convenience in place of intulērunt socerī.

25 raptae: the abducted Sabine women. mātrum . . . habēbant: they had borne children to their abductors. 26 trāctaque . . . morā: *and the wars between relatives had been drawn*

Mars in repose; at his feet is Cupid, son of Venus. Museum of the Baths of Diocletian, Rome.

Alinari, Fototeca Unione

' aspice dē cannā strāminibusque domum.
In stipulā placidī capiēbat mūnera somnī
    et tamen ex illō vēnit in astra torō.
Iamque locō maius nōmen Rōmānus habēbat,
    nec coniūnx illī nec socer ūllus erat.   10
Spernēbat generōs inopēs vīcīnia dīves,
    et male crēdēbar sanguinis auctor ego.
In stabulīs habitāsse et ovēs pāvisse nocēbat
    iūgeraque incultī pauca tenēre solī.
Cum pare quaeque suō coeunt volucrēsque feraeque,   15
    atque aliquam dē quā prōcreet anguis habet.
Extrēmīs dantur cōnūbia gentibus, at quae
    Rōmānō vellet nūbere, nūlla fuit.

"Romulus took my advice and gained by force the wives that his citizens wanted. A long war with neighboring peoples was the outcome."

Indoluī patriamque dedī tibi, Rōmule, mentem:
    "Tolle precēs," dīxī, "Quod petis, arma dabunt.   20
Fēsta parā Cōnsō." Cōnsus tibi cētera dīcet
    illō gesta diē, cum sua sacra canēs.
Intumuēre Curēs et quōs dolor attigit īdem;
    tum prīmum generīs intulit arma socer.
Iamque ferē raptae mātrum quoque nōmen habēbant,   25

53

nūpta, married woman, wife
dictus, appointed
Iūnō, -ōnis, f. Juno
aedēs, -is, f. temple
nurus, -ūs, f. daughter-in-law
° audeō, -ēre, ausus sum, *semi-dep.* dare, venture
pariter, equally, at the same time
quoniam, since
ultrā, beyond, further
lentē, slowly, calmly, indifferently
° pius, dutiful, loyal, good

° ēligō, -ere, ēlēgī, ēlēctus, pick out, choose
° hinc, from here, on this side
viduus, widowed
orbus, orphaned
° pāreō, -ēre, -uī, -itum, obey
° crīnis, -is, m. hair
resolvō, -ere, -solvī, -solūtus, loosen, undo

maestus, sad, sorrowful
fūnereus, funereal, of mourning
° tegō, -ere, tēxī, tēctus, hide, cover

° ferrum, iron, sword
lituus, trumpet
sinus, -ūs, m. bosom, breast, arms
pignus, -noris, n. pledge, security
° cārus, dear, loved

scissus, torn, disheveled
° tangō, -ere, tetigī, tāctus, touch, reach
° capillus, hair
prōcumbō, -ere, -cubuī, -cubitum, fall forward, bend down
genū, genūs, n. knee
° quasi, as if
blandus, winning, endearing
° nepōs, -ōtis, m. grandson
tendō, -ere, tetendī, tentus (tēnsus), stretch, hold out
° avus, grandfather
bracchium, arm
° dēnique, at last

° removeō, -ēre, -mōvī, -mōtus, remove, put aside
° nāta, daughter
° scūtum, shield
dulcis, -e, sweet, welcome

out with long delay (= *had continued for a long time*); it was three years from the abduction to the peace. **27 dictam** = **condictam**: *into the agreed-upon temple* = *into the temple, as agreed.* **28 quās inter** = **inter quās. mea nurus**: Hersilia, the wife of Romulus. **29 raptae**: voc. **30 nōn ultrā**: *no longer.* **lentē**: *at leisure.* **piae**: the Roman concept of **pietās** required a woman to be loyal both to her father and to her husband.

31 utrā . . . rogandī: indir. question; in prose order, **prō utrā parte dī** (= **deī**) **rogandī sint. 33 Quaerendum est**: sc. **vōbīs**; *you must ask.* (**utrum**) **viduae . . . orbae**: indir. question.

35 Cōnsilium: Ovid creates suspense by not telling us what the advice was. **35-36 crīnēsque . . . tegunt**: signs of mourning. **37 ferrō mortīque**: dat. w. **parātae. 38 pugnae**: objective gen. w. **signa. 40 pignora**: in apposition w. **nātōs**; *their children as pledges of love.* **41 medium**: neuter of the adj., used as noun; *the middle.* **43 sentīrent**: subjv. in conditional clause of comparison; *as if they understood.* **44 avōs**: their Sabine grandfathers. **45 Quī**: sc. **is** as antecedent; *The one who could.* **vīsum**: sc. **esse**; *that then at last he had seen his grandfather.* **46 posse . . . erat**: by the coaxing of the mother; some have suggested that the mothers pinched their children so that they would cry Ah vae! (*"Oh woe!"*) = Ave! (*O grandfather!*).

47 virīs: dat. of reference; *of the men* or *from the men.* **animī**: of anger. **48 dant . . . manūs**: in token of reconciliation. **49 laudātās tenent natās** = **laudant et tenent natās. scūtō**: abl. of means; *in a shield.*

Model showing a portion of a triumphal procession, the climax of a Roman military victory.

trāctaque erant longā bella propinqua morā.

"The wives followed the advice of Hersilia, wife of Romulus."

> Conveniunt nūptae dictam Iūnōnis in aedem,
> quās inter mea sīc est nurus ausa loquī,
> "Ō pariter raptae, quoniam hoc commūne tenēmus,
> nōn ultrā lentē possumus esse piae.   *30*
> Stant aciēs, sed utrā dī sint prō parte rogandī,
> ēligite! Hinc coniūnx, hinc pater arma tenet.
> Quaerendum est, viduae fierī mālītis an orbae!
> Cōnsilium vōbīs forte piumque dabō."
> Cōnsilium dederat. Pārent crīnēsque resolvunt   *35*
> maestaque fūnereā corpora veste tegunt.

"When battle was about to begin, the women intervened and effected a reconciliation between husbands and fathers."

> Iam stābant aciēs ferrō mortīque parātae,
> iam lituus pugnae signa datūrus erat,
> cum raptae veniunt inter patrēsque virōsque
> inque sinū nātōs, pignora cāra, tenent.   *40*
> Ut medium campī scissīs tetigēre capillīs,
> in terram positō prōcubuēre genū,
> et quasi sentīrent, blandō clāmōre nepōtēs
> tendēbant ad avōs bracchia parva suōs.
> Quī poterat, clāmābat avum tunc dēnique vīsum,   *45*
> et quī vix poterat, posse coāctus erat.
> Tēla virīs animīque cadunt, gladiīsque remōtīs
> dant socerī generīs accipiuntque manūs,
> laudātāsque tenent nātās, scūtōque nepōtem
> fert avus: hic scūtī dulcior ūsus erat."   *50*
>
> FASTI III. 179–

Faustulus discovers the twins. Figures at left are local divinities. Rubens (1577-1640). Capitoline Gallery, Rome.

1-5

luō, -ere, luī, pay, undergo
Numitor, -ōris, *m.* king of Alba
° pāstor, -ōris, *m.* shepherd
geminus, twin
° vulgus, -ī, *n.* common people
° contrahō, -ere, -trāxī, -trāctus, draw together, assemble
agrestis, -is, *m.* person living in the country
° moenia, -ium, *n. pl.* fortifications, city walls, city
° convenit, -īre, -vēnit, -ventus, it is agreed
ambigō, -ere, argue, debate
° opus est, *w. abl.,* there is need of
certāmen, -minis, *n.* contest, struggle

6-10

° avis, -is, *f.* bird
experior, -īrī, -pertus sum, test, make trial of
nemorōsus, wooded, leafy
Palātium, the Palatine Hill
Aventīnus, of the Aventine

māne, in the morning, early
cacūmen, -minis, *n.* peak, summit
volucris, -is, *f.* bird
pactum, agreement
arbitrium, judgment, decision

11-15

° aptus, fit, suitable
° legō, -ere, lēgī, lēctus, pick, choose
° signō (1), mark, trace
° arātrum, plow
° sacra, -ōrum, *n. pl.* festival
Palēs, -is, *f.* goddess of shepherds
subsum, -esse, be underneath, be at hand
° fossa, ditch, trench
solidus, firm, solid
frūx, frūgis, *f.* fruit of the earth
° vīcīnus, neighboring, nearby
° solum, ground, soil
° repleō, -ēre, -plēvī, -plētus, fill again
° humus, -ī, *f.* earth, ground
° plēnus, full
° impōnō, -ere, -posuī, -positus, place upon
āra, altar

XI. KAL. MĀI. = ante diem ūndecimum Kalendās Māiās, *the eleventh day before the Kalends of May,* i.e., 21 April.

2 geminō sub duce = geminīs sub ducibus: Romulus and Remus. 3-4 utrīque: dat. w. convenit; *it is agreeable to each of the two = both agree.* 4 moenia . . . uter: indir. question;

56

The Founding of Rome

XI KAL. MĀI.

King Numitor of Alba Longa had been ousted by his brother Amulius. The usurper had cast Numitor's twin grandsons adrift on the Tiber. They were washed ashore, rescued by a she-wolf, and raised by a shepherd. When they grew up, they punished Amulius, restored Numitor to his throne as king of Alba Longa, and decided to found a city on the spot where they had been washed ashore.

With recourse to augury, Romulus wins the right to be the founder of the city.

> Iam luerat poenās frāter Numitōris, et omne
> pāstōrum geminō sub duce vulgus erat.
> Contrahere agrestēs et moenia pōnere utrīque
> convenit; ambigitur, moenia pōnat uter.
> "Nīl opus est," dīxit, "certāmine," Rōmulus, "ūllō.   5
> Magna fidēs avium est. Experiāmur avēs."
> Rēs placet. Alter init nemorōsī saxa Palātī,
> alter Aventīnum māne cacūmen init.
> Sex Remus, hic volucrēs bis sex videt ōrdine. Pactō
> stātur, et arbitrium Rōmulus urbis habet.   10

The ceremonial founding begins on the festival of Pales.

> Apta diēs legitur, quā moenia signet arātrō.
> Sacra Palis suberant: inde movētur opus.
> Fossa fit ad solidum, frūgēs iaciuntur in īma,
> et dē vīcīnō terra petīta solō.
> Fossa replētur humō, plēnaeque impōnitur āra,   15

---

which of the two is to establish the walls = *found the city.* **5 certāmine:** abl. of means w. **opus est;** *There is no need of any controversy.* **6 fidēs:** *reliability.* **Experiāmur:** hortatory subjv.; *Let us try.* The Romans used augury (observation of the flight of birds) to discover the will of the gods.

9 bis sex: as Romulus sees twice as many birds as his brother, he wins the right to found the city. **ōrdine:** *in a row.* **9-10 Pactō stātur:** impers. pass.; *They stand by the agreement.* **11 signet:** subjv. in rel. clause of purpose; *on which to mark out.* **arātrō:** It was the practice of the Romans in founding a city that the founder should mark out its boundaries with a bronze plow drawn by a white bull yoked with a white cow (the white color symbolized good fortune). This furrow had a magical significance: the **imperium** of an enemy could not cross it. In order to leave a space through which the Roman **imperium** could be carried against the foe, the plow was lifted at the sites of future gates. **12 Sacra Palis:** held on 21 April, the traditional date for the founding of Rome. **inde:** *from that date.* **movētur:** *begins.* **13 Fossa:** the **mundus,** a ritual pit dug on the spot where the first auguries were taken and the first surveys of the new city made. **fit ad solidum:** *is dug down to solid rock.* **īma:** used as noun, n. pl.; *the bottom.* **13-14 frūgēs, terra:** the grain represents "the first-fruits of all things either good by custom or necessary by nature; lastly, every man taking a small piece of earth of the country from whence he came, they all threw in promiscuously together." (Plutarch, *Life of Romulus,* Dryden's translation). **15 plēnae:** sc. **fossae,** dat. w. compound verb **impōnitur;** *and over the ditch, when filled in, is placed . . .* **16 accēnsō igne:** abl. w. **fungitur:** *serves the fire that has been kindled.*

* accendō, -ere, -cendī, -cēnsus, kindle, light
fungor, -ī, fūnctus sum, w. abl., perform, serve
focus, hearth, fireplace
stīva, plow handle
* dēsignō (1), mark off, trace out
sulcus, furrow, trench
albus, white
iugum, yoke
niveus, snowy, white
* bōs, bovis, m. bull
vacca, cow
* condō, -ere, -didī, -ditus, build, found
genitor, -ōris, m. father
Māvors, -ortis, m. old name for Mars
Vesta, goddess of the hearth

21-25

* pius, pious, devout
* adhibeō, -ēre, -hibuī, -hibitus, admit, summon
* advertō, -ere, -vertī, -versus, turn, attend
cūnctus, all, whole
auspex, -picis, m. and f. augur, protector
* surgō, -ere, surrēxī, surrēctum, rise
* domina, mistress
potentia, power
oriēns, -entis, rising, eastern
occiduus, setting, western
* precor (dep. 1), pray
tonitrus, -ūs, m. thunder
ōmen, ōminis, n. omen, sign, portent
laevus, left

26-30

fulmen, -minis, n. thunderbolt
polus, pole, sky
augurium, augury, omen
* laetus, happy, glad
fundāmen, -minis, n. foundation
exiguus, narrow, short, small
Celer, -eris, m. name of a knight of Romulus

urgeō, -ēre, ursī, push forward, urge on

31-35

nēve, and not
vōmer, -meris, m. plowshare
* audeō, -ēre, ausus sum, semi-dep. dare
* dēdō, -ere, -didī, -ditus, give up, devote
nex, necis, f. death
ignōrō (1), not know, be ignorant of
humilis, -e, low, humble
contemnō, -ere, -tempsī, -temptus, despise, scorn
trānsiliō, -īre, -siluī, jump across
rūtrum, spade

36-40

sanguinolentus, bloody
* discō, -ere, didicī, learn
intrōrsus, within
oborior, -īrī, -ortus sum, spring up
dēvorō (1), swallow, gulp down, repress
* pectus, -toris, n. chest, breast
* fleō, -ēre, flēvī, flētus, cry, weep (for)
palam, openly
* exemplum, pattern, example
* aiō, def. speak, say

41-45

exsequiae, -ārum, f. pl. funeral rites
suspendō, -ere, -pendī, -pēnsus, hang up, repress
* flētus, -ūs, m. weeping
* pietās, -ātis, f. piety, brotherly love
dissimulō (1), hide, dissemble
pateō, -ēre, -uī, be open, be evident
* ōsculum, kiss
applicō, -āre, -āvī (-uī), -ātus (-itus), apply, bring, add
* suprēmus, last, highest
feretrum, bier
* invītus, unwilling, reluctant
adimō, -ere, -ēmī, -ēmptus, take away
* ārdeō, -ēre, ārsī, ārsum, burn
artus, -ūs, m. limb
ungō, -ere, ūnxī, ūnctus, anoint

17-18 Inde . . . tulit: see note on line 11, arātrō. 19 Condentī: sc. mihi, dat. w. compound verb ades; *Help me while I found.* 19-20 Iuppiter, Māvors, Vesta: voc. case; but the verb is sing., agreeing with the last addressed. 21 quōs: antecedent is cūnctī; *all whom it is holy to invoke as gods.* Roman prayers usually included some such clause, to ensure that no interested gods would be offended by being omitted. 22 Auspicibus vōbīs: abl. abs. mihi: dat. of reference; *for me, of mine.* surgat: optative subjv.; *may this work rise.* 23 sit: optative subjv. huic dominae terrae: dat. of possession; *may there be for this ruling land (may this ruling land have).* -que: to be taken w. potentia. 24 oriēns . . . diēs: *the rising and the setting day = East and West.*

25 tonitrū laevō: omens on the augur's left (the east side) were regarded by the Romans as favorable. 27 Auguriō: abl. of cause w. laetī. 29 Celer: the head of the Celeres, knights who acted as the royal bodyguard. vocārat = vocāverat. 30 Sint: *Let those matters be your concern.* cūrae tuae: dat. of purpose. 31-32 nēve quis trānseat: jussive subj.; *and let no one*

et novus accēnsō fungitur igne focus.
Inde premēns stīvam dēsignat moenia sulcō;
alba iugum niveō cum bove vacca tulit.

Romulus prays that his city may endure and become great. Jupiter
shows his approval.

Vōx fuit haec rēgis: "Condentī, Iuppiter, urbem,
et genitor Māvors Vestaque māter, ades,   20
quōsque pium est adhibēre deōs, advertite, cūnctī!
Auspicibus vōbīs, hoc mihi surgat opus!
Longa sit huic aetās dominaeque potentia terrae,
sitque sub hāc oriēns occiduusque diēs!"
Ille precābātur; tonitrū dedit ōmina laevō   25
Iuppiter et laevō fulmina missa polō.

Remus leaps over the low city wall. Celer strikes him down.

Auguriō laetī iaciunt fundāmina cīvēs
et novus exiguō tempore mūrus erat.
Hoc Celer urget opus, quem Rōmulus ipse vocārat,
"Sint"que, "Celer, cūrae," dīxerat, "ista tuae,   30
nēve quis aut mūrōs aut factam vōmere fossam
trānseat! Audentem tālia dēde necī."
Quod Remus ignōrāns, humilēs contemnere mūrōs
coepit et, "Hīs populus," dīcere, "tūtus erit?"
Nec mora, trānsiluit. Rūtrō Celer occupat ausum.   35
Ille premit dūram sanguinolentus humum.

Romulus approves Celer's action but mourns for his brother. Remus is
given honorable burial.

Haec ubi rēx didicit, lacrimās intrōrsus obortās
dēvorat et clausum pectore vulnus habet.
Flēre palam nōn vult exemplaque fortia servat,
"Sīc"que "meōs mūrōs trānseat hostis," ait.   40
Dat tamen exsequiās nec iam suspendere flētum
sustinet, et pietās dissimulāta patet,
ōsculaque applicuit positō suprēma feretrō
atque ait, "Invītō frāter adēmpte, valē!"
Ārsūrōsque artūs ūnxit. Fēcēre, quod ille,   45

---

cross. **32 tālia:** direct object of **audentem. 33 Quod:** direct object of **ignōrāns;** *And not
knowing about this (command).* **34 Hīs:** sc. **mūrīs.**

35 Nec mora: sc. **erat** = **Sine morā** or **Statim. ausum:** sc. **eum;** *strikes him down when
he has dared to do this.* **39 exemplaque . . . servat:** *and maintains an example of fortitude.*
40 Sīc: *On these terms.* **trānseat:** optative subjv. **41 nec iam:** *and no longer.* **44 Invītō:**
sc. **mihi,** dat. w. **adēmpte** (voc. case); *Taken from me against my will.*

45 Ārsūrōs: *Destined to be cremated (on the funeral pyre).* **Fēcēre** = **Fēcērunt. quod:** sc.
idem as antecedent; *did the same as he.* **46 Faustulus et Acca:** the shepherd and his wife

46-48

maestus, sad, sorrowful

solvō, -ere, solvī, solūtus, set free, loosen

* iuvenis, -is, *m.* youth

* Quirītēs, -ium, *m. pl.* Roman citizens

plōrō (1), weep for, bewail

* subdō, -ere, -didī, -ditus, put under

rogus, funeral pyre

who had reared the twins. **comās**: acc. of respect w. **solūta**; *loosened as to her sad hair = sadly loosening her hair.* **47 nōndum**: modifies **factī. flēvēre = flēvērunt. Quirītēs**: subjective complement w. **factī**; *they, not yet called Quirites* (this name for Roman citizens was

1-5

Mercurius, Mercury

* vīcīnus, *w. dat.*, near, close to

Capēnus, of Capena

experior, -īrī, expertus sum, test, experience

* nūmen, -minis, *n.* divine power

incīnctus, girded

tunica, tunic

urna, water jar, urn

* pūrus, cleansed, undefiled, pure

suffītus, fumigated, perfumed

hauriō, -īre, hausī, haustus, draw, drain

* ūdus, wet, moist, soaked

* hinc, from here, hence, from this source

* laurus, -ī, *f.* laurel tree, laurel branch

* spargō, -ere, sparsī, sparsus, sprinkle, scatter

6-10

rōrō (1), bedew, wet

* capillus, hair

peragō, -ere, -ēgī, -āctus, finish, complete

solitus, accustomed

* fallō, -ere, fefellī, falsus, cheat, deceive

* prex, precis, *f.* prayer

abluō, -ere, -luī, -lūtus, wash away, remove

praeteritus, past, bygone

* periūrium, perjury

perfidus, treacherous, dishonest

11-15

* sīve ... sīve, whether ... or; if ... or if

* testis, -is, *m. and f.* witness

* falsō, falsely

citō, (1), cite, appeal to

* Iuppiter, Iovis, *m.* Jupiter

prūdēns, -entis, knowing, being aware

* dīva, goddess

* auferō, -ferre, abstulī, ablātus, carry away

improbus, wicked, dishonest

Notus, South Wind

pateō, -ēre, -uī, be open, be ready

Mercury in repose. National Museum, Naples.

ĪD. MĀI. = ĪDŪS MĀIAE: *Ides of May;* 15 May, the date for the dedication of the temple to Mercury, the god of trade and profit, became a festival day for merchants.

1 aqua: a fountain near the temple of Mercury which was on the Aventine overlooking the Circus Maximus. The spring was near the Porta Capena (from which the Via Appia ran as the main route to southern Italy) and was popularly supposed to wash away perjury so that the perjurer could make a fresh start. **2 iuvat**: impers.; sc. **vōs**, *if it pleases you* (= *if you care*) *to believe those who have tested it.* **3 incīnctus tunicā**: *with his tunic girded up*

Faustulus et maestās Acca solūta comās.
Tum iuvenem nōndum factī flēvēre Quirītēs.
Ultima plōrātō subdita flamma rogō est.

FASTI IV. 809–

not adopted until the union between the Romans and the Sabines). **48 plōrātō rogō:** dat. w.
the compound verb **subdita est;** *was put under the funeral pyre when the mourning was
ended.*

The Lying Merchant Prays to Mercury

ĪD. MĀI.

It is the festival of Mercury on the Ides of May. Near the Porta Capena
a typical merchant sprinkles himself and his merchandise with hal-
lowed water and offers a prayer to Mercury.

Est aqua Mercuriī portae vīcīna Capēnae;
    sī iuvat expertīs crēdere, nūmen habet.
Hūc venit incīnctus tunicā mercātor et urnā
    pūrus suffītā quam ferat haurit aquam.
Ūda fit hinc laurus, laurō sparguntur ab ūdā   5
    omnia quae dominōs sunt habitūra novōs.
Spargit et ipse suōs laurō rōrante capillōs,
    et peragit solitā fallere vōce precēs.

"Forget and forgive, O Mercury, my lies and crooked dealings in the
past. Cleanse me of all iniquity, and give me license to cheat and trick
in the days ahead."

"Ablue praeteritī periūria temporis," inquit,
    "Ablue praeteritae perfida verba diē!   10
Sīve ego tē fēcī testem falsōve citāvī
    nōn audītūrī nūmina magna Iovis,
sīve deum prūdēns alium dīvamve fefellī,
    abstulerint celerēs improba verba Notī,
et pateant veniente diē periūria nōbīs,   15

(*so that he will be free for action*). **tunicā:** abl. of specification. **4 suffītā:** the water jar has
already been purified. **quam ferat:** rel. clause of characteristic; *to carry.*

5 hinc = **ex aquā. laurus:** the laurel branch is used to sprinkle and purify the goods that
the merchant wants to sell. **7 Spargit . . . capillōs:** the merchant purifies his own person
before making his prayer. **solitā fallere:** *accustomed to deceive* = *trained in deceit.*

10 diē: gen. sing. (alternative form). **12 nōn audītūrī** = **quī nōn audiet,** since Jupiter
refuses to lend himself to crooked dealings. **13 prūdēns:** an adj. modifying the subject often
is equivalent to an adv.; *cleverly.* **14-16 abstulerint pateant, cūrent:** optative subjvs.; *may
the swift winds have taken away,* etc. **14 Notī:** specific winds, used to indicate winds
generally. **15 nōbīs** = **mihi. 16 sī qua:** *if any things (whatever things).* **18 fac ut:** *do so*

61

* **superī** (*sc.* deī), *m. pl.* the gods above
* **modo,** only, just
  lucrum, gain, profit
* **gaudium,** joy, pleasure
* **ēmptor, -ōris,** *m.* buyer
  verba dare, *w. dat.,* cheat, trick

* **poscō, -ere, poposcī,** demand, pray for
* **rīdeō, -ēre, rīsī, rīsus,** laugh at, smile upon
  altum, height, heaven
  memor, -oris, mindful, remembering
  Ortygius, Ortygian, Delian, of Apollo
  surripiō, -ere, -ripuī, -reptus, take away
  secretly, steal
* **bōs, bovis,** *m. and f.* ox, cow

that = *grant that.* **verba dedisse: verba dare,** i.e., *to give words* (*empty promises, instead of deeds*) is an idiom for *cheat.* **iuvet:** sc. **mē;** *it may give me joy.*

19 Tālia poscentēs = **Eōs quī tālia poscunt:** *Those who make prayers of this kind.* **rīdet:** affectionately; he is amused rather than shocked. **20 memor:** *remembering* = *because he*

  coniugium, marriage
* **scelus, -leris,** *n.* crime
  mercēs, -cēdis, *f.* pay, reward
  peragō, -ere, -ēgī, -āctus, carry through, complete
* **soleō, -ēre, solitus sum,** be accustomed
* **dictum,** word, remark
  exstimulō (1), goad on
* **pius,** dutiful, loyal, devoted
* **coniūnx, -iugis,** *m. and f.* husband, wife
  dōtālis, -e, dotal, of a dowry
* **parēns, -entis,** *m. and f.* parent, father, mother
  exigō, -ere, -ēgī, -āctus, demand, claim
  dōs, dōtis, *f.* dowry
* **opēs, opum,** *f. pl.* wealth, resources
* **rēgius,** royal, regal

  socer, -erī, *m.* father-in-law
  necō (1), kill
* **patrius,** of a father
  tingō, -ere, tīnxī, tīnctus, dip, stain
  īnstīnctus, goaded, incited
  solium, throne
  prīvātus, lacking official office, private person
  attonitus, bewildered, thunderstruck
* **vulgus, -ī,** *n.* the common people
  ruō, -ere, ruī, rutum, rush
* **hinc,** hence, from this
  cruor, -ōris, *m.* bloodshed
  īnfirmus, weak
  scēptrum, scepter, kingship
  gener, -erī, *m.* son-in-law
  Esquiliae, *f. pl.* the Esquiline Hill
* **rēgia** (*sc.* domus), royal palace

III ĪD. IŪN. = **ante diem tertium Īdūs Iūniās:** *the third day before the Ides of June,* i.e., 11 June. The story of the death of Servius Tullius and the naming of the Street of Crime (**Vīcus Scelerātus**), here recounted in swift, graphic style, is given in more detail by Livy (I. 46-48).

1 Tullia: daughter of the king, Servius Tullius. **mercēde:** in apposition w. **coniugiō. 2 virum:** *her husband,* Lucius Tarquinius, the future Tarquinius Superbus (last of Rome's seven kings). **3 Quid . . . parēs:** *What pleasure does it give you and me to be marriage-partners?* **nostrae** = **meae. 5 Vīvere dēbuerant:** *ought to have stayed alive.* **6 ausūrī erāmus:** fut. periphrastic; *we meant to venture on.*

7 dōtāle: used as a noun, predicate acc. w. **faciō;** *I make both the life and the kingdom of my father my dowry* = *I am offering as dowry the life of my father and his kingdom too.* **8 ī:** imper. of **eō. dictās opēs:** *the promised power.* **9 Rēgia . . . est:** *The crime is a kingly deed.* **Socerō necātō:** abl. abs.

11-14 Ovid compresses into four lines what Livy relates in detail: Tarquin with an armed band had gone to the forum, sat on the royal throne, summoned a meeting of the senate, and denounced Servius Tullius as a usurper (Tarquin was the son, Servius only the adopted son, of Tarquinius Priscus, the previous king). During an angry dispute between Servius and Tarquin, the latter flung the king down the steps of the senate house. The king returned

nec cūrent superī sī qua locūtus erō!
Dā modo lucra mihī, dā factō gaudia lucrō
et fac ut ēmptōrī verba dedisse iuvet!"

Mercury smilingly approves, for this is a merchant after his own heart.

Tālia Mercurius poscentēs rīdet ab altō,
sē memor Ortygiās surripuisse bovēs.   *20*

FASTI V. 673–

remembers. **Ortygiās:** *Delian = of Apollo.* Mercury (Hermes to the Greeks) was only one day old when he drove off fifty cows belonging to Apollo, and then returned to his cradle. Naturally he became the god of all who delight in trickery.

How the Vicus Sceleratus Received Its Name

III ĪD. IŪN.

Tullia, daughter of King Servius Tullius, murdered her husband and persuaded her husband's brother, Lucius Tarquinius, to murder his wife (Tullia's own sister) so that they would be free to marry.

Tullia now goads her new husband to further crime. She urges him to kill the king (her own father) and reign in his stead.

Tullia coniugiō sceleris mercēde perāctō
    hīs solita est dictīs exstimulāre virum,
"Quid iuvat esse parēs, tē nostrae caede sorōris
    mēque tuī frātris, sī pia vīta placet?
Vīvere dēbuerant et vir meus et tua coniūnx,   *5*
    sī nūllum ausūrī maius erāmus opus.
Et caput et rēgnum faciō dōtāle parentis!
    Sī vir es, ī, dictās exige dōtis opēs.
Rēgia rēs scelus est! Socerō cape rēgna necātō
    et nostrās patriō sanguine tinge manūs!"   *10*

Lucius Tarquinius rouses the people and dethrones Servius. The king's dead body is left on the road near the Esquiline.

Tālibus īnstīnctus soliō prīvātus in altō
    sēderat; attonitum vulgus in arma ruit.
Hinc cruor et caedēs, īnfirmaque vincitur aetās;
    scēptra gener socerō rapta Superbus habet.
Ipse sub Esquiliīs, ubi erat sua rēgia, caesus   *15*

home, only to be murdered by Tarquin's followers; his body was thrown into the street. Tullia drove to the senate house to be the first to hail her husband as king. **11 prīvātus:** *though a private person = though not the king.* **13 Hinc:** sc. **sunt. īnfirma aetās:** Servius Tullius had been king for 43 years at the time of the murder. **14 socerō:** abl. of separation w. **rapta.**

63

* concidō, -ere, -cidī, fall, collapse
sanguinolentus, bloody
* humus, -ī, f. ground
carpentum, two-wheeled carriage
penātēs, -ium, m. pl. household gods, home
altus, tall, arrogant, haughty
ferōx, -ōcis, spirited, insolent
* aspiciō, -ere, -spexī, -spectus, gaze at
aurīga, -ae, m. groom, driver
* profundō, -ere, -fūdī, -fūsus, pour forth, shed
resistō, -ere, -stitī, stop, halt
corripiō, -ere, -ripuī, -reptus, catch up, reprimand

sonus, sound, tone, effect

vādō, -ere, go on
an, or
* pretium, price, reward, payment
* pietās, -ātis, f. duty, piety, pity, devotion
amārus, bitter
inquam, def. say
* invītus, unwilling, reluctant
* ōs, ōris, n. mouth, face
rota, wheel
* factum, action, deed
* scelerātus, wicked, criminal
vīcus, street, quarter
* aeternus, eternal, everlasting
nota, mark, sign, stigma

---

15 Esquiliīs: the Esquiline Hill had been incorporated into the city by Servius. 17 penātēs = domum (metonymy); Tullia wastes no time in moving into the palace of the dead king, her father. 18 mediās . . . viās: emphasizing her arrogance. 20 corripit: *she upbraids.* 22 invītās: emphatic; *whether they want to go or not.* 23-24 Certa, dictus, pressa: sc. est w. each.

Īdūs, -uum, f. pl. the Ides
Aprīlis, -e, (of) April
nefāstus, wicked, unlucky

1-5

exigō, -ere, -ēgī, -āctus, demand, require
raptus, -ūs, m. kidnaping
* ēdō, -ere, ēdidī, ēditus, put out, relate
* recognōscō, -ere, -nōvī, -nitus, recollect
scopulus, cliff, crag
vāstus, vast, immense
* prōcurrō, -ere, -currī, -cursum, run out
* aequor, -oris, n. level surface, sea
Trīnacris, -idis, (lit. with three promontories) Sicilian
positus, -ūs, m. position

* adipīscor, -ī, adeptus sum, get, obtain
* Cerēs, Cereris, f. Ceres, goddess of agriculture
* possideō, -ēre, -sēdī, -sessus, possess

6-10

* colō, -ere, coluī, cultus, till, cultivate
fertilis, -e, able to produce, fertile
* solum, ground, soil
* frīgidus, chill, cold
caelestis, -is, m. and f. god, goddess
flāvus, yellow, golden
daps, dapis, f. feast, meal
cōnsuētus, customary, usual
comitātus, accompanied, attended
prātum, meadow, field

Heading. Tertius diēs ante Īdūs Aprīlēs. Nefāstus: *11 April. Unlucky* (i.e., unsuitable for legal or legislative business).

1 locus: i.e., in the calendar. raptūs . . . ēdam: indir. command w. exigit. 2 plūra: *more things = the greater part.* recognōscēs: Ovid assumes that his Roman reader will know most of the story; it is told in the Homeric *Hymn to Demeter* and by Ovid himself in *Metamorphoses* (V. 385-661). pauca: object of docendus; doceō takes two objects and retains one in the passive. 3 scopulīs: abl. of means w. prōcurrit; the three angles of the triangular island of Sicily. 4 Trīnacris: adj., modifies terra. ā positū: *from the shape.* nōmen: direct object of adepta. 5 Cererī: dat. w. grāta. possidet: because she was worshipped as the chief goddess in these cities. Henna: town in central Sicily. 7 caelestum mātrēs: *mothers of the gods,* a periphrasis for *goddesses.* Arethūsa: the nymph of a spring

concidit in dūrā sanguinolentus humō.

On her way to the palace Tullia forces the driver of her carriage to drive over the dead body of the king, her own father. Her impious deed gives the street its name, *Vicus Sceleratus.*

Fīlia carpentō, patriōs initūra penātēs,
    ībat per mediās alta ferōxque viās.
Corpus ut aspexit, lacrimīs aurīga profūsīs
    restitit; hunc tālī corripit illa sonō,   20
"Vādis an exspectās pretium pietātis amārum?
    Dūc, inquam, invītās ipsa per ōra rotās!"
Certa fidēs factī: dictus Scelerātus ab illā
    vīcus, et aeternā rēs ea pressa notā.

                          FASTI VI. 587–

23 Scelerātus: the name *Street of Crime* was given to a street on the Esquiline, and Ovid's account in the *Fasti* gives June 11 as the day from which it took its name. **24 pressa:** *branded.*

Ceres Searches for Persephone

111 ĪD. APR. N.

The date records the abduction of Persephone. To the familiar story a few details will be added. Ceres had been invited to attend a festival arranged by Arethusa.

Exigit ipse locus, raptūs ut virginis ēdam;
    plūra recognōscēs, pauca docendus eris.
Terra tribus scopulīs vāstum prōcurrit in aequor
    Trīnacris, ā positū nōmen adepta locī,
grāta domus Cererī. Multās ibi possidet urbēs,   5
    in quibus est cultō fertilis Henna solō.
Frīgida caelestum mātrēs Arethūsa vocārat;
    vēnerat ad sacrās et dea flāva dapēs.

Persephone came too, and her girl companions. Happily they gathered flowers in a valley near Henna.

Fīlia, cōnsuētīs ut erat comitāta puellīs,
    errābat nūdō per sua prāta pede.   10

on the island of Ortygia in the harbor of Syracuse. Her story is told in *Arethusa.* (See page 111.) **vocārat = vocāverat:** *had invited.* **8 et:** *also.* **dea flāva:** Ceres.

9 Fīlia: Persephone. **10 per sua prāta:** the meadows of Henna were sacred to Ceres and

° vallēs, -is, *f.* valley
umbrōsus, shaded
aspergō, -ginis, *f.* sprinkling, spray
ūvidus, wet, moist
dēsiliō, -īre, -siluī, -sultum, leap down
° tot . . . quot, as many as
° illīc, there
pictus, painted, colorful
niteō, -ēre, shine, be bright
° humus, -ī, *f.* earth, ground
° aspiciō, -ere, -spexī, -spectus, look at, see
° comes, -mitis, *m. and f.* companion

° plēnus, full
° sinus, -ūs, *m.* fold, bosom, lap
puellāris, -e, girlish
prōlectō (1), allure, entice
inānis, -e, empty, carefree
sēdulitās, -ātis, *f.* diligence, being busy
° impleō, -ēre, -plēvī, -plētus, fill up
° lentus, pliant, bending, tough
calathus, (wicker) basket
vīmen, -minis, *n.* osier
nexus, woven
° gremium, bosom, lap
laxus, loose
dēgravō (1), weigh down, burden

° legō, -ere, lēgī, lēctus, pick, choose
caltha, marigold
violārium, bed of violets
papāvereus, of poppies
subsecō, -āre, -secuī, -sectus, cut off

° unguis, -is, *m.* fingernail
° coma, hair, foliage
hyacinthus, iris, hyacinth
amarantus, amaranth
° moror (*dep.* 1), delay, attract
thymum, thyme
rōs, rōris, *m.* dew; rōs (marīnus), rosemary
melilōtos, -ī, *m.* melilot, kind of clover

crocus, saffron, crocus
tenuis, -e, thin, slender
līlium, lily
° albus, white
° carpō, -ere, carpsī, carptus, pick, gather
° paulātim, gradually
patruus, uncle
° vēlōciter, swiftly
caeruleus, dark blue, dark

iō, cry to attract attention
° cārus, dear
° abscindō, -ere, -scidī, -scissus, tear away, rend
° pandō, -ere, pandī, passus, spread, open
° Dīs, Dītis, *m.* Dis, Pluto
° diurnus, daily, of the day
° lūmen, -minis, *n.* light
inadsuētus, unaccustomed
chorus, group of attendants
aequālis, -e, equal, of the same age
cumulō (1), heap, pile up
ministra, attendant, maid

Persephone. **11-12 aspergine . . . aquae:** *freshened by the copious spray from water leaping down from a height.* **14 picta:** modifies **humus. dissimilī = variō. flōre:** collective sing. for **flōribus. 15 Quam simul = Et simul ac eam** (**humum**).

19-22 haec, haec, illa, illa, huic, illa: of individual girls. **23-26 hās, illās, pars, pars:** of different groups; and finally **ipsa** of Persephone herself. **20 gremium:** the skirt of the loose tunic, picked up and held like an apron for gathering the flowers. **sinūs:** the top part of the tunic, hanging down over the girdle. **23 hyacinthe, amarante:** for even greater variety in his description Ovid has recourse to the voc. case and talks to the flowers! **25 rosa:** collective sing.

27 Carpendī: gerund, objective gen. w. **studiō. longius:** *rather far, too far.* **ītur:** impers. use of the intrans. **eō;** *there is a going = she goes* (the context shows that Persephone is meant). **28 secūta:** sc. **est. 29-30 Hanc . . . equīs:** with dramatic suddenness Pluto takes Persephone to Hades; in the *Metamorphoses* V. 395 the abduction is even swifter, **paene simul vīsa est dīlēctaque** (*loved*) **raptaque Dītī. 29 patruus:** Pluto was the brother of Jupiter, Persephone's father. **32 suōs:** placed next to **ipsa** for emphasis. **abscideratque:** in prose the **-que** would be attached to the first word in the clause. **sinūs:** folds of her dress, which she rends in the agony of her fear. **33 Panditur Dītī:** *is opened for Dis* (*Pluto*); through a deep cave which leads into Hades.

Pluto abducts Persephone. Woodcut illustrating Book Five of the *Metamorphoses*. French edition, Paris, 1539. Metropolitan Museum of Art, N.Y.C.

Valle sub umbrōsā locus est aspergine multā
    ūvidus ex altō dēsilientis aquae.
Tot fuerant illīc quot habet nātūra colōrēs,
    pictaque dissimilī flōre nitēbat humus.
Quam simul aspexit, "Comitēs, accēdite!" dīxit,   *15*
    "et mēcum plēnōs flōre referte sinūs!"
Praeda puellārēs animōs prōlectat inānēs,
    et nōn sentītur sēdulitāte labor.
Haec implet lentō calathōs ē vīmine nexōs,
    haec gremium, laxōs dēgravat illa sinūs;   *20*
illa legit calthās, huic sunt violāria cūrae,
    illa papāvereās subsecat ungue comās;
hās, hyacinthe, tenēs, illās, amarante, morāris;
    pars thyma, pars rōrēs et melilōton amat;
plūrima lēcta rosa est, sunt et sine nōmine flōrēs;   *25*
    ipsa crocōs tenuēs līliaque alba legit.

Persephone, who had strayed from her companions, was seen by Dis and carried off to Hades despite her cries for help.

Carpendī studiō paulātim longius ītur,
    et dominam cāsū nūlla secūta comes.
Hanc videt et vīsam patruus vēlōciter aufert,
    rēgnaque caeruleīs in sua portat equīs.   *30*
Illa quidem clāmābat, "Iō, cārissima māter,
    auferor!" ipsa suōs abscideratque sinūs.
Panditur intereā Dītī via, namque diurnum
    lūmen inadsuētī vix patiuntur equī.

Attracted by the cries of Persephone's companions, Ceres searched and called in vain for her lost daughter.

At chorus aequālis, cumulātae flōre ministrae,   *35*

36-40

* sileō, -ēre, -uī, be silent
  ululātus, -ūs, m. cry, shout
  feriō, -īre, beat, strike
  maestus, sad, sorrowful
* pectus, -toris, n. breast, chest
  attonitus, thunderstruck, stunned
  plangor, -ōris, m. lamentation, wailing
* modo, just, recently, now

41-45

* quācumque, in whatever direction
* ingredior, -ī, -gressus sum, enter, proceed
* cūnctus, the whole, all
  querēla, complaint, lament
* gemō, -ere, -uī, -itus, groan, sigh for, lament
  āles, ālitis, m. and f. bird
  per vicēs = alternīs, by turns, alternately
  cieō, -ēre, cīvī, citus, stir up, call

46-50

* pereō, -īre, -iī, -itum, be lost, perish
* Iuppiter, Iovis, m. Jupiter; sub Iove, in the open
  dūrō (1), harden, endure
* immōtus, unmoved
  pluviālis, -e, rainy, of rain
* fors, fortis, f. chance, luck
* quisque, quae-, quid- (quod-), each
  Cereālis, -e, of Ceres
* rūs, rūris, n. country, farm
* senex, senis, m. old man

51-55

  glāns, glandis, f. acorn, nut
  excutiō, -ere, -cussī, -cussus, shake off
  mōrum, blackberry
  rubētum, thicket of bramble bushes
* ārdeō, -ēre, ārsī, ārsum, be on fire, burn
* āridus, dry

  lignum, wood, log
* focus, hearth, fireplace
* redigō, -ere, -ēgī, -āctus, drive back
  capella, she-goat
  tener, -era, -erum, tender, delicate, young
  cūnae, f. pl. cradle
  aiō, def. say; ait, says

56-60

  sōlus, gen. -īus, alone, lonely
  incomitātus, unaccompanied
  resistō, -ere, -stitī, stop, halt
* senior, -ōris, m. the older one, old man
* quamvīs, although
* onus, oneris, n. load, burden
  urgeō, -ēre, ursī, press, weigh down
* tēctum, roof, house
* subeō, -īre, -iī, -itus, go under, enter
  quantuluscumque, however small
* casa, hut, cottage
* simulō (1), pretend, imitate
  anus, -ūs, f. old woman
  mitra, cap, bonnet
* capillus, hair
  īnstō, -stāre, -stitī, press, urge

61-65

* sōspes, -pitis, safe, fortunate
* parēns, -entis, m. and f. parent
* heu, alas!
  sors, sortis, f. fate, lot, destiny
* lacrimō (1), shed tears
* dēcidō, -ere, -cidī, fall down
* tepidus, warm
  lūcidus, clear, shining
  gutta, drop
* fleō, -ēre, flēvī, flētus, weep
* pariter, equally, at the same time
  mollis, -e, soft, gentle, kind

---

35 flōre: collective sing. **36 dōna:** the flowers. **38 feriunt pectora:** a sign of mourning among the Romans. **39 modo . . . Hennam:** *she had just come to Henna;* with names of towns the prep. is omitted. **40 nec mora:** sc. est; *nor is there delay = at once.* **Mē:** acc. of exclamation. **42 ut cum:** *just as when.* **āles:** (for the story of Procne and her son Itys v. I.P.N. Itys). **Ityn:** Greek acc. **44 clāmat:** repeated to indicate that the mother called again and again. **46 audit . . . perit:** the line corresponds in structure to l. 44. **perit:** i.e., receives no answer.

47 Sub Iove = Sub caelō. diēbus: abl. of time within which where we would express duration; *for many days.* **48 lūnae patiēns:** *enduring the moon = enduring sleepless nights.* **lūnae, aquae:** objective genitives w. patiēns. **49 locō:** dat. of possession; *Every place has its own destiny.* **Eleusis:** Eleusis in Attica was for centuries famous for the mysteries celebrating the cult of Demeter (Ceres) and her daughter. **50 hoc:** antecedent for **Quod. fuēre = fuērunt:** agreeing w. the complement **rūra.**

51 Ille: the old man, Celeus. **52 ārsūrīs focīs:** *for the hearths about to burn = to make a fire*

"Persephonē," clāmant, "ad tua dōna venī!"
Ut clāmāta silet, montēs ululātibus implent
et feriunt maestā pectora nūda manū.
Attonita est plangōre Cerēs—modo vēnerat Hennam—
nec mora, "Mē miseram! Fīlia," dīxit, "ubi es?"   40
Quācumque ingreditur, miserīs loca cūncta querēlīs
implet, ut āmissum cum gemit āles Ityn,
perque vicēs modo "Persephonē!" modo "Fīlia!" clāmat,
clāmat et alternīs nōmen utrumque ciet,
sed neque Persephonē Cererem, nec fīlia mātrem   45
audit, et alternīs nōmen utrumque perit.

Inconsolable, Ceres wandered without sleep and came to Eleusis,
where she was persuaded to enter the cottage of Celeus, whose young
son was gravely ill.

Sub Iove dūrāvit multīs immōta diēbus
et lūnae patiēns et pluviālis aquae.
Fors sua cuique locō est. Quod nunc Cereālis Eleusis
dīcitur, hoc Celeī rūra fuēre senis.   50
Ille domum glandēs excussaque mōra rubētīs
portat et ārsūrīs ārida ligna focīs:
fīlia parva duās redigēbat monte capellās,
et tener in cūnīs fīlius aeger erat.
"Māter," ait virgō—mōta est dea nōmine mātris—   55
"quid facis in sōlīs incomitāta locīs?"
Restitit et senior, quamvīs onus urget, et ōrat
tēcta suae subeat quantulacumque casae.
Illa negat. (Simulārat anum mitrāque capillōs
presserat.) Īnstantī tālia dicta refert,   60
"Sōspes eās semperque parēns! Mihi fīlia rapta est.
Heu! melior quantō sors tua sorte meā est!"
Dīxit et ut lacrimae—neque enim lacrimāre deōrum est—
dēcidit in tepidōs lūcida gutta sinūs.
Flent pariter mollēs animīs virgōque senexque,   65

---

on his hearth. **55 Māter:** used by the little girl to address the goddess. **57 et:** *also.* **quamvīs . . .
urget:** *although his load is heavy.* **ōrat:** sc. *ut* for the indir. command; *begs that she go under
the roof, however small, of his cottage* = *invites her to find shelter in his cottage, humble
though it is.*

59 Simulārat (= **Simulāverat**) **anum:** *She had assumed the appearance of an old woman.*
mitrā: *characteristic of old women.* **60 Īnstantī:** sc. *eī,* dat., indir. obj. of **refert**; *When he
insisted* (lit. *To him insisting*) *she answered as follows.* **61 eās:** optative subjv; *may you go.*
62 quantō: abl. of degree of difference w. **melior. sorte:** abl. of comparison. **63 ut lacrimae:**
just as tears (*do*). **deōrum:** predicate gen.; *to shed tears is not* (*characteristic*) *of gods* =
gods cannot shed tears.

65 animīs: abl. of specification w. **mollēs. 66 ē quibus:** expressing a partitive idea w. **senis;**

* surgō, -ere, surrēxī, surrēctum, rise, get up
  exiguus, small, humble
* dēspiciō, -ere, -spexī, -spectus, despise, look down on
* quā, in what way, how
  levō (1), lift, raise
* subsequor, -ī, -secūtus sum, follow closely

* somnus, sleep
  invigilō (1), stay awake
  sopōrifer, -era, -erum, sleep-producing
* penātēs, -ium, m. pl. household gods, home
* colligō, -ere, -lēgī, -lēctus, gather, collect
* agrestis, -e, of the field, countryside
  lēnis, -e, gentle, soft
* papāver, -eris, n. poppy
  oblītus, having forgotten, forgetting, forgetful
  gustō (1), taste
  palātum, palate

  imprūdēns, -entis, unaware, thoughtless
  exsolvō, -ere, -solvī, -solūtus, undo, end
* famēs, -is, f. hunger, fasting
* prīncipium, beginning
* ieiūnium, fasting, fast
  mysta, -ae, m. priest of the mysteries, initiate
* sīdus, -deris, n. star
* līmen, -minis, n. threshold, entrance
  lūctus, -ūs, m. mourning, grief

* salūtō (1), greet
  dignor (dep. 1), deign, see fit
  puerīlis, -e, boyish, of the boy
  pallor, -ōris, m. paleness
* subitus, sudden, suddenly gained
* caelestis, -e, divine, heavenly
* laetus, joyful, happy

* nāta = fīlia
* mox, soon, shortly
* epulae, f. pl. feast, banquet
  liquefactus, melted
  coāgulum, rennet
* lac, lactis, n. milk
* pōmum, fruit, apple
  cēra, wax
  aureus, golden, yellow
  mel, mellis, n. honey
  abstineō, -ēre, -uī, -tentum, hold off, abstain
* bibō, -ere, -ī, drink

* placidus, peaceful, calm
* silentium, silence
* tollō, -ere, sustulī, sublātus, lift, raise
* ter, three times
  permulceō, -ēre, -mulsī, -mulsus, soothe, caress
* carmen, -minis, n. song, hymn
  sonus, sound, noise
  favīlla, ashes

the words of the good old man of them = of the two of them, it was the good old man who said. **66 fuēre** = fuērunt. **67 Sīc:** often used to introduce a wish, the fulfillment of which is conditioned by a second clause; *So may your daughter be safe (as) you get up and show no scorn for. . . .* Such conditional wishes survive in English only in *So help me God.* **sit:** optative subjv.

69 Dūc: imper. of dūcō. **Scīstī** = Scīvistī. **quā . . . possēs:** indir. question; *how you could compel (me),* i.e., by expressing a wish for her daughter's safety.

71 comitī: Ceres. **71-72 quam . . . malīs:** indir. question; *how his son is ill, does not sleep, and is restless because of his illness.* **73 sopōriferum:** modifies papāver. **initūra penātēs:** *about to enter the cottage;* **penātēs** by metonymy for casam. **75 fertur:** *she is said.* **gustāsse** = gustāvisse. **76 exsoluisse:** instead of exsolvisse, for metrical reasons. **famem:** she had intended to fast until she found her daughter. **77 Quae:** modifies ieiūnia, the object of **posuit** (= dēposuit); *And because she ended this fast.* **78 habent:** *hold, consider.* **mystae:** initiates in the celebration of the Eleusinian mysteries; Ovid is explaining their custom of fasting until nightfall. **sīdera vīsa:** *the seen stars = the time when the stars are seen; the initiates hold that the time for food is the time when the stars are seen.*

79 lūctūs: partitive gen. w. plēna. **80 in puerō:** *in the boy's case.* **82 iungere . . . suō:** *she deigned to join the boy's mouth to hers = she graciously kissed the child.* **85-86 Tōta domus**

ē quibus haec iūstī verba fuēre senis,
"Sīc tibi, quam raptam quaeris, sit fīlia sōspes,
surge nec exiguae dēspice tēcta casae."
Cui dea, "Dūc!" inquit, "Scīstī quā cōgere possēs,"
sēque levat saxō subsequiturque senem.   70
Dux comitī nārrat, quam sit sibi filius aeger
nec capiat somnōs invigiletque malīs.
Illa sopōriferum, parvōs initūra penātēs,
colligit agrestī lēne papāver humō.
Dum legit, oblītō fertur gustāsse palātō   75
longamque imprūdēns exsoluisse famem.
Quae quia prīncipiō posuit iēiūnia noctis,
tempus habent mystae sīdera vīsa cibī.

Ceres restored the child to health and would have made him immortal
but for the intervention of Metanira, the mother. The goddess however
promised that he would become a benefactor of mankind, and continued her search.

Līmen ut intrāvit, lūctūs videt omnia plēna:
iam spēs in puerō nūlla salūtis erat.   80
Mātre salūtātā—māter Metanīra vocātur—
iungere dignāta est ōs puerīle suō.
Pallor abit, subitāsque vident in corpore vīrēs;
tantus caelestī vēnit ab ōre vigor.
Tōta domus laeta est, hoc est, māterque paterque   85
nātaque: trēs illī tōta fuēre domus.
Mox epulās pōnunt, liquefacta coāgula lacte
pōmaque et in cērīs aurea mella suīs.
Abstinet alma Cerēs, somnīque papāvera causās
dat tibi cum tepidō lacte bibenda, puer.   90
Noctis erat medium placidīque silentia somnī:
Triptolemum gremiō sustulit illa suō
terque manū permulsit eum, tria carmina dīxit,
carmina mortālī nōn referenda sonō,
inque focō corpus puerī vīvente favīllā   95

... fuēre (= fuērunt) domus: in some forms of the myth Celeus and Metanira were king
and queen, with a large family; Ovid is at pains to indicate that it was a humble home and
a small family. The "feast" about to be served is also plain homegrown food.

89 somnī causās: *as a soporific.* 90 tibi, puer: apostrophe. bibenda: modifies papāvera;
poppies to be drunk. 91 medium: n. of adj. used as noun; *the middle.* 92 Triptolemum:
the name of the little boy who had been ill. In the lines that follow Demeter is interrupted
in the ceremony of making Triptolemus immortal; however, he became a hero, teaching
men the art of agriculture as the foundation of peace and civilization. gremiō suō: *in her lap;*
abl. of means. 94 carmina . . . sonō: *charms not to be repeated by human voice.* 95 vīvente
favīllā: *with hot ashes.* 96 hūmānum onus: *the burden of his mortality (which prevents
his soul from becoming immortal).*

71

96-100

obruō, -ere, -ruī, -rutus, cover over
pūrgō (1), cleanse, purify
* pius, devoted, loving
āmēns, -entis, wild, frantic
* membrum, limb, member
* scelerātus, wicked, criminal
inritus, useless, in vain
* metus, -ūs, *m.* fear

101-105

* arō (1), plough
serō, -ere, sēvī, satus, sow, plant
* nūbēs, -is, *f.* cloud
dracō, -ōnis, *m.* serpent
ālifer, -era, -erum, winged
axis, -is, *m.* axis, axle, chariot
immūnis, -e, *w. gen.,* free from, not sharing
   in
* pontus, sea

106-110

* adloquor, -ī, -locūtus sum, address
gelidus, cold, chill
signum, -ī, *n.* mark, sign, constellation
Parrhasis, -idis, Parrhasian, Arcadian

* nōscō, -ere, nōvī, nōtus, get to know
aequoreus, of the sea

111-115

* crīmen, -minis, *n.* charge, guilt
vacuus, *w. abl.,* free from, without
* cōnsulō, -ere, -suluī, -sultus, consult
* adeō, -īre, -iī, -itus, approach
vānus, vain, empty, fruitless
* nūbō, -ere, nūpsī, nūptus, *w. dat.,* marry
queror, -ī, questus sum, complain
adfor (*dep.* 1), address, speak to
Tonāns, -antis, *m.* the Thunderer

116-120

* vultus, -ūs, *m.* expression, face
* doleō, -ēre, -uī, -itus, sorrow, grieve
memor, -oris, remembering, able to remember
dīmidium, half
* orbis, -is, *m.* circle, world
* pererrō (1), wander through
iniūria, wrong, injustice
* commissum = factum, action, deed
* raptor, -ōris, *m.* robber, abductor

Demeter (Ceres), Triptolemus and Persephone. Relief from Eleusis. Fifth century, B.C. National Museum, Athens.

Alinari, Fototeca Unione

obruit, hūmānum pūrget ut ignis onus.
Excutitur somnō subitō pia māter, et āmēns
   "Quid facis?" exclāmat membraque ab igne rapit.
Cui dea, "Dum nōn vīs," dīxit, "scelerāta fuistī;
   inrita māternō sunt mea dōna metū.   *100*
Iste quidem mortālis erit, sed prīmus arābit
   et seret et cultā praemia tollet humō."
Dīxit et ēgrediēns nūbem trahit inque dracōnēs
   trānsit et āliferō tollitur axe Cerēs.

The stars of the Great Bear informed Ceres that they knew nothing
about the abduction and referred her to the Sun god since the crime
was committed in daylight. The Sun informed Ceres that Persephone
was now wedded to Dis and queen of the Underworld. Ceres com-
plained to Jupiter, father of Persephone.

Errat et in caelō, liquidīque immūnia pontī   *105*
   adloquitur gelidō proxima signa polō,
"Parrhasidēs stellae—namque omnia nōsse potestis,
   aequoreās numquam cum subeātis aquās—
Persephonēn nātam miserae mōnstrāte parentī!"
   Dīxerat. Huic Helicē tālia verba refert,   *110*
"Crīmine nox vacua est. Sōlem dē virgine raptā
   cōnsule, quī lātē facta diurna videt."
Sōl aditus, "Quam quaeris," ait, "nē vāna labōrēs,
   nūpta Iovis frātrī tertia rēgna tenet."
Questa diū sēcum sīc est adfāta Tonantem,   *115*
   maximaque in vultū signa dolentis erant,
"Sī memor es, dē quō mihi sit Prōserpina nāta,
   dīmidium cūrae dēbet habēre tuae.
Orbe pererrātō, sōla est iniūria factī
   cognita; commissī praemia raptor habet.   *120*

---

99 Dum nōn vīs: *While not wanting* (*to be wicked*). **101 prīmus arābit:** *he will be the first
to plow.* **102 cultā humō:** *from the cultivated soil.* **103 nūbem trahit:** *she draws a cloud*
(*behind her, to make herself invisible*). **103-104 inque . . . Cerēs:** Ceres rode through the
air in a snakedrawn chariot. **104 axe** = **currū** (metonymy).

105 immūnia pontī: these constellations are so described because they do not set, being so
near the North Pole. **106 polō:** dat. w. **proxima;** *closest to the chill pole.* **107 Parrhasidēs:** so
called because Callisto and her son, who became the constellations of the two Bears, were
Arcadian. **nōsse** = **nōvisse.** **109 Persephonēn:** Greek acc. **110 Helicē:** Ursa Major, so
named (**helicē** in Greek means *winding, circling*) because it revolves around the pole star.
111 Crīmine . . . est: the night cannot be accused of allowing the kidnaping to occur.
112 facta diurna: *the deeds of daytime.* **113 Quam:** sc. **ea** as antecedent and subject of
tenet. 114 tertia rēgna: Jupiter ruled the sky; Neptune, the sea; and Pluto, Hades. **tenet:**
inhabits.

115 sēcum: *to herself.* **116 dolentis:** used as a noun; *of a mourner.* **117 dē . . . nāta:**
indir. question depending on **memor;** Demeter's way of reminding Jupiter that he is
Persephone's father and should show parental concern. **118 dēbet:** subject is *she* (*Persephone*). **119-120 Orbe . . . cognita:** *The world having been wandered through, only the injustice of the deed has been learned* = *The sole result of my world-wide search is the*

Ursa minor

Ursa maior

The Great Bear and the Little Bear.
Woodcut from an edition of Hyginus,
Poetica Astronautica, Venice, 1482.
Metropolitan Museum of Art, N.Y.C.

121-125

* **dignus**, *w. abl.*, worthy of, deserving
praedō, -ōnis, *m.* pirate, robber
marītus, husband
* **gener, -erī**, *m.* son-in-law
lēniō, -īre, -iī, -ītus, soothe, calm
pudendus, to be ashamed of, shameful
* **nōbilis, -e**, noble, illustrious
* **rēgia**, palace, royal dwelling

126-130

chaos, *n.* the Lower World
* **forte**, by chance
mūtābilis, -e, changeable, subject to change
* **semel**, once, once and for all
* **vinc(u)lum**, bond, tie
torus, couch, bed
siquidem, if in fact
iēiūnus, fasting, without food
remaneō, -ēre, -mānsī, -mānsum, remain
īnfernus, below, of the Lower World
* **uxor, -ōris**, *f.* wife

131-135

Tartara, -ōrum, *n. pl.* Tartarus, the Lower World
Cādūcifer, -erī, *m.* the wand bearer, Mercury
* **āla**, wing

* **cito**, quickly
grānum, seed, grain
pūnicus, reddish, purple
cortex, -ticis, *m.* bark
* **tegō, -ere, tēxī, tēctus**, cover, hide
secus, otherwise
indolēscō, -ere, -doluī, feel grief

136-140

* **reficiō, -ere, -fēcī, -fectus**, restore, revive
habitābilis, -e, habitable
Taenarius, of Taenarus
pacīscor, -ī, pactus sum, arrange, agree

141-145

dēmum, at length
spīceus, of ears of grain, spiky
sertum, wreath, garland
largus, generous, bountiful
cessātus, left idle
messis, -is, *f.* harvest, crop
arvum, plowed land, field
* **congerō, -ere, -gessī, -gestus**, heap up
ārea, threshing floor
* **opēs, -um**, *f. pl.* wealth, bounty
* **deceō, -ēre, -uī**, be becoming to, suit
Cereālia, -ium, *n. pl.* festival of Ceres

146

pullus, dark-colored
vellus, -leris, *n.* fleece, wool

---

knowledge that a wrong has been done. **122 nec . . . erat:** *and we did not need to get a son-in-law this way.*

123 factumque . . . amōre: *and pleads love as an excuse for the deed.* **124 Nec = et 'Nōn.'
Nec . . . ait:** *and says, "We do not need to be ashamed of him as son-in-law."* **125 caelō:** abl.
of place where without prep. **126 alter, alter:** i.e., Neptune and Pluto. **128 statque . . . torī:**
and it is your firm purpose (stat) to break the bonds of a marriage (torī; metonymy) once

At neque Persephonē digna est praedōne marītō,
nec gener hōc nōbīs mōre parandus erat."

Jupiter attempted to console Ceres and sent Mercury to Hades to inquire whether Persephone had fasted. But Persephone had eaten three
pomegranate seeds and had to remain as wife of Pluto.

Iuppiter hanc lēnit factumque excūsat amōre.
"Nec gener est nōbīs ille pudendus," ait,
"Nōn ego nōbilior. Posita est mihi rēgia caelō,   *125*
  possidet alter aquās, alter ināne chaos.
Sed sī forte tibī nōn est mūtābile pectus
  statque semel iūnctī rumpere vincla torī,
hoc quoque temptēmus, siquidem iēiūna remānsit;
  sī minus, īnfernī coniugis uxor erit."   *130*
Tartara iussus adit sūmptīs Cādūcifer ālīs,
  spēque redit citius vīsaque certa refert.
"Rapta tribus," dīxit, "solvit iēiūnia grānīs,
  pūnica quae lentō cortice pōma tegunt."

To console Ceres, Jupiter decreed that Persephone should spend half
the year with her mother.

Nōn secus indoluit quam sī modo rapta fuisset   *135*
  maesta parēns, longā vixque refecta morā est
atque ita, "Nec nōbīs caelum est habitābile!" dīxit,
  "Taenariā recipī mē quoque valle iubē!
Et factūra fuit, pactus nisi Iuppiter esset,
  bis tribus ut caelō mēnsibus illa foret.   *140*

Ceres was now happy and harvests again were bountiful. White is appropriate for the feast of Ceres.

Tum dēmum vultumque Cerēs animumque recēpit
  imposuitque suae spīcea serta comae,
largaque prōvēnit cessātīs messis in arvīs,
  et vix congestās ārea cēpit opēs.
Alba decent Cererem: vestēs Cereālibus albās   *145*
  sūmite! Nunc pullī velleris ūsus abest.

FASTI IV. 417–

---

it has been made (semel iūnctī). **129 temptēmus:** hortatory subjv.; *let us try.* **130 sī minus:**
if not. **131 Tartara:** *to Tartarus;* prep. is omitted as w. names of towns. **132 spē:** abl. of comparison; *sooner than expected.* **vīsa certa:** *facts that he had witnessed.*

133 Rapta: used as a noun; *The kidnaped girl.* **134 pūnica pōma:** *pomegranates.* **135 Nōn
secus quam sī:** *Not otherwise than if = Exactly as if.* **fuisset:** subjv. in past contrary-to-fact
condition. **139 factūra:** *intending to do* (*it*). **pactus esset:** subjv. in past contrary-to-fact
condition. **140 caelō:** abl. of place where without prep., = **sub caelō. mēnsibus:** for case,
compare **diēbus** (l. 47).

141 vultumque . . . recēpit: *Ceres recovered both cheerful expression and spirit = showed
the relief that she felt in her heart.* **142 comae:** dat. w. compound verb **imposuit;** *placed in
her hair.* **146 sūmite:** addressed to the poet's Roman readers. It is now time to wear clothes
of a lighter color.

75

Apollo and dancing girl. House of the Vettii, Pompeii. National Museum, Naples.

Anderson, Fototeca Unione

METAMORPHOSES

spargō, -ere, sparsī, sparsus, spread, scatter
* fulmen, -minis, *n.* thunderbolt
* forte, by chance, perhaps
* aethēr, -eris, *m.* sky, heaven, upper air
* concipiō, -ere, -cēpī, -ceptus, seize, grasp, take
ārdēscō, -ere, begin to burn, take fire
axis, -is, *m.* axis, pole, sky
* repōnō, -ere, -posuī, -positus, put back, lay aside
fabricō (1), make, forge
Cyclōps, -ōpis, *m.* Cyclops, one-eyed giant
dīversus, diverse, different, opposite
* mortālis, -e, mortal
sub, *with abl.* beneath, below
* unda, wave

* perdō, -ere, -didī, -ditus, lose, destroy
* nimbus, violent rain, rain cloud
* dēmittō, -ere, -mīsī, -missus, send down
* prōtinus, at once, straightway
Aeolius, Aeolian, belonging to Aeolus, the king of the winds
Aquilō, -ōnis, *m.* the north wind
* claudō, -ere, clausī, clausus, enclose
antrum, cave
* quīcumque, quae-, quod-, whoever, whatever
fugō (1), rout, put to flight
* indūcō, -ere, -dūxī, -ductus, bring in, overlay
flāmen, -minis, *n.* (= ventus) wind, blast
* nūbēs, -is, *f.* (= nimbus, nebula, nūbilum) cloud
* ēmittō, -ere, ēmīsī, ēmissus, let go out, release
Notus, south wind
madidus, wet, dripping

ēvolō (1), fly out
* āla, wing, pinion
piceus, of pitch, pitch black
* tegō, -ere, tēxī, tēctus, cover, conceal
cālīgō, -ginis, *f.* mist, fog
* vultus, -ūs, *m.* face, expression

barba, beard
cānus, gray, hoary
fluō, -ere, flūxī, flūxum, flow, float
* capillus, hair
frōns, frontis, *f.* forehead, brow
rōrō (1), distil dew, be wet
* penna, feather, wing
sinus, -ūs, *m.* curve, fold, breast
* ut, *w. indic.* as, when
pendeō, -ēre, pependī, overhang, hover
* premō, -ere, pressī, pressus, press, squeeze, overwhelm
fragor, -ōris, *m.* crash, roar
* fundō, -ere, fūdī, fūsus, pour, produce
nūntia, messenger
Iūnō, -ōnis, *f.* Juno
induō, -ere, -duī, -dūtus, put on, assume

Īris, Iridis, *f.* Iris, goddess of the rainbow
alimentum, food, nourishment
* sternō, -ere, strāvī, strātus, lay low, destroy
* seges, -getis, *f.* field of grain, crop
dēplōrō (1), weep bitterly, mourn for
colōnus, farmer, settler
* vōtum, vow, prayer
* iaceō, -ēre, -uī, lie prostrate, be ruined
* pereō, -īre, -iī, -itum, perish, be lost
inritus, useless, vain
* Iuppiter, Iovis, *m.* Jupiter
* caeruleus, dark blue
* iuvō, -āre, iūvī, iūtus, help, aid
auxiliāris, -e, helping, assistant

---

1 erat: the subject is Jupiter. **sparsūrus:** *on the point of scattering.* **2 sacer:** because the gods lived there. **4 Tēla:** i.e., fulmina. **6 perdere . . . dēmittere:** a reversal of the logical order of ideas, for which the technical term is *hysteron proteron.* Both infinitives are in apposition with **poena.**

7 Aquilōnem claudit: because it usually brings clear, dry weather. **8 quaecumque flāmina** = omnia flāmina quae. **10 vultum:** acc. of respect w. perf. pass. participle; lit. *having been covered as to face,* i.e., *his face covered.*

11 barba: sc. est. **capillīs:** abl. of place where without a prep.; so also with **fronte.** **13-14 Utque . . . fit fragor:** the poet describes how thunder occurs. **14 dēnsī funduntur nimbī:** *thick rain clouds are poured;* i.e., *floods of rain pour forth from the clouds in heaven.* **15 colōrēs:** acc. with **indūta,** *clothed in various colors;* cf. line 10, tēctus vultum. **17 dēplōrāta:** by a metonymy of the effect for the cause, this participle often means *lost; the farmer's prayers lie there lost.* **18 vōta:** another metonymy; the crops lie flat, and with them the farmer's hopes for a good harvest.

19 caelō suō: because when Jupiter divided the universe with his brothers, the sky was his portion, as Neptune's was the sea. **20 caeruleus frāter:** Neptune. **21 amnēs:** in Roman mythology, Neptune controlled not only the seas, but all bodies of water. **Quī postquam** =

THE FLOOD

In the Golden Age men were good and happy with their lot. But in time they turned to every form of wickedness. Angered by their crimes, Jupiter decides to destroy the human race.

> Iamque erat in tōtās sparsūrus fulmina terrās;
> sed timuit nē forte sacer tot ab ignibus aethēr
> conciperet flammās, longusque ārdēsceret axis.
> Tēla repōnuntur manibus fabricāta Cyclōpum;
> poena placet dīversa: genus mortāle sub undīs   5
> perdere, et ex omnī nimbōs dēmittere caelō.
> Prōtinus Aeoliīs Aquilōnem claudit in antrīs
> et quaecumque fugant inductās flāmina nūbēs,
> ēmittitque Notum, Madidīs Notus ēvolat ālīs,
> terribilem piceā tēctus cālīgine vultum;   10
> barba gravis nimbīs, cānīs fluit unda capillīs,
> fronte sedent nebulae, rōrant pennaeque sinūsque.
> Utque manū lātā pendentia nūbila pressit,
> fit fragor; hinc dēnsī funduntur ab aethere nimbī.
> Nūntia Iūnōnis variōs indūta colōrēs   15
> concipit Īris aquās, alimentaque nūbibus adfert
> Sternuntur segetēs, et dēplōrāta colōnī
> vōta iacent, longīque perit labor inritus annī.

He is aided by Neptune, who orders the rivers to flood.

> Nec caelō contenta suō est Iovis īra, sed illum
> caeruleus frāter iuvat auxiliāribus undīs.   20

Neptune. Copy of a famous work of the fourth century, B.C. National Museum, Athens.

Alinari, Fototeca Unione

21-25

* amnis, -is, m. river
* tēctum, roof, dwelling
* intrō (1), enter
hortāmen, -minis, n. exhortation, harangue
* vīrēs, -ium, f. pl. strength, powers
effundō, -ere, -fūdī, -fūsus, pour out, release
* opus, operis, n. work, necessity
* aperiō, -īre, -uī, -tus, open
mōlēs, -is, f. bulk, barrier, bar
* immittō, -ere, -mīsī, -missus, let in, let loose
habēnae, f. pl. reins

26-30

fōns, fontis, m. spring, source
* ōs, ōris, n. mouth, opening, face
relaxō (1), release, free, undo
dēfrēnātus, unbridled, unchecked
* volvō, -ere, volvī, volūtus, roll
* aequor, -oris, n. level expanse, sea
* cursus, -ūs, m. rush, speed, course
tridēns, -entis, m. trident
* percutiō, -ere, -cussī, -cussus, strike, smite
intremō, -ere, -tremuī, tremble (at)
* mōtus, -ūs, m. movement
* patefaciō, -ere, -fēcī, -factus, open up
exspatior (dep. 1), wander off course, spread out
* ruō, -ere, ruī, rutus, rush

31-35

satum, a crop
arbustum, orchard, plantation; pl. trees
pecus, pecudis, f. sheep, head of cattle
penetrālia, -ium, n. pl. inner room, sanctuary
sacra, -ōrum, n. pl. sacred objects
* indēiectus, not thrown down, not destroyed
* malum, evil, harm, misfortune
* culmen, -minis, n. peak, pinnacle, roof
* lateō, -ēre, -uī, lie hidden
gurges, gurgitis, m. flood

36-40

* tellūs, -ūris, f. earth, land
discrīmen, -minis, n. difference, distinction
* pontus, sea
* dēsum, deesse, dēfuī, dēfutūrus, w. dat. be lacking

cumba, skiff, boat
aduncus, curved
* illīc, there, in that place
nūper, lately, recently
arō (1), plow
* mergō, -ere, mersī, mersus, sink

41-45

piscis, -is, m. fish
dēprゥ ndō, -ere, -prēndī, -prēnsus, catch
ulゥaus, -ī, f. elm
* fīgō, -ere, fīxī, fīxus, fix, set, make fast
viridis, -e, green
* fors, fortis, f. chance, luck, accident
prātum, field, meadow
* subiectus, placed beneath, lying below
terō, -ere, trīvī, trītus, rub, scrape, graze, wear away
vīnētum, vineyard
carīna, keel
* modo, recently, just now, only
gracilis, -e, slender, lean, thin
grāmen, -minis, n. grass
carpō, -ere, carpsī, carptus, pluck, graze
capella, nanny goat
dēfōrmis, -e, shapeless, ungainly
phōca, seal

46-50

lūcus, grove
Nēreis, -idis, f. a Nereid, daughter of the sea god, Nereus; sea nymph
delphīn, -īnis, m. dolphin
* incursō (1), w. dat. keep running against
rāmus, branch
* agitō (1), trouble, disturb, shake
rōbur, roboris, n. oak
* pulsō (1), keep striking, batter
nō (1), swim
* lupus, wolf
ovis, ovis, f. sheep
fulvus, yellow, tawny
* vehō, -ere, vexī, vectus, carry
* leō, leōnis, m. lion
tigris, -is, m. and f. tiger
fulmen, fulminis, n. thunderbolt
aper, aprī, m. boar

Et postquam eī. 21-22 tyrannī suī, *of their master*, i.e., Neptune. 22 intrāvēre = intrāvērunt. 22-23 est ūtendum: pass. periphrastic; sc. mihi, *I must use*. 24 mōle: i.e., river banks, dikes, etc. 25 tōtās immittite habēnās, *give free rein;* a metaphor from horse racing, continued in dēfrēnātō cursū. 26 Iusserat: as often with the perfect tenses, the completion of the action is emphasized; *He finished giving his orders*. fontibus: dat. of reference; fontibus ōra relaxant, *open the sluice gates*.

28 Ipse: Neptune. 29 motū: dat. case, *for the movement (tumult) of the water*. 30-32 Exspatiāta ruunt . . . penetrālia sacrīs: notice the effect created by the separation of exspatiāta from flūmina and of apertōs from campōs, the alliteration, the repeated -que, and the dactylic rhythm. 32 sacrīs: i.e., the Penates, the family gods worshipped in the penetrālia.

80

Convocat hic amnēs. Quī postquam tēcta tyrannī
intrāvēre suī, "Nōn est hortāmine longō
nunc,"ait, "ūtendum. Vīrēs effundite vestrās.
Sīc opus est. Aperīte domōs ac mōle remōtā
flūminibus vestrīs tōtās immittite habēnās."   25
Iusserat. Hī redeunt ac fontibus ōra relaxant
et dēfrēnātō volvuntur in aequora cursū.
    Ipse tridente suō terram percussit, at illa
intremuít mōtūque viās patefēcit aquārum.
Exspatiāta ruunt per apertōs flūmina campōs;   30
cumque satīs arbusta simul pecudēsque virōsque
tēctaque cumque suīs rapiunt penetrālia sacrīs.

The flood submerges everything.

    Sī qua domus mānsit potuitque resistere tantō
indēiecta malō, culmen tamen altior huius
unda tegit, pressaeque latent sub gurgite turrēs.   35
Iamque mare et tellūs nūllum discrīmen habēbant:
omnia pontus erant; deerant quoque lītora pontō.
Occupat hic collem, cumbā sedet alter aduncā
et dūcit rēmōs illīc ubi nūper arābat;
ille super segetēs aut mersae culmina vīllae   40
nāvigat, hic summā piscem dēprēndit in ulmō.
Fīgitur in viridī (sī fors tulit) ancora prātō,
aut subiecta terunt curvae vīnēta carīnae.
Et, modo quā gracilēs grāmen carpsēre capellae,
nunc ibi dēfōrmēs pōnunt sua corpora phōcae.   45
Mīrantur sub aquā lūcōs urbēsque domōsque
Nēreides, silvāsque tenent delphīnes et altīs
incursant rāmīs agitātaque rōbora pulsant.
Nat lupus inter ovēs; fulvōs vehit unda leōnēs;
unda vehit tigrēs. Nec vīrēs fulminis aprō,   50

33 **Sī qua:** qua for aliqua, *If any house was left.* 34 **huius:** to be taken with **culmen,** *its roof.*
37 **Omnia pontus erant:** an effective phrase. **pontō:** dat. of the possessor; *the sea had no shores.*

38-41 hic ... alter ... ille .. hic: *one man ... another ... another ... yet another.* 39 **dūcit rēmōs:** *plies his oars.* 41 **summā in ulmō:** *on the top of an elm tree.* 42 **sī fors tulit:** *if it so happened.* 44 **modo quā:** *where just recently.* Notice the alliteration in this line.

47 **Nēreides, delphīnes:** for words of Greek origin Ovid prefers Greek case endings; hence the short **e.** 48 **agitāta rōbora pulsant** = rōbora agitant et pulsant. 49-50 **vehit unda, unda vehit:** Ovid likes to repeat phrases; cf. lines 70-71.

50 **fulminis:** used figuratively, *destructive power.* **aprō:** dat. w. **prōsunt;** *his destructive violence is of no use to the boar.* 51 **crūra ... cervō:** in prose order, nec crūra vēlōcia ablātō cervō prōsunt. 52 **dētur:** subjv. in a rel. clause of characteristic; *where it (the wandering bird) may be allowed to perch;* sistere is the subject, and the dative (**volucrī vagae**) is implied. 56 **Maxima pars:** sc. hominum. 57 **inopī vīctū:** *food being insufficient = through lack of food.*

Fountain of Triton by Bernini (1598-1680). Piazza Berberini, Rome.

51-55

crūs, crūris, *n.* leg

° auferō, auferre, abstulī, ablātus, carry away

° prōsum, prōdesse, prōfuī, *w. dat.* be useful to

vēlōx, -ōcis, swift

cervus, stag, deer

sistō, -ere, stitī, statum, stand, stop, rest

lassō (1), tire, weary

volucris, -is, *f.* bird

vagus, wandering, roaming

° dēcidō, -ere, -cidī, fall down

obruō, -ere, -ruī, -rutus, cover over, bury

tumulus, mound, hill

immēnsus, boundless, limitless

licentia, freedom, license

° montānus, of the mountains

° cacūmen, -minis, *n.* peak, summit

56-60

° parcō, -ere, pepercī, parcitum, *w. dat.*, spare

domō, -āre, domuī, domitus, overcome, subdue

inops, -opis, weak, needy, destitute, insufficient

iēiūnium, fasting, hunger

vīctus, -ūs, *m.* food, diet, fare

sēparō (1), separate, divide

Āonius, Aonian, Boeotian

Oetaeus, of Oeta, mountain range in Thessaly

Phōcis, -idis, *f.* Phocis, district west of Boeotia; Mt. Parnassus and Delphi are in Phocis

arvum, plowed land, field

ferāx, -ācis, fertile

° dum, *w. indic.* while, as long as

° subitus, sudden

61-65

vertex, -ticis, *m.* peak, point

arduus, steep, high

astrum, star

Parnāsus, Parnassus

° cēterus, the rest, the other

cōnsors, -sortis, *m. and f.* partner

torus, bed, couch

ratis, -is, *f.* raft, boat

adhaereō, -ēre, -haesī, -haesum, cling to, run aground

Cōrycis, -idis, of Corycium, cave on Mt. Parnassus

° nympha, nymph

° nūmen, -minis, *n.* deity, divine will

° adōrō (1), worship, pray to

58 Sēparat . . . arvīs: *Phocis separates the Aonians from the fields of Oeta;* i.e., separates Boeotia from Thessaly. **60 pars:** sc. **erat.**

64 cōnsorte torī: his wife. **66 Themin:** the Greek form of the acc. **ōrācla** = **ōrācula. 67 illō:**

82

Model of the Theater of Marcellus, which was undertaken by Caesar and carried out by Augustus as an homage to his nephew. It could hold about twenty thousand spectators. Museum of Roman Civilization, Rome.

crūra nec ablātō prōsunt vēlōcia cervō.
Quaesītīsque diū terrīs ubi sistere dētur,
in mare lassātīs volucris vaga dēcidit ālīs.
Obruerat tumulōs immēnsa licentia pontī,
pulsābantque novī montāna cacūmina flūctūs.   55
Maxima pars undā rapitur; quibus unda pepercit,
illōs longa domant inopī iēiūnia vīctū.

Deucalion and Pyrrha

Deucalion and Pyrrha reach the peaks of Parnassus.

Sēparat Āoniōs Oetaeīs Phōcis ab arvīs,
terra ferāx dum terra fuit, sed tempore in illō
pars maris et lātus subitārum campus aquārum.   60
Mōns ibi verticibus petit arduus astra duōbus,
nōmine Parnāsus, superantque cacūmina nūbēs.
Hīc ubi Deucaliōn (nam cētera tēxerat aequor)
cum cōnsorte torī parvā rate vectus adhaesit,
Cōrycidas nymphās et nūmina montis adōrant   65

83

fātidicus, prophetic
Themis, -idis, f. Themis, goddess of justice and prophecy
° tunc, then
° ōrāc(u)lum, oracle, prophecy
° aequum, fairness, justice
metuō, -ere, -uī, fear, reverence
° liquidus, clear, liquid
stāgnō (1), flood, overflow
° palūs, ūdis, f. swamp, pool
° orbis, -is, m. circle, world
supersum, -esse, -fuī, -futūrus, be left, survive

71-75
innocuus, harmless, innocent
° ambō, -ae, -ō, both
cultor, -ōris, m. worshiper
° disiciō, -ere, -iēcī, -iectus, scatter
° ostendō, -ere, -tendī, -tentus, show, reveal
tricuspis, -idis, three-pointed

76-80
° mulceō, -ēre, mulsī, mulsus, soothe, calm
° rēctor, -ōris, m. ruler
pelagus, -ī, n. sea
profundum, the deep (sea)
exstō, -āre, stand out
° umerus, shoulder
° innātus, inborn, native
mūrex, mūricis, m. shell fish, purple dye
Trītōn, -ōnis, m.Triton, sea-god
concha, shell, conch
sonō, -āre, -uī, -itum, sound
īnspīrō (1), blow into
° cavus, hollow

būcina, horn, trumpet
81-85
tortilis, -e, twisted, curved
turbō, -binis, m. spiral, whorl
° crēscō, -ere, crēvī, crētum, grow, increase
° āēr, āeris, m. air
° repleō, -ēre, -plēvī, -plētus, fill up
° uterque, utraque, utrumque, each (of two)
° iaceō, -ēre, -uī, lie, be situated
Phoebus, the sun, Phoebus
° madidus, wet, dripping
° contingō, -ere, -tigī, -tāctus, touch
° canō, -ere, cecinī, cantus, sing, sound
īnflō (1), blow into
receptus, -ūs, m. retreat, withdrawal
86-90
° coerceō, -ēre, -uī, -itus, check, confine
° plēnus, full
alveus, hollow, channel, river bed
subsīdō, -ere, -sēdī, -sessum, settle, subside
° surgō, -ere, surrēxī, surrēctum, rise up
° humus, -ī, f. ground, earth
° dēcrēscō, -ere, -crēvī, -crētum, decrease, grow less

91-95
° nūdō (1), lay bare, expose
līmus, mud, slime
frōns, frondis, f. leaf, foliage
° inānis, -e, void, empty
dēsōlō (1), abandon, forsake
° silentium, silence
° lacrima, tear
adfor, -fārī, -fātus sum, address
oborior, -īrī, -ortus sum, rise, spring up

abl. of comparison, as is **illā** in the following line. **67-68 aequī, deōrum**: objective genitives, *more devoted to justice, more god-fearing.* **69 ut**: with **videt**, *When Jupiter sees. . .* **stāgnāre orbem**: the first of three indirect statements governed by **videt**. **70-71 superesse . . . ūnum, superesse . . . ūnam**: to emphasize that they are the sole survivors, united by a common destiny. **74 aethera**: Greek acc. sing. ending.

75 positō = **dēpositō. tricuspide tēlō**: his trident. **76 rēctor pelagī**: Neptune. **profundum**; as substantive, *the deep.* **77 exstantem, tēctum**: modifying **Trītōna** (the -a is again the Greek acc. ending). **umerōs**: acc. of respect with **tēctum**; compare **vultum** in line 10. The phrase will be somewhat as follows: *and he calls sky-blue Triton, towering over the deep, his shoulders covered . . .* **innātō mūrice**: *with the shellfish that grow there;* but since the phrase could, by metonymy, also mean *with a cloak of native purple,* a pun is doubtless intended, with, as often in Ovid, a sly satiric glance at his own day, as if to say, "Triton did not have to buy his mantle of murex; it grew naturally on his shoulders." Garments dyed in the blood of the murex, a spiky mollusk common near the Levantine shore of the Mediterranean, were extremely expensive and hence a mark of great wealth; the rank of the Roman Knights and Senators was indicated by the width of the purple stripe on their togas and tunics. The color was not in fact what we know as "purple," but a brownish crimson. **78 conchae sonantī**: indir. object of **īnspīrāre**, *blow upon his echoing horn.* Read Wordsworth's sonnet, "The world is too much with us." **79-80 signō datō**: abl. of means, *by giving a signal.* **80 būcina**: the conch-shell mentioned in l. 78. **illī**: dat. of agent. **81 in lātum . . . ab īmō**: *which increases in* (lit. *into*) *width, starting with its smallest whorl.* **82 āera**: *the air,* i.e., Triton's breath; the ending -a is Greek acc. sing. **pontō**: abl. of place

fātidicamque Themin, quae tunc ōrācla tenēbat.
Nōn illō melior quisquam nec amantior aequī
vir fuit, aut illā metuentior ūlla deōrum.

Jupiter decides to save them.

Iuppiter ut liquidīs stāgnāre palūdibus orbem
et superesse virum dē tot modo mīlibus ūnum   70
et superesse videt dē tot modo mīlibus ūnam,
innocuōs ambōs, cultōrēs nūminis ambōs,
nūbila disiēcit; nimbīsque Aquilōne remōtīs,
et caelō terrās ostendit et aethera terrīs.
Nec maris īra manet; positōque tricuspide tēlō   75
mulcet aquās rēctor pelagī, suprāque profundum
exstantem atque umerōs innātō mūrice tēctum
caeruleum Trītōna vocat, conchaeque sonantī
īnspīrāre iubet, flūctūsque et flūmina signō
iam revocāre datō. Cava būcina sūmitur illī   80
tortilis, in lātum quae turbine crēscit ab īmō,
būcina quae, mediō concēpit ubi āera pontō,
lītora vōce replet sub utrōque iacentia Phoebō.
Tunc quoque, ut ōra deī madidā rōrantia barbā
contigit et cecinit iussōs īnflāta receptūs,   85
omnibus audīta est tellūris et aequoris undīs;
et quibus est undīs audīta, coercuit omnēs.
Iam mare lītus habet, plēnōs capit alveus amnēs,
flūmina subsīdunt, collēsque exīre videntur,
surgit humus, crēscunt loca dēcrēscentibus undīs;   90
postque diem longam nūdāta cacūmina silvae
ostendunt, līmumque tenent in fronde relictum.
Redditus orbis erat.

They realize that they are the only survivors.

Quem postquam vīdit inānem
et dēsōlātās agere alta silentia terrās,
Deucaliōn lacrimīs ita Pyrrham adfātur obortīs: 95

where without the preposition. **83 sub utrōque Phoebō:** i.e., under both the eastern and the western sun.

84 ut: *when.* **ōra . . . barbā:** *the god's lips bedewed by his dripping beard;* notice the interlocking word order. **85-86 contigit, cecinit, audīta est:** the subject is still **būcina. 85 cecinit iussōs receptūs:** a military idiom, *sounded the retreat as ordered.* **87 quibus undīs omnēs =** omnēs undās quibus. **88 plēnōs . . . amnēs:** *the river beds contain the rivers, full though they are.* **89 videntur:** *are seen,* not *seem.*

91 diem: feminine, when used loosely for an indefinite period of time. **nūdāta:** *clear (of the water).* **91-92 cacūmina silvae ostendunt:** *the forests show the tree-tops.*

93 Quem = Et eum (orbem): *And when he saw that it was void.* **94 agere:** this verb is often used, together with its object, as a circumlocution for another verb; here **agere silentia = silēre. 94 silentia:** n. pl. of -um nouns is frequently used in preference to the sing. in order to get the short syllable. **96 soror:** here perhaps as a term of affection; she was actually his

* coniŭnx, -iugis, m. and f. husband, wife
superstes, -stitis, surviving
* commūnis, -e, common, shared
patruēlis, -e, of a cousin
orīgō, -ginis, f. origin, source, descent
* occāsus, -ūs, m. the setting, sunset
* ortus, -ūs, m. the rising, dawn
turba, crowd
possideō, -ēre, -sēdī, -sessus, own, possess

* adhūc, hitherto, so far
fīdūcia, confidence, assurance
nūbilum, cloud
* fātum, fate
* ēripiō, -ere, ēripuī, ēreptus, snatch away, rescue
miserandus, pitiable, unhappy
cōnsōlor (dep. 1), comfort, console
doleō, -ēre, -uī, -itum, grieve, sorrow

namque, for, indeed
* utinam: introducing a wish
reparō (1), restore, renew
* paternus, of a father, paternal
* ars, artis, f. art, skill
* anima, breath, spirit
fōrmō (1), shape, form
* īnfundō, -ere, -fūdī, -fūsus, pour in
restō, -āre, -stitī, rest, remain

* superī, -ōrum, m. pl. the gods above
* exemplum, example, pattern
fleō, -ēre, flēvī, flētum, weep
* placet, -ēre, -uit, -itum, it pleases, is decided
caelestis, -e, heavenly
* precor (dep. 1), pray to
* sors, sortis, f. lot, fortune, prophecy, oracle
* pariter, equally, side by side
Cēphīsis, -idis, of Cephisus, river rising in Mt. Parnassus

secō, -āre, secuī, sectus, cut, cleave

lībō (1), sip, gather, draw
inrōrō (1), bedew, wet, sprinkle
liquor, -ōris, m. liquid, water
* flectō, -ere, flexī, flexus, turn, direct, bend
* vēstīgium, footstep
* sānctus, sacred, holy
dēlūbrum, shrine, sanctuary
fastīgium, gable, summit
palleō, -ēre, -uī, be pale, be discolored
muscus, moss
* āra, altar
* templum, temple
* tangō, -ere, tetigī, tāctus, touch
* gradus, -ūs, m. step
prōcumbō, -ere, -cubuī, -cubitum, fall forward

prōnus, sloping, forward
gelidus, cold
paveō, -ēre, pāvī, shake with fear
* ōsculum, kiss
* prex, precis, f. prayer
remollēscō, -ere, become softened
damnum, loss
* reparābilis, -e, able to be restored
(ops), opis, f. help
* mītis, -e, mild, gentle, kind

* vēlō (1), veil, hide
* cingō, -ere, cīnxī, cīnctus, gird, encircle
* resolvō, -ere, -solvī, -solūtus, undo, loosen
* os, ossis, n. bone
* iactō (1), keep throwing, toss
* parēns, -entis, m. and f. parent
obstipēscō, -ere, -stipuī, become dumbfounded
* prior, prius, earlier, first
* iussum, order, bidding
recūsō (1), refuse

cousin; hence **patruēlis**. 98 torus: *couch;* by metonymy, *marriage.* 99 terrārum; with **turba** of line 100. 100 turba: render by *crowd* or *throng,* or some such word to bring out the oxymoron of **duo turba.**

101-102 Haec . . . satis: *Even this assurance of our living is not as yet very strong.* 103 Quis (= Quī): modifying **animus**; *What would now be your feeling* . . . 104 miseranda: voc. case, *unhappy woman.* foret = esset. Quō: with modō, *How.* 105 possēs, dolērēs: like foret, main verbs in the conditional sentence. Quō cōnsōlante: abl. abs., *With whom consoling would you grieve?* = *Who would console your grief?* 107 quoque pontus habēret: repeated to indicate unanimity.

108 utinam possem: *if only I could;* utinam w. imperfect subjv. of a wish impossible of fulfillment. paternīs: i.e., of his father Prometheus, the creator of mankind. 111 vīsum est: because vīsum est is used with its indir. object to introduce decrees, resolutions, etc. (e.g., vīsum est Senātuī, *it has seemed best to the Senate that.* . .), we may translate it here as *So the gods above have decreed.*

112 Placuit: this verb, like vīsum est, is commonly used to introduce decrees and resolutions; *It pleased them to pray* = *They decided to pray.* 114 Cēphīsidas: as a Greek acc. pl. the -as is short. The river was about fifteen miles from Delphi. 115 ut . . . sīc: *although* . . .

"Ō soror, Ō coniūnx, Ō fēmina sōla superstes,
quam commūne mihī genus et patruēlis orīgō,
deinde torus iūnxit, nunc ipsa perīcula iungunt,
terrārum, quāscumque vident occāsus et ortus,
nōs duo turba sumus. Possēdit cētera pontus.   *100*
Haec quoque adhūc vītae nōn est fīdūcia nostrae
certa satis; terrent etiam nunc nūbila mentem!
Quis tibi, sī sine mē fātīs ērepta fuissēs,
nunc animus, miseranda, foret? Quō sōla timōrem
ferre modō possēs? Quō cōnsōlante dolērēs?   *105*
Namque ego, crēde mihī, sī tē quoque pontus habēret,
tē sequerer, coniūnx, et mē quoque pontus habēret.
Ō utinam possem populōs reparāre paternīs
artibus atque animās fōrmātae īnfundere terrae!
Nunc .genus in nōbīs restat mortāle duōbus   *110*
(sīc vīsum est superīs!) hominumque exempla manēmus."
Dīxerat, et flēbant.

They decide to consult the oracle of Themis.

                    Placuit caeleste precārī
nūmen, et auxilium per sacrās quaerere sortēs.
Nūlla mora est; adeunt pariter Cēphīsidas undās,
ut nōndum liquidās, sīc iam vada nōta secantēs.   *115*
Inde ubi lībātōs inrōrāvēre liquōrēs
vestibus et capitī, flectunt vēstīgia sānctae
ad dēlūbra deae, quōrum fastīgia turpī
pallēbant muscō, stābantque sine ignibus ārae.
Ut templī tetigēre gradūs, prōcumbit uterque   *120*
prōnus humī, gelidōque pavēns dedit ōscula saxō.
Atque ita, "Sī precibus," dīxērunt, "nūmina iūstīs
victa remollēscunt, sī flectitur īra deōrum,
dīc, Themi, quā generis damnum reparābile nostrī
arte sit, et mersīs fer opem, mītissima, rēbus."   *125*

The oracle replies, and they interpret the response.

                    Mōta dea est, sortemque dedit: "Discēdite templō,
et vēlāte caput, cīnctāsque resolvite vestēs,
ossaque post tergum magnae iactāte parentis."
Obstipuēre diū; rumpitque silentia vōce
Pyrrha prior, iussīsque deae pārēre recūsat: *130*

---

yet. **116 Inde:** translate with **lībātōs; inde** is the equivalent of **ex quibus** (referring to **undās** in l. 114). **116-117 ubi . . . capitī:** to purify themselves before entering the presence of the goddess. **116 inrōrāvēre** = **inrōrāvērunt. 117 flectunt vēstīgia:** like the English idiom, *to bend one's steps.* **118-119 quōrum . . . ārae:** details to remind of the recent flood.

121 humī: locative case, *on the ground.* **123 flectitur:** *is averted.* **124 Themi:** voc. case (Greek form) of **Themis. quā:** to be taken with **arte,** introducing the indir. question, which depends on **dīc,** *tell us by what device.* **generis:** to be construed with **rēbus** as well as with **damnum.**

126 sortem dedit: *delivered a prophecy.* **127 vēlāte, resolvite:** Plutarch explains the Roman practice of veiling the head at religious rites as either expressing the humility of the

87

venia, pardon, forgiveness
pavidus, trembling, fearful
* laedō, -ere, laesī, laesus, harm, injure
* māternus, of a mother
* umbra, shade, ghost
* repetō, -ere, -īvī, -ītus, seek again, repeat,
  go over
caecus, blind, unseeing, unseen
* obscūrus, dark, obscure
* latebrae, f. pl. hiding place, riddle
* volūtō (1), keep turning over
placidus, calm, gentle
* dictum, word

136-140

fallāx, -ācis, deceptive, false
sollertia, cleverness, intelligence
* pius, pious, devout
nefās, indecl. n. wickedness, sin
* suādeō, -ēre, suāsī, suāsus, counsel, advise
reor, rērī, ratus sum, think, suppose
augurium, augury, interpretation
* quamquam, conj. although
Tītānia, descendant of a Titan, Pyrrha

141-145

* dubium, doubt, uncertainty
adeō, adv. to such an extent
diffīdō, -ere, -fīsus sum, w. dat. distrust

* monitum, warning, instruction
tunica, tunic
recingō, -ere, -cīnxī, -cīnctus, ungird,
  loosen
testis, -is, m. and f. witness, evidence
* vetustās, -ātis, f. antiquity, tradition

146-150

dūritiēs, -ēī, f. hardness
rigor, -ōris, m. stiffness, hardness
molliō, -īre, -iī, -ītus, soften
* fōrma, shape, outline
* mox, adv. soon
* contingō, -ere, -tigī, -tāctum, fall to, come
  upon
* manifestus, clear, plain
marmor, -moris, n. marble

151-155

exāctus, worked out, clearly outlined
* rudis, -e, rough, unworked, unformed
* ūmidus, damp, moist
sūcus, juice, moisture
* terrēnus, of earth, earthy
* solidus, firm, solid
nequeō, -īre, -iī, -itum, be unable
* mūtō (1), change
* vēna, vein

priest or preventing ill-omened sounds from coming to his ears; while the Vergilian commentator Servius tells us that all knots had to be untied at sacrifices (this is perhaps based on the notion that knots would, on the principle of sympathetic magic, hinder the gods in performing whatever was asked). **128 iactāte:** imp. of the frequentative **iactō**, *keep throwing.* **131 det:** subjv. in an indir. command; the implied subject is **dea;** *and with trembling lips she asks the goddess to forgive her.* **132 laedere:** with **pavet,** on the analogy of infinitives with **timet. laedere . . . umbrās:** *to offend her mother's spirit.* Pyrrha takes the oracle literally.

133-134 repetunt . . . volūtant: *they go over again together the words of the oracle given them, lurking in blind riddles, and ponder them together.* **134 sēcum:** *to themselves.* **inter sē:** here, as usual, reciprocal, *with each other.* **135 Epimēthida:** Greek acc. form (the nom. is **Epimēthis**). **137 sunt:** the subject is **ōrācula. nūllum . . . suādent:** *the oracles give no wicked counsel.* **138-139 Lapidēs . . . dīcī:** *"I think that stones are meant by 'bones' in the body of the earth."*

140-141 in dubiō = dubia: *uncertain.* **142 quid temptāre nocēbit:** *what harm will it do to try?* **temptāre** is the subject, **quid** the internal object of **nocēbit. 143-144 Discēdunt . . . mittunt:** compare carefully with lines 126-128.

145 crēdat, sit: here, as frequently in poetry, the present subjv. is used for a present contrary-to-fact conditional sentence; *who would believe it if the ancient tradition did not vouch for it?* **146 pōnere = dēpōnere:** *to put aside.* **coepēre = coepērunt. 147 morā:** *with delay = gradually.* **mollīta:** in agreement with **saxa,** *and, when softened, to take shape.* **149-151 ut quaedam . . . signīs:** *though not yet clear, still some shape of a man can be seen, but as if begun in marble, not very sharply defined and very similar to statues in the rough.*

152 illīs: i.e., **lapidibus. aliquō ūmida sūcō:** *damp with some moisture.* **152-153 quae pars fuit = pars quae fuit. 156 superōrum nūmine:** *by the will of the gods.* **157 trāxēre = trāxērunt:** *assumed the appearance of men.* **158 fēmina:** *womankind.* **iactū:** with **dē** and **fēmineō,** *from the throwing that the woman did.* **159 Inde:** *Consequently.* **experiēns labōrum:** *capable of enduring hardships.* **160 orīgine:** abl. of source.

detque sibī veniam, pavidō rogat ōre; pavetque
laedere iactātīs māternās ossibus umbrās.
Intereā repetunt caecīs obscūra latebrīs
verba datae sortis sēcum, inter sēque volūtant.
Inde Promēthīdēs placidīs Epimēthida dictīs   *135*
mulcet; et, "Aut fallāx," ait, "est sollertia nōbīs,
aut (pia sunt nūllumque nefās ōrācula suādent)
'magna parēns' terra est. Lapidēs in corpore terrae
ossa reor dīcī. Iacere hōs post terga iubēmur."
    Coniugis auguriō quamquam Tītānia mōta est,   *140*
spēs tamen in dubiō est; adeō caelestibus ambō
diffīdunt monitīs. Sed quid temptāre nocēbit?

The stones which they throw become human beings.

    Discēdunt, vēlantque caput, tunicāsque recingunt,
et iussōs lapidēs sua post vēstīgia mittunt.
Saxa (quis hoc crēdat, nisi sit prō teste vetustās?)   *145*
pōnere dūritiem coepēre suumque rigōrem,
mollīrīque morā, mollītaque dūcere fōrmam.
Mox ubi crēvērunt, nātūraque mītior illīs
contigit, ut quaedam, sīc nōn manifesta, vidērī
fōrma potest hominis, sed utī dē marmore coepta,   *150*
nōn exācta satis rudibusque simillima signīs.
Quae tamen ex illīs aliquō pars ūmida sūcō
et terrēna fuit, versa est in corporis ūsum.
Quod solidum est flectīque nequit, mūtātur in ossa.
Quae modo vēna fuit, sub eōdem nōmine mānsit,   *155*

**Deucalion and Pyrrha repopulate the earth. An illustration by Hendrik
Goltzius, Netherlands, 1589. Metropolitan Museum of Art, N.Y.C.**

* faciēs, -ēī, f. face, appearance
* trahō, -ere, trāxī, trāctus, draw, take on
* fēmineus, of a woman
* reparō (1), remake, restore
  iactus, -ūs, m. throwing, cast
* dūrus, rough, tough, unfeeling
  experiēns, -entis, w. gen., used to, experienced in
* documentum, proof
* nāscor, -ī, nātus sum, be born

* sponte, voluntarily; sponte suā, of its own accord
  pariō, -ere, peperī, partus, bring forth
* ūmor, -ōris, m. liquid, moisture
  percalēscō, -ere, -caluī, become very warm
* sōl, sōlis, m. sun
  caenum, mud
  ūdus, wet, damp
  intumēscō, -ere, -tumuī, begin to swell
* aestus, -ūs, m. heat, tide
  fēcundus, fruitful, fertile
  sēmen, -minis, n. seed
  vīvāx, -ācis, enduring, quickening
* nūtriō, -īre, -iī, -ītus, nourish, nurture
* solum, ground, soil
  ceu, just as, as if
  alvus, -ī, f. belly, womb

  dēserō, -ere, -seruī, -sertus, desert, leave
  septemfluus, flowing, seven-fold
  Nīlus, the Nile
  alveus, hollow, channel, river-bed
  aetherius, heavenly, of the air
* recēns, -entis, fresh, new, recent
  exārdēscō, -ere, -ārsī, -ārsum, kindle, take fire, break out

  sīdus, -deris, n. star, constellation
  līmus, mud, slime
* plūrimus, most, very much, very many
* cultor, -ōris, m. cultivator, farmer
  glaeba, sod, clod of earth

* imperfectus, unfinished, incomplete
  truncus, maimed, deprived of, lacking
  quippe, certainly, indeed
  temperiēs, -ēī, f. blending, tempering
  calor, -ōris, m. warmth, heat

* cūnctus, all, entire
* pugnāx, -ācis, fond of fighting, hostile
  vapor, -ōris, m. steam, heat
* creō (1), create, beget, produce
  discors, -cordis, discordant
* concordia, harmony, concord, union
  fētus, -ūs, m. birth, growth, offspring
* aptus, fit, suitable, right
  dīluvium, flood, deluge
  lutulentus, muddy
* almus, nourishing, kind
  recandēscō, -ere, -canduī, become hot (again), glow

* ēdō, -ere, ēdidī, ēditus, put forth, give out
  innumerus, countless
* speciēs, -ēī, f. sight, appearance, species
* partim, partly
* figūra, form, shape, kind
  mōnstrum, portent, monster, marvel
  Pȳthōn, -ōnis, m. Python, serpent
  gignō, -ere, genuī, genitus, beget, produce
* incognitus, unknown
  serpēns, -entis, m. and f. snake, serpent

161 dīversīs formīs: abl. of description. **165** solō: the noun, not the adjective. **166** faciem aliquam: i.e., *some shape or other;* Ovid implies that the kind is not predetermined by the sēmina.

167-178 This passage is introduced by way of example: in antiquity it was believed that when the Nile receded from its annual inundation it left behind numerous animals, spontaneously generated from the fertile soil of Egypt by the fecundating waters of the river. The belief in spontaneous generation was held even by the learned until the seventeenth century. **167** septemfluus: the Nile is so called because of its seven mouths. **168** flūmina: used here in its original sense of *flowings.* alveō: indir. object; the -eō is taken as one syllable. **169** aetheriō exārsit sīdere: *has dried out* (lit. *has been burned*) *from the sun in the sky.* **171** sub: here (as often w. the acc. in expressions of time) the meaning is *just after; some only begun, just after the actual moment of birth.* **173** numerīs: abl. of separation; trunca numerīs: *lacking parts.* vident: the subject is still cultōrēs. **175** temperiem sūmpsēre (= sūmpsērunt): *have taken on the right proportions.* **176** concipiunt: *they conceive, they become pregnant.* **177** cum: *although.* aquae: dat. w. pugnāx. **178** discors concordia: the oxymoron refers to the union of the apparently irreconcilable elements fire and water (or heat and moisture), which the ancients thought to be the source of life.

inque brevī spatiō superōrum nūmine saxa
missa virī manibus faciem trāxēre virōrum,
et dē fēmineō reparāta est fēmina iactū.
Inde genus dūrum sumus experiēnsque labōrum
et documenta damus, quā sīmus orīgine nātī.   *160*

Python

Other living creatures are born from the earth by spontaneous generation.

Cētera dīversīs tellūs animālia fōrmīs
sponte suā peperit, postquam vetus ūmor ab igne
percaluit sōlis, caenumque ūdaeque palūdēs
intumuēre aestū, fēcundaque sēmina rērum
vīvācī nūtrīta solō, ceu mātris in alvō,   *165*
crēvērunt, faciemque aliquam cēpēre morandō.
Sīc ubi dēseruit madidōs septemfluus agrōs
Nīlus, et antīquō sua flūmina reddidit alveō,
aetherīōque recēns exārsit sīdere līmus,
plūrima cultōrēs versīs animālia glaebīs   *170*
inveniunt; et in hīs, quaedam modo coepta sub ipsum
nāscendī spatium, quaedam imperfecta suīsque
trunca vident numerīs; et eōdem in corpore saepe
altera pars vīvit, rudis est pars altera tellūs.
Quippe ubi temperiem sūmpsēre ūmorque calorque,   *175*
concipiunt; et ab hīs oriuntur cūncta duōbus.
Cumque sit ignis aquae pugnāx, vapor ūmidus omnēs
rēs creat; et discors concordia fētibus apta est.
Ergō ubi dīluviō tellūs lutulenta recentī
sōlibus aetheriīs almōque recanduit aestū,   *180*
ēdidit innumerās speciēs, partimque figūrās
rettulit antīquās, partim nova mōnstra creāvit.

One of the newly created monsters, Python, is killed by Apollo, who
then founds the Pythian Games.

Illa quidem nōllet, sed tē quoque, maxime Pȳthōn,
tum genuit; populīsque novīs, incognite serpēns,
terror erās, tantum spatiī dē monte tenēbās.   *185*

179 dīluviō: abl. of cause w. lutulenta. 180 sōlibus: *from the rays of the sun.*

183 Illa: i.e., Tellūs (now personified). nollet: supply genuisse, *She could have wished that
she had not given you* (tē) *birth;* potential subjv. 183-184 maxime Pȳthon, incognite serpēns:
voc. case; apostrophe. 184 populīs novīs: those just created by Deucalion and Pyrrha.
185 tantum spatiī dē monte: *so large an area of the mountain;* dē monte = montis.

91

arcitenēns, -entis, carrying the bow, archer
dāma, deer
caprea, roe, she-goat
fugāx, -ācis, swift, fleet, fleeing
exhauriō, -īre, -hausī, -haustus, drain off,
  empty
* pharetra, quiver
* niger, -gra, -grum, black
venēnum, poison, venom
nēve, and in order that . . . not
* dēleō, -ēre, -ēvī, -ētus, destroy, blot out

celeber, -bris, -bre, thronged, famous
* certāmen, -minis, n. contest, struggle
Pȳthia, -ōrum, n. pl. the Pythian games
perdomō, -āre, -uī, -itus, tame thoroughly,
  overcome
* iuvenis, -is, m. youth, young man
* quīcumque, quae-, quod-, whoever, whatever
* -ve, enclitic, or
rota, wheel, car, chariot
aesculeus, of oak
* frōns, frondis, f. leaf, foliage, garland
* honōs (honor), -ōris, m. honor, distinction, award
* laurus, -ī, f. laurel
decēns, -entis, appropriate, handsome
crīnis, -is, m. hair

tempus, -poris, n. time, temple of the head

* cingō, -ere, cīnxī, cīnctus, surround, encircle
* quīlibet, quae-, quod-, any you like, any
  at all
Phoebus, Phoebus, Apollo, god of light
  and prophecy
Daphnē, -ēs, f. Daphne, daughter of the
  river god Peneus
Pēnēius, of Peneus
* ignārus, ignorant, unaware
saevus, cruel, fierce
Cupīdō, -dinis, m. Cupid, god of love
Dēlius, Delian, of Delos
* nūper, recently, lately
* superbus, proud, haughty
* addūcō, -ere, -dūxī, -ductus, draw toward,
  draw tight, stretch
* cornū, -ūs, n. horn, wing, tip (of a bow)
nervus, sinew, bowstring

lascīvus, playful, sportive
decet, -ēre, -uit, suit, be appropriate for
gestāmen, -minis, n. a thing carried, load,
  weapon
* fera, wild beast
pestifer, -era, -erum, pestilential, destructive
iūgerum, iugerum, land measure, roughly
  ⅝ of an acre
* venter, -tris, m. stomach, belly
innumerus, countless
tumidus, swollen

---

186 deus arcitenēns: Apollo. et: and yet. armīs: abl. w. ūsus. 186-187 arcitenēns . . . ūsus: *carrying a bow, yet never before having used such weapons except on fallow-deer and swift goats.* 188 gravem: modifying Hunc (l. 186). mīlle gravem tēlīs: *heavy from the thousand weapons = encumbered by the countless arrows (from the archer-god Apollo).* 189 perdidit: the subject is deus, the object Hunc.

190 Nēve . . . vetustās: purpose clause. 192 Pȳthia: predicate noun after lūdōs dictōs, *games called the Pythia.* perdomitae: notice that serpēns is now changed to feminine gender. 193 Hīs: the antecedent is lūdōs. iuvenum: partitive gen. w. quīcumque. manū pedibusve rotāve: i.e., in wrestling, boxing, throwing, etc., in running, and in chariot-racing. The Pythian games were similar to the Olympic. 194 capiēbat honōrem: *used to win a prize.* 195 crīne: abl. of means w. decentia. 196 quālibet: *any at all,* almost our colloquial *any old.* The laurel, Apollo's sacred tree, did not yet exist (its origin is explained in the next story), and so he did not care from what tree he took his garlands.

197 Prīmus . . . Pēnēia: sc. erat. 199 Dēlius: Apollo, who was born on the island of Delos. hunc: the antecedent is Cupīdinis. victō serpente: abl. of cause explaining superbus, *proud of having recently conquered the serpent.* 201 -que: joining vīderat and dīxerat. tibi: dat. of possession. Quid tibi: sc. est, *What business have you?*

202 nostrōs = meōs. In poetry and colloquial Latin the first person plural is often used for the singular. So, too, possumus and strāvimus below. 203 quī: the antecedent is the first person plural in nostrōs, as though it were *of us* rather than *our.* certa: modifies vulnera; certa vulnera is to be taken with both dare's. 205 innumerīs: indicating the severity of the struggle. tumidum: i.e., with poison. Pȳthōna: Greek acc. sing. ending. 206 face: torch to

Hunc deus arcitenēns, et numquam tālibus armīs
ante, nisi in dāmīs capreīsque fugācibus, ūsus,
mīlle gravem tēlīs (exhaustā paene pharetrā)
perdidit, effūsō per vulnera nigra venēnō.
Nēve operis fāmam posset dēlēre vetustās,   *190*
īnstituit sacrōs celebrī certāmine lūdōs,
Pȳthia perdomitae serpentis nōmine dictōs.
Hīs iuvenum quīcumque manū pedibusve rotāve
vīcerat, aesculeae capiēbat frondis honōrem.
Nōndum laurus erat, longōque decentia crīne   *195*
tempora cingēbat dē quālibet arbore Phoebus.

Apollo and Daphne

Exulting in his victory, Apollo taunts Cupid with lack of skill in
archery. In revenge Cupid lets fly two arrows. One causes Apollo to fall
in love with Daphne, daughter of the river god Peneus; the other
causes Daphne to rebuff all suitors.

Prīmus amor Phoebī Daphnē Pēnēia, quem nōn
fors ignāra dedit, sed saeva Cupīdinis īra.
Dēlius hunc, nūper victō serpente superbus,
vīderat adductō flectentem cornua nervō,   *200*
"Quid"que "tibī, lascīve puer, cum fortibus armīs?"
dīxerat, "Ista decent umerōs gestāmina nostrōs,
quī dare certa ferae, dare vulnera possumus hostī,
quī modo pestiferō tot iūgera ventre prementem
strāvimus innumerīs tumidum Pȳthōna sagittīs.   *205*

Apollo and Daphne. The river god in the lower right hand
corner is her father. Poussin (1594-1665). Louvre, Paris.

* fax, facis, f. flame, torch
* contentus, content, satisfied
  irrītō (1), arouse, stir up
* laus, laudis, f. praise, glory
  adserō, -serere, -seruī, -sertus, aspire to, claim
* Venus, -neris, f. Venus, goddess of love
  arcus, -ūs, m. bow

211-215

ēlīdō, -ere, ēlīsī, ēlīsus, dash out, force out
impiger, -gra, -grum, active, vigorous, nimble
* umbrōsus, shady, shaded
cōnsistō, -ere, -stitī, take a position, alight
* arx, arcis, f. height, summit, citadel
sagittifer, -era, -erum, carrying arrows
prōmō, -ere, prōmpsī, prōmptus, take out
aurātus, golden
cuspis, -pidis, f. point
fulgeō, -ēre, fulsī, glow, gleam, shine
* acūtus, sharp

216-220

obtūsus, blunt, dull
harundō, -dinis, f. reed, shaft
plumbum, lead
Pēnēis, -idis, of Peneus; as f. noun, daughter of Peneus
Apollineus, of Apollo
* trāiciō, -ere, -iēcī, -iectus, throw across, pierce
medulla, marrow, pith
* fugiō, -ere, fūgī, fugitus, flee (from), shun

exuviae, -ārum, f. pl. spoils
* gaudeō, -ēre, gāvīsus sum, rejoice, exult in
innūptus, unwed, maiden
aemula, rival
Phoebē, -ēs, f. Diana, sister of Phoebus Apollo
vitta, fillet, headband
āversor (dep. 1), turn away, rebuff
impatiēns, -entis, impatient
expers, -ertis, w. gen., having no part in, scornful of
nemus, -moris, n. grove
āvius, untrodden, remote
lūstrō (1), traverse, roam over
Hymēn, -menis, m. Hymen, god of marriage
* cōnūbium, marriage, wedlock

226-230

gener, -erī, m. son-in-law
* nāta, daughter
* nepōs, -ōtis, m. grandson
* velut, as though, as if
* crīmen, -minis, n. accusation, crime, fault
taeda, pine torch, torch
exōsus, detesting, loathing
iugālis, -e, of the yoke, nuptial
verēcundus, modest, bashful
* suffundō, -ere, -fūdī, -fūsus, suffuse, overspread
rubor, -ōris, m. redness, blush
blandus, flattering, caressing
* haereō, -ēre, haesī, haesum, cling
* cervīx, -vīcis, f. neck
* lacertus, upper part of arm, arm

---

kindle the flame of love. nescio quōs: together serving as an indefinite adj., indicating contempt or lack of interest; *some loves or other; loves, whatever they are.* estō: future imperative of sum, *you shall be.* 207 tuā: modifies face (l. 206). adsere: in poetry prohibitions are sometimes expressed by the imperative with nē (here combined with -que to make nec) instead of the usual periphrases (nōlī adserere or cavē nē adserās.)

208 Fīlius Veneris: Cupid. Fīgat: ordinary jussive subjv. with tuus (arcus), and as jussive of proviso with meus arcus, *Let your bow wound everything, Phoebus, provided that mine wounds you.* 209-210 cēdunt deō = minōra sunt quam deus. quantō: abl. of degree of difference, as is tantō below; quantō . . . tantō, *as much as all living creatures are inferior to a god.* 210 nostrā: see note on l .202.

211 ēlīsō, percussīs: the violence in these words expresses the force of Cupid's wrath. 212 arce: abl. of place where without a preposition. 213 ēque = ē + que. 214 diversōrum operum: gen. of description, *serving opposite purposes.* 217 Hoc, illō: *The latter, with the former.*

220 latebrīs: depending on gaudēns in the next line. 221 Phoebēs: gen. sing. (a Greek form) of Phoebē. 222 sine lēge: *without order (casually).* 223 petiēre = petiērunt. petentēs: *suitors.* 224 expers virī: *wanting no part of marriage.*

228 taedās: direct object of exōsa. 229 ōra: acc. of respect w. suffunditur; *is covered as to pretty face = has her pretty face covered.* 230 inque = in + que. cervīce: w. the prep. in.

The transformation of Daphne into laurel.
Statue by Bernini in the Villa Borghese, Rome.

Gabinetto, Fototeca Unione

Tū face nescio quōs estō contentus amōrēs
irrītāre tuā, nec laudēs adsere nostrās."
    Fīlius huic Veneris, "Fīgat tuus omnia, Phoebe,
tē meus arcus," ait, "quantōque animālia cēdunt
cūncta deō, tantō minor est tua glōria nostrā."   *210*
Dīxit, et ēlīsō percussīs āere pennīs
impiger umbrōsā Parnāsī cōnstitit arce,
ēque sagittiferā prōmpsit duo tēla pharetrā
dīversōrum operum: fugat hoc, facit illud amōrem.
Quod facit aurātum est et cuspide fulget acūtā;   *215*
quod fugat obtūsum est et habet sub harundine plumbum.
Hoc deus in nymphā Pēnēide fīxit, at illō
laesit Apollineās trāiecta per ossa medullās.

Daphne scorns all suitors.

    Prōtinus alter amat. Fugit altera nōmen amantis,
silvārum latebrīs captīvārumque ferārum   *220*
exuviīs gaudēns, innūptaeque aemula Phoebēs.
Vitta coercēbat positōs sine lēge capillōs.
Multī illam petiēre. Illa āversāta petentēs
impatiēns expersque virī nemora āvia lūstrat;
nec quid Hymēn, quid Amor, quid sint cōnūbia, cūrat.   *225*
Saepe pater dīxit, "Generum mihi, fīlia, dēbēs,"
saepe pater dīxit, "Dēbēs mihi, nāta, nepōtēs."
Illa, velut crīmen taedās exōsa iugālēs,
pulchra verēcundō suffunditur ōra rubōre,
inque patris blandīs haerēns cervīce lacertīs,   *230*

* perpetuus, lasting, perpetual
* genitor, -ōris, *m.* father
* cārus, dear
  virginitās, -ātis, *f.* virginity
* fruor, -ī, frūctus sum, *w. abl.,* enjoy
  obsequor, -ī, -secūtus sum, yield, comply
* decor, -ōris, *m.* grace, beauty
* optō (1), desire, pray for
* vetō, -āre, -uī, -itus, forbid, prevent
  repugnō (1), *w. dat.,* conflict with, oppose

236-240

* fallō, -ere, fefellī, falsus, deceive, betray, fail
* ut, *correl. w.* sīc, just as . . . so
* levis, -e, light
  stipula, stalk, stubble, reed
  dēmō, -ere, dēmpsī, dēmptus, take away, remove
  adoleō, -ēre, -uī, burn
  arista, ear of grain
  saepēs, -is, *f.* a hedge
  ārdeō, -ēre, ārsī, ārsum, burn, blaze
  viātor, -ōris, *m.* wayfarer, traveler
  vel . . . vel, either . . . or
  nimis, too, too much
* pectus, -toris, *n.* breast, heart

241-245

  ūrō, -ere, ussī, ustus, burn
  sterilis, -e, sterile, barren
  nūtriō, -īre, -iī, -ītus, nurture, nourish
* inōrnātus, unadorned
* collum, neck
* pendeō, -ēre, pependī, hang
  cōmō, -ere, cōmpsī, cōmptus, comb, dress
  micō, -āre, -uī, flash, shine
* sīdus, sīderis, *n.* star

* ōsculum, *dimin. of* ōs, little mouth, lip, kiss
* digitus, finger

246-250

  bracchium, arm
* ōcior, -ius, swifter
  aura, air, breeze
  resistō, -ere, -stitī, halt, stop
* īnsequor, -ī, -secūtus sum, pursue
  cerva, hind, deer

251-255

* aquila, eagle
* trepidō (1), tremble, quiver
  columba, dove
* quisque, quaeque, quidque (quodque), each
  prōnus, forward, headlong
* indignus, not deserving
  crūs, crūris, *n.* leg
  notō (1), mark, scratch
  sentis, -is, *m.* briar, bramble
* asper, -era, -erum, rough, harsh
  quā, where
* properō (1), hurry, hasten
  moderātē, with moderation, moderately

256-260

  inhibeō, -ēre, -hibuī, -hibitus, check, restrain
* inquīrō, -ere, -quīsīvī, -quīsītus, ask, inquire
* incola, -ae, *m.* inhabitant
* pāstor, -ōris, *m.* shepherd
  armentum, herd
  grex, gregis, *m.* flock
  horridus, rough, shaggy
  temerārius, rash, impulsive
  ideō, *adv.* on that account
  Delphicus, of Delphi

231-232 Dā mihi fruī: *Permit* (lit. *Give*) *me to enjoy;* fruī is the direct object of Dā. **232 pater:** Jupiter.

233 quidem, sed: the use of these words in coordinate clauses gives a kind of concessive meaning to the first clause; *Although he gave in, nevertheless that beauty . . .* or *He gave in, all right, but that beauty. . .* tē: Ovid apostrophizes Daphne. **quod:** sc. *id, what you pray for.* **234 vōtō:** dat., indir. object of repugnat. **235 Daphnēs:** gen. sing. (a Greek form). **236 quod:** supply id as antecedent and direct object of spērat. ōrācula: Apollo was the god of prophecy.

237-238 Ut, ut; introducing two similes; the comparison is made by sīc in l. 240. **237 stipulae:** after the grain was harvested the farmers burnt off the stubble. **238-239 ut . . . relīquit:** the simile is of a hedge carelessly ignited by the torch of a passer-by who has allowed it to brush the hedge or has abandoned it with the coming of daylight. **239 nimis:** modifies the adverbial sense of the prefix ad- of admōvit, *has brought too near.* **240 in flammās abiit:** a common metaphor applied to those in love.

242 collō: abl. of place where without a prep. **244 quae:** direct object of vīdisse. **246 plūs:** acc. of extent. **parte:** abl. of comparison. **247 sī qua:** *if any things = whatever.* **248 resistit:** *stops and looks back.*

"Dā mihi perpetuā, genitor cārissime," dīxit,
"virginitāte fruī. Dedit hoc pater ante Diānae."

Apollo falls in love with Daphne.

Ille quidem obsequitur, sed tē decor iste quod optās
esse vetat, vōtōque tuō tua fōrma repugnat.
   Phoebus amat, vīsaeque cupit cōnūbia Daphnēs,   *235*
quodque cupit spērat; suaque illum ōrācula fallunt.
Utque lévēs stipulae dēmptīs adolentur aristīs,
ut facibus saepēs ārdent, quās forte viātor
vel nimis admōvit vel iam sub lūce relīquit,
sīc deus in flammās abiit, sīc pectore tōtō   *240*
ūritur, et sterilem spērandō nūtrit amōrem.
Spectat inōrnātōs collō pendēre capillōs
et "Quid sī comantur?" ait. Videt igne micantēs
sīderibus similēs oculōs; videt ōscula, quae nōn
est vīdisse satis; laudat digitōsque manūsque   *245*
bracchiaque et nūdōs mediā plūs parte lacertōs;
sī qua latent meliōra putat.

She flees; Apollo tries to call her back by listing his many attributes.

               Fugit ōcior aurā
illa levī, neque ad haec revocantis verba resistit:
"Nympha, precor, Pēnēi, manē! Nōn īnsequor hostis.
Nympha, manē! Sīc agna lupum, sīc cerva leōnem,   *250*
sīc aquilam pennā fugiunt trepidante columbae,
hostēs quaeque suōs; amor est mihi causa sequendī!
Mē miserum! Nē prōna cadās, indignave laedī
crūra notent sentēs, et sim tibi causa dolōris!
Aspera quā properās loca sunt. Moderātius, ōrō,   *255*
curre, fugamque inhibē; moderātius īnsequar ipse.
Cui placeās inquīre tamen: nōn incola montis,
nōn ego sum pāstor, nōn hīc armenta gregēsque
horridus observō. Nescīs, temerāria, nescīs
quem fugiās, ideōque fugis. Mihi Delphica tellūs   *260*

249 Pēnēi: voc. case (Greek form) of **Pēnēis,** *daughter of Peneus.* **hostis:** in apposition with the subject, *as an enemy.* **252 quaeque:** in partitive apposition with **columbae. 253 Mē miserum:** acc. of exclamation. **indignave: -ve** (*or*) serves as connective but the negative **nē** goes also with **notent. 253-254 cadās, notent:** optative subjv., *May you not fall . . . may the brambles not scratch.* **254 sim:** potential subjv., *I would be.*

255 quā: modifies **viā** understood, *the way you are hurrying.*

255-256 Moderātius . . . īnsequar ipse: the god gallantly offers to "deescalate" if she will do likewise. **257 Cui placeās:** indir. question with **inquīre. 260-267 Mihi . . . nōbīs:** Apollo lists his powers. **261 Claros, Tenedos:** nom. sing. (Greek ending). **Patarēa:** adj. w. **rēgia;** *my palace at Patara.* Patara and Claros are towns on the southwest coast of Asia Minor; Tenedos is an island off the coast of Troy.

* rēgia (*sc.* domus), palace
* serviō, -īre, -iī, -ītum, *w. dat.*, be subject to
* pateō, -ēre, -uī, lie open, be revealed
  concordō (1), harmonize, be in tune with
* carmen, -minis, *n.* poem, song
  nervus, sinew, string
* vacuus, empty, vacant, carefree

* inventum, discovery, invention
* medicīna, art of healing, medicine
  opifer, -era, -erum, bringer of help
* herba, herb, plant, grass
* subiciō, -ere, -iēcī, -iectus, put under, make subject
* potentia, power, efficacy
  ei, *interj.* oh! ah!
* sānābilis, -e, curable
  Pēnēia, daughter of Peneus, Daphne
  cursus, -ūs, *m.* running, race, course

* imperfectus, unfinished
  decēns, -entis, attractive, graceful
* nūdō (1), lay bare, expose
  obvius, in the way, opposing, meeting
  adversus, facing, opposing
  vibrō (1), shake, flutter
  flāmen, -minis, *n.* blowing, breeze, wind
* impellō, -ere, -pulī, -pulsus, strike against
* retrō, back, backwards
* augeō, -ēre, auxī, auctus, increase
* sustineō, -ēre, -tinuī, -tentus, support, endure
  ultrā, further, longer

  blanditia, flattery, blandishment
* passus, -ūs, *m.* pace; admissō passū, swiftly
* canis, -is, *m. and f.* dog
  lepus, -poris, *m.* hare
  arvum, field
* alter . . . alter, the one . . . the other
  inhaereō, -ēre, -haesī, -haesum, cling to

  extentus, outstretched
  stringō, -ere, strīnxī, strictus, scrape, graze, touch
* rōstrum, beak, muzzle, snout
  ambiguus, doubtful, uncertain
  an, whether
  comprēndō, -ere, -prēndī, -prēnsus, seize, grasp
  morsus, -ūs, *m.* act of biting, bite
  virgō, -ginis, *f.* maiden, girl
* adiuvō, -āre, -iūvī, -iūtus, aid

* requiēs, -ētis (*acc.* -ētem *or* -em), *f.* rest, repose
  fugāx, -ācis, fleeing, running away
  immineō, -ēre, -uī, *w. dat.*, lean over, threaten
* crīnis, -is, *m.* hair
  adflō (1), breathe upon
* absūmō, -ere, -sūmpsī, -sūmptus, use up
  expallēscō, -ere, -palluī, turn very pale
  citus, swift, rapid
  Pēnēis, -idis, of Peneus
  (ops), opis, *f.* help, aid

---

262 Per mē: as god of prophecy and as god of music. **264 nostra:** supply **sagitta. nostrā:** abl. of comparison. **ūna sagitta:** i.e., Cupid's. **265 vacuō:** *unoccupied;* hence, *unattached.*

266 orbem: sc. **terrārum; orbis terrārum,** *the circle of lands* (around the Mediterranean) comes to mean *the inhabited world.* **267 dīcor:** *I am called.* **subiecta:** sc. **est. 268 Ei:** interj. of dismay. **268-269 quod . . . artēs:** quod-substantive clause with verbs of feeling (**Ei mihi, Woe is me = Doleō**).

270 locūtūrum with **eum** implied, *fled from him as he was about to say.* **271 cum ipsō:** note that the Latin inverts the normal English construction, which would be *left him with his words unsaid.* **272 vīsa:** sc. **est,** *she looked* (*she appeared*). **corpora = corpus:** the plural is often used for the singular in poetry. **273 obviaque . . . vestēs:** a "golden line," i.e., "two substantives and two adjectives, with a verb between them to keep the peace." The next line is also "golden" if we take **retrō dabat** (*blew back*) as a verb; cf. l .229. **276 utque: ut** here is *because* but in l. 278 **Ut** will mean *Just as,* introducing the simile. **monēbat:** sc. **eum;** *advised him.*

278 canis . . . leporem: these words belong in the **cum**-temporal clause; the **cum** has been displaced for reasons of meter and emphasis. **canis Gallicus:** the Gallic hound (a kind of greyhound) typifies a swift hunting dog. **279 pedibus:** probably chosen for alliteration; translate *by running.* **280 inhaesūrō similis:** *like one about to cling = quasi inhaesūrus, almost going to catch.* **282 alter . . . comprēnsus:** a close call! **an sit comprēnsus:** *whether he has been caught.* **284 sīc:** *in the same way,* resuming after the long simile.

285 Quī: supply **ille** as antecedent. **287 crīnem:** object of **adflat. cervīcibus:** abl. of place

et Claros et Tenedos Patarēaque rēgia servit.
Iuppiter est genitor. Per mē quod eritque fuitque
estque patet. Per mē concordant carmina nervīs.
Certa quidem nostra est—nostrā tamen ūna sagitta
certior, in vacuō quae vulnera pectore fēcit.   265
Inventum medicīna meum est, opiferque per orbem
dīcor, et herbārum subiecta potentia nōbīs.
Ei mihi, quod nūllīs amor est sānābilis herbīs,
nec prōsunt dominō quae prōsunt omnibus artēs!"

The pursuit continues.

Plūra locūtūrum timidō Pēnēia cursū   270
fūgit, cumque ipsō verba imperfecta relīquit,
tum quoque vīsa decēns. Nūdābant corpora ventī,
obviaque adversās vibrābant flāmina vestēs,
et levis impulsōs retrō dabat aura capillōs,
auctaque fōrma fugā est. Sed enim nōn sustinet ultrā   275
perdere blanditiās iuvenis deus; utque monēbat
ipse amor, admissō sequitur vēstīgia passū.
     Ut canis in vacuō leporem cum Gallicus arvō
vīdit, et hic praedam pedibus petit, ille salūtem
(alter inhaesūrō similis iam iamque tenēre   280
spērat et extentō stringit vēstīgia rōstrō;
alter in ambiguō est, an sit comprēnsus, et ipsīs
morsibus ēripitur tangentiaque ōra relinquit),
sīc deus et virgō. Est hic spē celer, illa timōre.
Quī tamen īnsequitur, pennīs adiūtus amōris,   285
ōcior est, requiemque negat tergōque fugācis
imminet, et crīnem sparsum cervīcibus adflat.

Daphne prays to Peneus, her river-god father, for help, and receives it.

Vīribus absūmptīs expalluit illa; citaeque
victa labōre fugae, spectāns Pēnēidas undās,
"Fer, pater," inquit, "opem, sī flūmina nūmen habētis!   290

Slaying of Python, quarrel of
Apollo and Cupid, pursuit and
transformation of Daphne.
Woodcut from an edition of the
Metamorphoses, Venice, 1501.

The Metropolitan Museum of Art,
Rogers Fund, 1922

291-295

nimium, too much
* mūtō (1), change, alter
* figūra, shape, beauty
* finiō, -īre, -iī, -ītus, complete, end
  torpor, -ōris, m. numbness, torpor
  artus, -ūs, m. limb
  tenuis, -e, thin, delicate
  praecordia, -ōrum, n. pl. heart
  liber, -brī, m. bark (of a tree)
* rāmus, branch
  vēlōx, -ōcis, quick, swift
  piger, -gra, -grum, slow, sluggish
* rādīx, -īcis, f. root

296-300

nitor, -ōris, m. bright beauty, brightness
stīpes, -pitis, m. tree trunk
cortex, -ticis, m. bark (of a tree)
* complector, -ī, -plexus sum, embrace, enfold
* membrum, limb

301-305

lignum, wood
refugiō, -ere, -fūgī, flee from, shun
* quoniam, since
* arbor, -oris, f. tree
* certē, certainly, at least
* coma, hair, foliage
  cithara, lyre, cithara

Latius, of Latium
* adsum, -esse, -fuī, -futūrus, w. dat., be present with, attend
* laetus, happy, joyful, glad
* triumphus, triumph

306-312

* canō, -ere, cecinī, cantus, sing
  vīsō, -ere, vīsī, go to see, behold
  Capitōlium, the Capitoline Hill, the Capitol
  pompa, procession, parade
  postis, -is, m. door post
* augustus, -a, -um, venerable, august; Augustan, imperial
* fīdus, loyal, faithful
* custōs, -ōdis, m. and f. guard, protector
  foris, -is, f. door, entrance
* tueor, -ērī, tūtus sum, keep safe, defend
* quercus, -ūs, f. oak
  intōnsus, unshorn, uncut
  iuvenālis, -e, youthful
* honor, -ōris, m. honor, distinction
  Paeān, -ānis, epithet of Apollo as god of healing
  laureus, of laurel; laurea (arbor), laurel tree
  adnuō, -ere, -nuī, -nūtum, nod approval
* agitō (1), sway, toss
  cacūmen, cacūminis, n. summit, top

Door with oak wreath. House of the Civic Crown, a wreath of oak leaves given for saving a citizen's life in battle, Pompeii.

Fototeca Unione

Quā nimium placuī, mūtandō perde figūram."
Vix prece fīnītā, torpor gravis occupat artūs;
mollia cinguntur tenuī praecordia librō;
in frondem crīnēs, in rāmōs bracchia crēscunt;
pēs, modo tam vēlōx, pigrīs rādīcibus haeret;   295
ōra cacūmen habet. Remanet nitor ūnus in illā.

Apollo decrees that the laurel will be sacred to him, will crown the
brow of triumphant Roman generals, and will stand at the entrance to
the Emperor's palace.

Hanc quoque Phoebus amat, positāque in stīpite dextrā
sentit adhūc trepidāre novō sub cortice pectus;
complexusque suīs rāmōs, ut membra, lacertīs   300
ōscula dat lignō—refugit tamen ōscula lignum.
Cui deus, "At quoniam coniūnx mea nōn potes esse,
arbor eris certē," dīxit, "mea. Semper habēbunt
tē coma, tē citharae, tē nostrae, laure, pharetrae.
Tū ducibus Latiīs aderis, cum laeta triumphum   305
vōx canet, et vīsent longās Capitōlia pompās.
Postibus augustīs eadem fīdissima custōs
ante forēs stābis, mediamque tuēbere quercum.
Utque meum intōnsīs caput est iuvenāle capillīs,
tū quoque perpetuōs semper gere frondis honōrēs."   310
Fīnierat Paeān. Factīs modo laurea rāmīs
adnuit, utque caput vīsa est agitāsse cacūmen.

METAMORPHOSES I. 253–567

where without a prep. **289 Pēnēidas:** Greek acc. pl.: hence the short a. **291 Quā:** the antecedent is **figūram.**

292 Vix: w. the abl. abs.; *Hardly was her prayer finished when . . .* **293 librō:** *with bark;*
this is the original meaning of **liber,** which later came to mean *book* because the ancients
first wrote on the inner bark of a tree. Similarly the English word *book* at first meant *beech
tree.* **296 ūnus = sōlus.**

305-306 Tū . . . pompās: the laurel crown was worn by a general celebrating a triumph.
306 Capitōlia: the triumphal procession crossed the Forum and ascended the Capitoline
Hill, where the triumphing general made his offering to Jupiter.
307 augustīs: i.e., belonging to the Emperor Augustus. The reference is to the laurel wreath
displayed at Augustus' doorway in commemoration of his triumph over Cleopatra.
308 quercum: a wreath of oak leaves was also hung at Augustus' door, the *corona cīvica,*
the reward for saving a fellow-citizen's life in battle. This was among the honors granted to
him by the Senate. **312 utque . . . cacūmen:** *and seemed to sway its crest as though nodding
its head.*

Europa and the bull. Red chalk drawing. Bologna, seventeenth century. Metropolitan Museum of Art, N.Y.C.

*The Metropolitan Museum of Art,
Gift of Mrs. John H. Wright, 1949*

1-5

fallāx, -ācis, deceptive
* imāgō, -ginis, *f.* likeness, appearance
* taurus, bull
* cōnfiteor, -ērī, -fessus sum, admit, confess
Dictaeus, of Dicte, a mountain in Crete
* rūs, rūris, *n.* countryside
ignārus, unaware, not knowing
* perquīrō, -ere, -quīsīvī, -quīsītus, search thoroughly
exsilium, exile
* factum, action, deed
pius, pious, devout, devoted
scelerātus, wicked, criminal

6-10

* orbis, -is, *m.* circle, ring, world
pererrō (1), wander through
dēprēndō, -ere, -ēndī, -ēnsus, detect, discover
fūrtum, theft, robbery
* Iuppiter, Iovis, *m.* Jupiter
profugus, fugitive, exiled
vītō (1), avoid, shun
Agēnoridēs, -ae, *m.* son of Agenor, Cadmus
* ōrāculum, oracle
supplex, -plicis, suppliant
* cōnsulō, -ere, -suluī, -sultus, consult, ask advice of
* tellūs, -ūris, *f.* earth, land
requīrō, -ere, -quīsīvī, -quīsītus, search for, inquire
* bōs, bovis, *m. and f.* ox, heifer, cow
aiō: *def.,* say; ait, says

* sōlus, -a, -um (*gen.* -īus), alone, lonely, deserted
* occurrō, -ere, -currī, cursum, *w. dat.,* meet
* arvum, field

11-15

iugum, yoke
immūnis, -e, *w. gen.,* free from, unburdened by
* arātrum, plow
carpō, -ere, carpsī, carptus, pick, take, choose
* requiēscō, -ere, -quiēvī, -quiētum, rest
* moenia, -ium, *n. pl.* town walls, city
* condō, -ere, -didī, -ditus, found, establish, hide
Boeōtius (*lit.* of the cow), Boeotian
Castalius, of Castalia
* antrum, cave
incustōdītus, unguarded
lentē, slowly
iuvenca, heifer

16-20

* servitium, slavery
* cervīx, -īcis, *f.* neck
* subsequor, -ī, -secūtus sum, follow closely
* legō, -ere, lēgī, lēctus, pick, choose
vēstīgium, footstep
* auctor, -ōris, *m.* author, adviser
* taciturnus, silent
Cēphīsus, river in Boeotia
Panopē, -ēs, *f.* Panope
ēvādō, -ere, ēvāsī, ēvāsus, escape from, go past
speciōsus, handsome, attractive

1 deus: Jupiter. positā = dēpositā. 2 sē . . . erat: i.e., had revealed his identity. Dictaea rūra: in a cave on Mt. Dicte Jupiter as an infant had been hidden from his father Cronos. tenēbat: *was staying in.* 3 pater: Agenor. ignārus: not knowing what had happened to his daughter.

102

Cadmus and the Founding of Thebes

Jupiter, disguised as a white bull, has abducted Europa, daughter of
the Phoenician king Agenor, and has carried her away over the waters
to the island of Crete. Agenor orders his son Cadmus to find the girl or
not to come back home.

> Iamque deus, positā fallācis imāgine taurī,
> sē cōnfessus erat, Dictaeaque rūra tenēbat,
> cum pater ignārus Cadmō perquīrere raptam
> imperat et poenam, sī nōn invēnerit, addit
> exsilium, factō pius et scelerātus eōdem. 5

Cadmus searches everywhere and, unable to find his sister, consults the
oracle at Delphi; Apollo tells him to follow a cow and build a city
where the cow first stops.

> Orbe pererrātō (quis enim dēprēndere possit
> fūrta Iovis?) profugus patriamque īramque parentis
> vītat Agēnoridēs, Phoebīque ōrācula supplex
> cōnsulit et quae sit tellūs habitanda requīrit.
> "Bōs tibi," Phoebus ait, "sōlīs occurret in arvīs, 10
> nūllum passa iugum curvīque immūnis arātrī;
> hāc duce carpe viās et, quā requiēverit herbā,
> moenia fac condās Boeōtiaque illa vocātō."

Cadmus obeys instructions, offers thanks to Apollo, and sends his companions to fetch water so that he may sacrifice to Jupiter.

> Vix bene Castaliō Cadmus dēscenderat antrō,
> incustōdītam lentē videt īre iuvencam, 15
> nūllum servitiī signum cervīce gerentem.
> Subsequitur pressōque legit vēstīgia passū
> auctōremque viae Phoebum taciturnus adōrat.
> Iam vada Cēphīsī Panopēsque ēvāserat arva:
> bōs stetit et, tollēns speciōsam cornibus altīs 20

---

perquīrere = ut perquīreret. **raptam:** used as a noun, *the kidnaped girl.* **4 poenam:** in apposition w. exsilium. **invēnerit:** subjv. in subordinate clause in indir. discourse (**poenam addit** =
poenam futūram esse dīcit). **5 factō . . eōdem:** i.e., his **pietās** regarding his daughter made
him **scelerātus** toward his son.

6 possit: potential subjv. *would be able.* **7 fūrta:** i.e., acts which he wishes to conceal.
8 Agēnoridēs: patronymic, *son of Agenor,* used for variety; so too **Agēnore nātus** (1.51)
and **Sīdōnius hospes** (1. 129). **Phoebī ōrācula:** the oracle at Delphi served as an information center for the ancient world. **9 sit habitanda:** sc. sibi; pass. periphrastic, *what land
he should inhabit.* **11 iugum:** dir. obj. of passa. **12 quā herbā:** *on whatever grass* (= meadow-
land). **13 fac (ut) condās:** *see to it that you found.* **Boeōtia:** from **bōs. illa:** antecedent is
moenia. vocātō: fut. imper., *you shall call them Boeotian;* Boeotia was actually the name
of the district; the citadel of Thebes was in fact called Cadmea, after its founder.

14 bene: *completely;* modifies **dēscenderat. Castaliō antrō:** abl. of place from which
without prep.; the grotto of the Castalian spring is near the temple of Apollo, high above
the valley of the Pleistus on the southern slope of Mt. Parnassus. **16 servitiī signum:** i.e.,
the mark of the yoke. **17 pressō passū:** *with heavy tread* = *slowly.* **19 Panopēs:** Greek gen.

21-25

° **frōns, frontis,** *f.* brow, forehead
mūgītus, -ūs, *m.* lowing, bellowing
° **impellō, -ere, -pulī, -pulsus,** smite, strike
° **respiciō, -ere, -spexī, -spectus,** look behind at
prōcumbō, -ere, -cubuī, -cubitum, fall forward
° **tener, -era, -erum,** soft, tender
° **submittō, -ere, -mīsī, -missus,** let down, lower
grātēs agere, render thanks
peregrīnus, foreign, strange
° **ōsculum,** kiss
° **fīgō, -ere, fīxī, fīxus,** fix, implant
° **ignōtus,** unknown
° **salūtō** (1), hail, greet

26-30

sacrum, offering, sacrifice
° **minister, -trī,** *m.* servant, attendant
vīvus, living, running (of water)
lībō (1), sip, offer, draw
fōns, fontis, *m.* fountain, spring, source
violō (1), violate, profane
secūris, -is, *f.* axe
specus, -ūs, *m.* cave
virga, green twig
vīmen, -minis, *n.* pliant shoot, osier
humilis, -e, low
compāgēs, -is, *f.* fitting together, structure
° **arcus, -ūs,** *m.* arch, bow, curve

31-35

über, *gen.* **-eris,** fertile, rich, plentiful
fēcundus, fertile, abundant
° **Mārtius,** of Mars
anguis, -is, *m.* snake, dragon
crista, crest, plume
praesignis, -e, clearly marked, conspicuous
micō, -āre, -uī, flash, glitter
° **tumeō, -ēre, -uī,** swell
° **venēnum,** poison
vibrō (1), vibrate, flicker
triplex, -icis, triple, threefold
° **dēns, dentis,** *m.* tooth

Tyrius, Tyrian, of Tyre
lūcus, grove, wood

36-40

īnfaustus, unlucky
gradus, -ūs, *m.* step, tread, pace
° **urna,** urn, water vessel
sonitus, -ūs, *m.* sound, noise
° **efferō, -ferre, extulī, ēlātus,** carry out, lift up
caeruleus, dark blue, dark, livid
° **serpēns, -entis** = **anguis**
° **horrendus,** awe-inspiring, dreadful
sībilum, a hissing sound
effluō, -ere, -flūxī, flow out, escape
attonitus, thunderstruck, dumbfounded
° **subitus,** sudden
artus, -ūs, *m.* limb

41-45

volūbilis, -e, turning, circling
squāmōsus, scaly
nexus, -ūs, *m.* clasp, embrace, entwining
° **torqueō, -ēre, torsī, tortus,** twist, turn
saltus, -ūs, *m.* leap, springing
sinuō (1), wind, curve, writhe
ērēctus, directed upward, rearing high
° **dēspiciō, -ere, -spexī, -spectus,** look down at
° **nemus, -moris,** *n.* grove, wood
geminī, -ae, -a, twin
° **sēparō** (1), separate, keep apart
Arctus, -ī, *f.* bear, Great Bear; Little Bear

46-50

Phoenīces, -um, *m. pl.* Phoenicians
° **sīve . . . sīve,** whether . . . or
° **uterque, utra-, utrum-,** each of two, both
morsus, -ūs, *m.* biting, bite
complexus, -ūs, *m.* encircling, embrace
necō (1), kill
adflō (1), breathe upon, blast
fūnestus, deadly, fatal
tābēs, -is, *f.* wasting, decay, plague
exiguus, small, slight
umbra, shadow, shade

---

sing. ending; Ovid here indicates the route toward Thebes, crossing the Cephisus and skirting the village of Panope, from Delphi to Thebes a distance of about 55 miles. **22 comitēs:** i.e., Cadmus and his followers. **terga:** pl. for sing., as often w. parts of the body. **24 terrae:** indir. obj. of fīgit (= dat); it was a Roman custom to kiss the earth, on returning home from abroad, as an act of worship of the *Lar* or *Genius Loci.* Cadmus thus signifies that this is to be his home. **26 factūrus erat:** *he intended to make.* **27 vīvīs:** *running;* stagnant water could not be used in religious ceremonies. **lībandās:** fut. pass. participle, *for making a libation.*

29 specus: i.e., the entrance to the cave; antrum (1. 31) is the actual cave. **31 fēcundus:** modifies **specus. 32 Mārtius:** the dragon was said to be the offspring of Mars and one of the Furies; its death foreboded trouble for Cadmus and his descendants. **cristīs et aurō:** *with golden crest;* hendiadys. **33-34 Igne . . dentēs:** Ovid describes as briefly as possible; hence there are no connectives.

35 Quem postquam lūcum = Et postquam eum lūcum. **Tyriā dē gente profectī:** *those who*

104

ad caelum frontem, mūgītibus impulit aurās
atque ita, respiciēns comitēs sua terga sequentēs,
prōcubuit tenerāque latus submīsit in herbā.
Cadmus agit grātēs peregrīnaeque ōscula terrae
fīgit et ignōtōs montēs agrōsque salūtat.   25
Sacra Iovī factūrus erat: iubet īre ministrōs
et petere ē vīvīs lībandās fontibus undās.

A cave in the primeval forest nearby abounds in springs, but a fearful
dragon, sacred to Mars, has made its lair in this cave.

Silva vetus stābat, nūllā violāta secūrī,
et specus in mediā, virgīs ac vīmine dēnsus,
efficiēns humilem lapidum compāgibus arcum,   30
ūberibus fēcundus aquīs, ubi conditus antrō
Mārtius anguis erat, cristīs praesignis et aurō.
Igne micant oculī, corpus tumet omne venēnīs,
trēs vibrant linguae, triplicī stant ōrdine dentēs.

The dragon destroys all the followers of Cadmus when they come to
get water.

Quem postquam Tyriā lūcum dē gente profectī   35
īnfaustō tetigēre gradū, dēmissaque in undās
urna dedit sonitum, longum caput extulit antrō
caeruleus serpēns horrendaque sībila mīsit.
Efflūxēre urnae manibus, sanguisque relinquit
corpus et attonitōs subitus tremor occupat artūs.   40
Ille volūbilibus squāmōsōs nexibus orbēs
torquet, et immēnsōs saltū sinuātur in arcūs
ac, mediā plūs parte levēs ērēctus in aurās,
dēspicit omne nemus tantōque est corpore quantō,
sī tōtum spectēs, geminās quī sēparat Arctōs.   45
Nec mora, Phoenīcas, sīve illī tēla parābant
sīve fugam, sīve ipse timor prohibēbat utrumque,
occupat. Hōs morsū, longīs complexibus illōs,
hōs necat adflātōs fūnestī tābe venēnī.

Vowing to avenge his companions, Cadmus hurls a great rock; but the
dragon is uninjured.

Fēcerat exiguās iam sōl altissimus umbrās.   50

---

had set out from the nation of Tyre (*in Phoenicia*) = **Cadmī comitēs** or **sociī**; the phrase
is used for variety. **36 tetigēre** = **tetigērunt. 41-42 volūbilibus . . . arcūs:** details to emphasize the writhing, sinuous convolutions of the dragon. **43 plūs:** acc. of respect w. **ērēctus;**
raised as to more than the middle part = *towering for more than half its length.* **parte:** abl.
of comparison. **44 corpore, quantō:** abl. of description, *of as great bulk* (= *as huge*) *as is
the one which separates the twin Bears.* **45 spectēs:** subjv. in fut. less vivid condition, *if you
were to look at.* **quī:** sc. **is** as antecedent, *the one which* (Ovid is thinking of the constellation Draco). **46 Nec mora:** sc. **erat;** the phrase = **statim. Phoenīcas:** Greek acc. pl. (short
a) direct object of **occupat. 47 prohibēbat utrumque:** *prevented* (*them from doing*)
either. **48-49 hōs, illōs, hōs:** *some, others, still others.*

105

Agēnor, -oris, m. Agenor, king of Phoenicia
vēstīgō (1), track, search for
tegumen, -minis, n. covering, protection
* dēripiō, -ere, -ripuī, -reptus, tear away from
* leō, -ōnis, m. lion
* pellis, -is f. skin, hide
splendeō, -ēre, shine, gleam
lancea, lance, spear
iaculum, dart, javelin
praestāns, -antis, excellent, outstanding
lētō (1), kill, slay

56-60

* suprā, adv. and prep. w. acc., over, above
* spatiōsus, spacious, large
* trīstis, -e, sad, sorrowful
* sanguineus, bloody
lambō, -ere, lick
ultor, -ōris, m. avenger
* fīdus, faithful, loyal
* inquam: def., say; inquit, says
molāris, -is, m. millstone, large rock
* tollō, -ere, sustulī, sublātus, raise, lift
cōnāmen, -minis, n. effort, exertion

61-65

impulsus, -ūs, m. push, thrust
arduus = celsus, high, lofty
lōrīca, breastplate
* squāma, scale
āter, ātra, ātrum, black, dark
dūritia, hardness, toughness
pellis, -is, f. hide
cutis, -is, f. skin
repellō, -ere, reppulī, repulsus, fend off
* ictus, -ūs, m. blow, stroke

66-70

lentus, pliant, supple
spīna, spine, backbone
curvāmen, -minis, n. curve, curvature
īlia, īlium, n. pl. abdomen, groin
ferōx, -ōcis, wild, fierce
retorqueō, -ēre, -torsī, -tortus, twist back
* aspiciō, -ere, aspexī, aspectus, look at
hastīle, -is, n. shaft (of a javelin)
mordeō, -ēre, momordī, morsus, bite
* vīs, acc. vim, abl. vī, f. force, violence
labefaciō, -ere, -fēcī, -factus, cause to totter, loosen

71-75

os, ossis, n. bone

haereō, -ēre, haesī, haesum, cling, stick
solitus, customary, usual
* recēns, -entis, fresh, new, recent
plēnus, full
* guttur, -uris, n. throat, neck
* vēna, vein
spūma, foam, froth
pestifer, -era, -erum, plague-bringing, pestilential
circumfluō, -ere, -flūxī, flow around
albidus, whitish
rictus, -ūs, m. open mouth, gaping jaw
rāsus, scraped, grazed
sonō, -āre, -uī, -itum, sound, resound
hālitus, -ūs, m. breath

76-80

* niger, -gra, -grum, black
Stygius, Stygian, of the Styx
vitiō (1), make faulty, defile, pollute
īnficiō, -ere, -fēcī, -fectus, stain, infect
* modo, now, only, just, just now
spīra, coil
* cingō, -ere, cīnxī, cīnctus, encircle, gird, coil
interdum, sometimes
trabs, trabis, f. beam, timber
* rēctus, straight, upright
(impes), impetis, m.; used only in gen. and abl. sing. = impetus, rush, attack
ceu, as though, as if, as
concitus, stirred up, swollen
imber, -bris, m. shower, rain
amnis, -is, m. river, stream
* obstō, -āre, -stitī, -stātum, stand in the way, obstruct
prōturbō (1), overthrow, knock down

81-85

spolium, skin, hide, booty
incursus, -ūs, m. attack, onrush
īnstō, -āre, -stitī, press on, threaten
* retardō (1), slow down, hamper
cuspis, -pidis, f. point of a spear
praetendō, -ere, -tendī, -tentus, stretch forth, extend
* furō, -ere, rave, rage
* inānis, -e, empty, ineffectual
acūmen, -minis, n. sharp point
venēnifer, -era, -erum, poison-bearing, poisonous
mānō (1), drip, flow
palātum, palate

---

50 sōl altissimus: i.e., at midday. **51** Quae . . . sociīs: indir. question w. mīrātur. Agēnore: abl. of source, of Agenor. **52-53** dērepta . . . pellis: the mark of a hero. **52** leōnī: dat. w. dērepta, from a lion. **53** tēlum: collective sing. for tēla; sc. erat. ferrō: abl. of material, of shining steel. **54** tēlō: abl. of comparison. **55** Ut: As, When (w. indic.). **56** victōrem: used as adj. suprā: adv., on top. corporis: gen. of description. **59-62** Dīxit . . . mānsit: notice the alliteration. **59** dextrā: sc. manū. **60** magnum: modifies molārem, big as it was, he threw . . . **62** mōta forent = mōta essent: potential subjv., would have been shaken. **63** lōrīcae modō:

Quae mora sit sociīs, mīrātur Agēnore nātus
vēstīgatque virōs. Tegumen dērepta leōnī
pellis erat, tēlum splendentī lancea ferrō
et iaculum, tēlōque animus praestantior omnī.
Ut nemus intrāvit lētātaque corpora vīdit   55
victōremque suprā spatiōsī corporis hostem
trīstia sanguineā lambentem vulnera linguā,
"Aut ultor vestrae, fīdissima corpora, mortis,
aut comes," inquit, "erō." Dīxit dextrāque molārem
sustulit et magnum magnō cōnāmine mīsit.   60
Illius impulsū cum turribus ardua celsīs
moenia mōta forent; serpēns sine vulnere mānsit,
lōrīcaeque modō squāmīs dēfēnsus et ātrae
dūritiā pellis validōs cute reppulit ictūs.

A violent struggle begins and Cadmus wounds the dragon with his
javelin, the iron head of which remains embedded in the wound.

At nōn dūritiā iaculum quoque vīcit eādem,   65
quod mediō lentae spīnae curvāmine fīxum
cōnstitit, et tōtum dēscendit in īlia ferrum.
Ille dolōre ferōx caput in sua terga retorsit
vulneraque aspexit fīxumque hastīle momordit
idque, ubi vī multā partem labefēcit in omnem,   70
vix tergō ēripuit; ferrum tamen ossibus haesit.
Tum vērō, postquam solitās accessit ad īrās
causa recēns, plēnīs tumuērunt guttura vēnīs,
spūmaque pestiferōs circumfluit albida rictūs,
terraque rāsa sonat squāmīs, quīque hālitus exit   75
ōre niger Stygiō vitiātās īnficit aurās.
Ipse modo immēnsum spīrīs facientibus orbem
cingitur, interdum longā trabe rēctior adstat,
impete nunc vāstō, ceu concitus imbribus amnis,
fertur et obstantēs prōturbat pectore silvās.   80

Finally Cadmus drives his spear through the dragon's throat and pins
the creature to an oak tree, where it gradually spends its strength.

Cēdit Agēnoridēs paulum, spoliōque leōnis
sustinet incursūs īnstantiaque ōra retardat
cuspide praetentā. Furit ille et inānia dūrō
vulnera dat ferrō fīgitque in acūmine dentēs.
Iamque venēniferō sanguis mānāre palātō   85

in the manner of a breastplate = *as though they were a breastplate*, referring to **squāmīs**
and **dūritiā**. 64 **cute**: *with its hide*.

65 **nōn vīcit**: *did not succeed against*. 66 **curvāmine**: abl. of place where without prep.
67 **ferrum**: i.e., the head or point. 70 **partem in omnem**: *in every direction*. 72 **solitās**: i.e.,
he was always ferocious, and more so now. 75 **squāmīs**: may be taken w. both **rāsa** and
sonat. **quīque hālitus** = et hālitus quī. 76 **vitiātās īnficit aurās** = īnficit et vitiat aurās
(prolepsis). 77 **Ipse**: the serpent. 77-79 **modo, interdum, nunc**: used for variety. 77 **orbem**:
dir. obj. of **facientibus**. 78 **cingitur** = sē cingit (middle passive). **trabe**: abl. of comparison.
79 **impete**: metrically more convenient than impetū. 80 **fertur**: *rushes* (middle passive).

viridis, -e, green
aspergō, -ginis, f. sprinkling
tingō, -ere, tīnxī, tīnctus, stain, dye, dip
° quia, because
° retrahō, -ere, -trāxī, -trāctus, draw back
laedō, -ere, laesī, laesus, hurt, injure
plāga, blow, stroke
arceō, -ēre, -uī, fend off, keep away
sinō, -ere, sīvī, situs, let, allow
dōnec, conj. until, while

usque, all the way, constantly
° quercus, -ūs, f. oak tree
° pariter cum, equally with, along with
rōbur, -boris, n. hard wood, oak, strength
pondus, -deris, n. weight
curvō (1), curve, bend
° īmus, lowest, very low, bottom
flagellō (1), whip, lash
gemō, -ere, -uī, -itus, groan
cauda, tail
cōnsīderō (1), examine, inspect

prōmptus, ready, quick, easy
perimō, -ere, -ēmī, -ēmptus, destroy, slay
pavidus, trembling with fear
° perdō, -ere, -didī, -ditus, lose, destroy
gelidus, cold, chilling
coma, hair
rigeō, -ēre, be stiff

° ecce, lo! behold!
fautrīx, -īcis; fem. of fautor, patroness
superus, above, upper
° dēlābor, -ī, -lāpsus sum, glide down
Pallas, -adis, f. Pallas
° suppōnō, -ere, -posuī, -positus, with acc.
  and dat., put . . . under
vīpereus, of a (the) snake
incrēmentum, growth, source of increase
° sulcus, furrow

patefaciō, -ere, -fēcī, -factus, open up,
  reveal
° spargō, -ere, sparsī, sparsus, spread, scatter, sow
humus, -ī, f. ground
° sēmen, -minis, n. seed

glaeba, lump of earth, clod
° appāreō, -ēre, -uī, appear, become evident
tegmen, -minis, (= tegumen), n. covering
pictus, painted, colored
nūtō (1), nod, sway
umerus, shoulder
cōnus, cone, crest
onerātus, laden, burdened
exsistō, -ere, -stitī, -stitum, stand out,
  spring up
seges, -getis, f. field of grain
clipeātus, shield-bearing

fēstus, festive, holiday
aulaeum, tapestry, curtain
° theātrum, theater
° surgō, -ere, surrēxī, surrēctum, rise up
° soleō, -ēre, solitus sum, be accustomed
° vultus, -ūs, m. expression, face
° paulātim, gradually
placidus, quiet, calm, peaceful
tenor, -ōris, m. course, movement
° pateō, -ēre, -uī, lie open, be evident
margō, -ginis, m. edge, border

° creō (1), create, produce
° cīvīlis, -e, civil
īnserō, -ere, -seruī, -sertus, put in, join in
terrigenus, earth-born
rigidus, hard, unbending
comminus, adv. in close combat
ēnsis, -is, m. sword
feriō, -īre, strike, smite
ēminus, adv. from a distance
lētum, death

---

83 cuspide: the point of the spear (lancea). 83-84 dūrō ferrō: ind. obj. of dat. 88 dabat
retrō: drew back. 88-89 plāgam sedēre arcēbat: prevented the blow from driving home.
91 cui: sc. eum as antecedent and object of sequēns; cui is dat. w. compound verb obstitit.
92 pariter cum: equally with, i.e., its neck and also the oak tree. 94 rōbora: subject of
flagellārī, groaned that its strength was being lashed. caudae: partitive gen. w. parte.

96 cognōscere: subject of erat. 97 Quid = Cūr. nāte: voc. 98 spectābere = spectāberis.
serpēns: misfortune dogged the members of Cadmus' family, and at the end of a long life he
expressed the wish to be changed into a serpent, if a serpent's life was so dear to the gods
(his misfortunes were a punishment for having slain the serpent of Mars); his wish was
granted. 102 Pallas: Athena, the patroness of heroes. mōtae suppōnere terrae = terram
movēre et terrae suppōnere: lines 104 and 105 show in more detail what is meant.
105 humī: loc. case, in the ground.

106 fidē: abl. of comparison, a thing greater than belief = something too strange to believe.
maius: in apposition w. the whole sentence. coepēre = coepērunt. 108 pictō cōnō: referring

coeperat et viridēs aspergine tīnxerat herbās.
Sed leve vulnus erat, quia sē retrahēbat ab ictū
laesaque colla dabat retrō plāgamque sedēre
cēdendō arcēbat nec longius īre sinēbat,
dōnec Agēnoridēs coniectum in gutture ferrum   90
usque sequēns pressit, cui retrō quercus euntī
obstitit et fīxa est pariter cum rōbore cervīx.
Pondere serpentis curvāta est arbor et īmā
parte flagellārī gemuit sua rōbora caudae.

Cadmus hears a mysterious voice prophesy that he will be transformed
into a serpent; then Pallas Athena instructs him to sow the dragon's
teeth.

Dum spatium victor victī cōnsīderat hostis,   95
vōx subitō audīta est (neque erat cognōscere prōmptum
unde, sed audīta est), "Quid, Agēnore nāte, perēmptum
serpentem spectās? Et tū spectābere serpēns."
    Ille diū pavidus pariter cum mente colōrem
perdiderat, gelidōque comae terrōre rigēbant.   100
Ecce, virī fautrīx, superās dēlāpsa per aurās,
Pallas adest, mōtaeque iubet suppōnere terrae
vīpereōs dentēs, populī incrēmenta futūrī.
Pāret et, ut pressō sulcum patefēcit arātrō,
spargit humī iussōs, mortālia sēmina, dentēs.   105

Gradually men grow up out of the earth, fully armed.

Inde (fidē maius) glaebae coepēre movērī,
prīmaque dē sulcīs aciēs appāruit hastae,
tegmina mox capitum pictō nūtantia cōnō,
mox umerī pectusque onerātaque bracchia tēlīs
exsistunt, crēscitque seges clipeāta virōrum.   110
Sīc, ubi tolluntur fēstīs aulaea theātrīs,
surgere signa solent prīmumque ostendere vultūs,
cētera paulātim, placidōque ēducta tenōre
tōta patent īmōque pedēs in margine pōnunt.

The newly created warriors fight among themselves until there are only
five left, who help Cadmus to found the city of Thebes.

Territus hoste novō Cadmus capere arma parābat.   115
"Nē cape," dē populō quem terra creāverat ūnus
exclāmat, "nec tē cīvīlibus īnsere bellīs."
Atque ita terrigenīs rigidō dē frātribus ūnum
comminus ēnse ferit; iaculō cadit ēminus ipse.
Hunc quoque quī lētō dederat, nōn longius illō   120

to the brightly colored plumes on the helmets. **111 aulaea:** in the Roman theater the curtain
was drawn up from a slot in the stage floor at the end of a play; hence the heads of figures
embroidered on the curtain would be seen first. **114 īmō in margine:** *on the very bottom*
(*of the curtain*).

* exspīrō (1), breathe out
* exemplum, pattern, example
  turba, crowd
* Mārs, Mārtis, m. Mars, god of warfare
* subitus, suddenly formed
  mūtuus, mutual, reciprocal
  sortior, -īrī, -ītus sum, obtain by lot
* iuventūs, -ūtis, f. youth
  sanguineus, bloodstained
  tepidus, warm
  plangō, -ere, -ānxī, -ānctus, strike, beat

superstes, -stitis, surviving
Echīōn, -onis, m. Echion
* monitus, -ūs, m. warning, instruction
  Trītōnis, -idis, f. Tritonian; epithet of
    Pallas Athene
* frāternus, fraternal
  Sīdōnius, Sidonian, of Sidon (in Phoe-
    nicia)
  hospes, -pitis, m. visitor, stranger
  Phoebēus, of Phoebus (Apollo)
  sors, sortis, f. lot, destiny, prophecy

116 Nē cape: a form of negative command commonly used in poetry, where prose would
have Nōlī capere or (Cavē) Nē capiās. 118 rigidō: modifies ēnse. 120 Hunc: object of
dederat; antecedent is ipse; illō refers to the same person. quī: sc. is as antecedent. longius
= diūtius. 121 modo: modifies accēperat. 122-123 suō Mārte: metonymy, *in a battle of
their own choosing*, but suggesting also that the war god was punishing them. 125 mātrem:

1-5

exigō, -ere, -ēgī, -āctus, drive out, inquire
* almus, nurturing, kindly, gracious
  Cerēs, Cereris, f. Ceres, goddess of agri-
    culture
  nāta, daughter
  sēcūrus, free from worry, calm
* fōns, fontis, m. fountain, spring
  conticēscō, -ere, -ticuī, become silent
* unda, wave
  viridis, -e, green
  siccō (1), dry
* capillus, hair
  Alphēus, river in the north-west of the
    Peloponnese; the god of the river
6-10
  nympha, nymph
  Achāis, -idis, f. Achaea, northern part of
    the Peloponnese
* studiōsē, eagerly
  saltus, -ūs, m. woodland, glade
* legō, -ere, lēgī, lēctus, pick, choose, roam,
    traverse
  cassēs, -ium, m. pl. hunting net, snare

quamvīs, although
* fōrma, grace, beauty
* fāma, report, reputation
* fortis, -e, strong, athletic
* fōrmōsus, beautiful
11-15
* faciēs, -ēī, f. face, appearance
  nimium, too much, too
* iuvō, -āre, iūvī, iūtus, help, please
  gaudeō, -ēre, gāvīsus sum, *semidep.* re-
    joice, be glad
  soleō, -ēre, solitus sum, *semidep.* be accus-
    tomed
* rūsticus, rustic, of the country
  dōs, dōtis, f. dowry, gift
  ērubēscō, -ere, ērubuī, blush at, be
    ashamed of
  crīmen, -minis, n. reproach, guilt
  lassus, tired, weary
* meminī, -isse, remember
  Stymphalis, -idis, of Stymphalus, a district
    in Arcadia
  geminō (1), double, intensify
  aestus, -ūs, m. heat, hot weather

Arethusa, a spring on the island of Ortygia (part of Syracuse in Sicily), was supposed to
be connected by an underground passage with the river Alpheus in Elis (in the Pelopon-
nese). Hence the myth of the nymph Arethusa.

1 nātā receptā: Ceres had learned from Arethusa where Persephone was, and Jupiter had
arranged that Persephone should remain with her mother for six months of the year (v. *Fasti*
IV, 417 ff.). 2 quae ... fugae: sc. sit. 3 Conticuēre = Conticuērunt. 4 viridēs: water deities
are often given green hair by the poets. capillōs: acc. of respect with pass. participle siccāta;
having been dried as to her green hair = having dried her green hair.

7 mē: abl. of comparison. Nec altera: *And no other (nymph).* 8 posuit cassēs: like their
leader Diana, the mountain nymphs were huntresses. 9 fōrmae fāma: *reputation for beauty.*

vīvit et exspīrat modo quās accēperat aurās,
exemplōque parī furit omnis turba, suōque
Mārte cadunt subitī per mūtua vulnera frātrēs.
Iamque brevis vītae spatium sortīta iuventūs
sanguineam tepidō plangēbat pectore mātrem,   125
quīnque superstitibus, quōrum fuit ūnus Echīōn.
Is sua iēcit humō monitū Trītōnidis arma,
frāternaeque fidem pācis petiitque deditque.
Hōs operis comitēs habuit Sīdōnius hospes,
cum posuit iussam Phoebēīs sortibus urbem.   130

METAMORPHOSES III. 1–

the earth. **126 quīnque superstitibus:** abl. abs.; the five survivors were the legendary ancestors of noble Theban families. **quōrum = ē quibus.** Echion, specially mentioned, later
married a daughter of Cadmus. **127 humō:** indir. obj. instead of acc. of place to which.
129 operis: the founding of Thebes. **Sīdōnius hospes:** Cadmus.

Arethusa and the River God

Ceres asks Arethusa to tell her story, how and why she was turned into
a fountain; Arethusa begins.

Exigit alma Cerēs, nātā sēcūra receptā,
quae tibi causa fugae, cūr sīs, Arethūsa, sacer fōns.
Conticuēre undae, quārum dea sustulit altō
fonte caput, viridēsque manū siccāta capillōs
flūminis Alphēī veterēs nārrāvit amōrēs.   5

"Hunting had always been my joy; I was indifferent to anything else."

"Pars ego nymphārum quae sunt in Achāide," dīxit,
"ūna fuī. Nec mē studiōsius altera saltūs
lēgit, nec posuit studiōsius altera cassēs.
Sed quamvīs fōrmae numquam mihi fāma petīta est,
quamvīs fortis eram, fōrmōsae nōmen habēbam.   10
Nec mea mē faciēs nimium laudāta iuvābat,
quāque aliae gaudēre solent, ego rūstica dōte
corporis ērubuī, crīmenque placēre putāvī.

"Weary from hunting one hot summer day, I was bathing in a deep,
shaded pool."

Lassa revertēbar, meminī, Stymphālide silvā.
Aestus erat, magnumque labor gemināverat aestum.   15

mihi: dat. of agent with **petīta est. 10 quamvīs fortis eram: fortitūdō** was not a quality
usually associated with feminine beauty. **12 quāque = quā + que:** the antecedent is **dōte;
quā** is abl. of place where w. **gaudēre:** *to rejoice in.* **rūstica:** *country-dwelling* came to mean
simple-minded or *prudish* just as *city-dwelling* (**urbānus**) meant *witty* or *broad-minded.*
13 crīmen . . . putāvī: sc. **esse;** the subject of the indir. statement is **placēre.**

111

16-20

vertex, -ticis, *m.* eddy, whirlpool, peak
° murmur, -uris, *n.* murmur
° perspicuus, transparent, clear
° humus, -ī, *f.* ground, earth
° numerābilis, -e, able to be counted
° altē, high up, deep down
calculus, pebble, stone
cānus, white, gray
salictum, thicket of willows
nūtriō, -īre, -iī, -ītus, nourish
pōpulus, -ī, *f.* poplar tree
° sponte suā, of their own accord, spontaneously
dēclīvis, -e, sloping, steep
° umbra, shadow, shade

21-25

° vēstīgium, step, trace, mark, sole
° tingō, -ere, tīnxī, tīnctus, stain, dip, wet
poples, -litis, *m.* knee
tenus, *prep. w. abl.* as far as, up to
° contentus, satisfied
recingō, -ere, -cīnxī, -cīnctus, ungird, undress
mollis, -e, soft
salix, -icis, *f.* willow tree
vēlāmen, -minis, *n.* covering, garment
° curvus, bending, curving
mergō, -ere, mersī, mersus, dip, plunge
feriō, -īre, strike, splash
° lābor, -ī, lāpsus sum, slip, glide
excutiō, -ere, -cussī, -cussus, shake, toss
bracchium, arm
° iactō (1), fling, throw

26-30

nescioquis, -quod, (-quid), some or other
gurges, -gitis, *m.* flood, deep water
īnsistō, -ere, -stitī, stand on
° propior, -ius, nearer
margō, -ginis, *m. and f.* edge, border
° properō (1), hurry
° iterum, again
raucus, hoarse
° ōs, ōris, *n.* mouth
° sīcut, just as

31-35

īnstō, -āre, -stitī, press on
ārdeō, -ēre, ārsī, ārsum, be on fire, be in love
placēns, -entis, pleasing
ferus, wild, fierce
premō, -ere, pressī, pressus, press after
accipiter, -tris, *m.* hawk
° penna, wing
trepidō (1), quiver, tremble
° columba, dove
trepidus, alarmed, frightened
urgeō, -ēre, ursī, press after, pursue

36-40

usque, all the way, right up to
° sinus, -ūs, *m.* fold, hollow, valley, bay
gelidus, cold, chilling
° vēlōx, -ōcis, swift
° tolerō (1), endure
impār, -paris, unequal, inferior
patiēns, -entis, *w. gen.,* able to endure

Fountain of Arethusa on the island of Ortygia, Syracuse.

Alinari, Fototeca Unione

Inveniō sine vertice aquās, sine murmure euntēs,
perspicuās ad humum, per quās numerābilis altē
calculus omnis erat, quās tū vix īre putārēs.
Cāna salicta dabant nūtrītaque pōpulus undā
sponte suā grātās rīpīs dēclīvibus umbrās.   20
Accessī, prīmumque pedis vēstīgia tīnxī,
poplite deinde tenus; neque eō contenta, recingor
molliaque impōnō salicī vēlāmina curvae
nūdaque mergor aquīs.

"I was startled by the hoarse voice of the river god Alpheus calling to
me, and took to flight."

                Quās dum feriōque trahōque,
mīlle modīs lābēns, excussaque bracchia iactō,   25
nescioquod mediō sēnsī sub gurgite murmur
territaque īnsistō propiōris margine rīpae.
"Quō properās, Arethūsa?" suīs Alphēus ab undīs,
"Quō properās?" iterum raucō mihi dīxerat ōre.
Sīcut eram, fugiō sine vestibus (altera vestēs   30
rīpa meās habuit). Tantō magis īnstat et ārdet,
et quia nūda fuī, sum vīsa placentior illī.
Sīc ego currēbam, sīc mē ferus ille premēbat,
ut fugere accipitrem pennā trepidante columbae,
ut solet accipiter trepidās urgēre columbās.   35

"The flight continued a long time; I grew tired and could feel that my
pursuer was gaining on me."

     Usque sub Orchomenon Psōphīdaque Cyllēnēnque
Maenaliōsque sinūs gelidumque Erymanthon et Ēlin
currere sustinuī, nec mē vēlōcior ille.
Sed tolerāre diū cursūs ego, vīribus impār,
nōn poteram; longī patiēns erat ille labōris.   40

---

14 silvā: abl. of place from which without a prep. **15 labor:** of hunting. **17 ad humum:** i.e.,
to the bottom. **altē:** i.e., on the bottom. **18 putārēs:** potential subjv.; *you would have thought.*
19 undā: abl. of means with nūtrīta. **20 rīpīs:** indir. obj. of dabant.

22 recingor: middle passive; *I ungird myself.* **13 salicī:** dat. w. compound verb impōnō.
24 mergor: middle passive; *I plunge myself.* **25 excussa bracchia iactō** = excutiō et iactō
bracchia. **26 nescioquod murmur:** *I know not what murmur* = *a vague murmur.*
27 margine: abl. of place where without a prep. **31 Tantō magis:** *So much the more.*

34 ut . . . columbae: sc. solent. **36-37 Orchomenon, Psōphīda, Cyllēnēn, Erymanthon,**
Ēlin: accusatives (Greek forms); for these places v. I.P.N. **38 currere:** objective infinitive
with sustinuī; *I managed to run.* **ille:** sc. erat. **40 labōris:** objective gen. w. patiēns (here
used as an adjective).

113

41-45

opertus, covered, hidden
rūpēs, -is, *f.* cliff, rock
* **quā,** where
* **praecēdō, -ere, -cessī, -cessum,** go ahead
* **certē,** certainly, at least
* **sonitus, -ūs,** *m.* sound
ingēns, -entis, huge, great

46-50

crīnālis, -e, for the hair
vitta, headband, ribbon
adflō (1), blow upon, breathe on
anhēlitus, -ūs, *m.* panting
fessus, tired, weary
(ops), opis, *f.* help, aid
dēprēndō, -ere, -prēndī, -prēnsus, seize, overtake
* **inquam,** *defective verb,* I say
armigera, armor bearer (female), attendant
Dictynna, a name for Diana
* **arcus, -ūs,** *m.* bow
* **inclūdō, -ere, -clūsī, -clūsus,** enclose, contain
pharetra, quiver
spissus, thick
* **nūbēs, -is,** *f.* cloud

51-55

* **super,** *prep. w. acc. and abl.,* above, over
* **iniciō, -ere, -iēcī, -iectus,** throw on
lūstrō (1), go around, traverse, examine
cālīgō, -ginis, *f.* mist, fog
* **tegō, -ere, tēxī, tēctus,** cover, hide
amnis, -is, *m.* river

ignārus, not knowing, unaware
nūbilum, cloud
īnscius, unknowing, unaware
ambiō, -īre, -iī, -ītus, go round
iō, *exclam. to attract attention*
anne, *interr. particle,* or
agna, ewe lamb

56-60

* **lupus,** wolf
stabulum, stable, stall
fremō, -ere, -uī, -itum, roar, howl
lepus, -poris, *m.* hare
veprēs, -is, *m.* bramble bush
* **lateō, -ēre, -uī,** lie hid, lurk
* **hostīlis, -e,** hostile
* **cernō, -ere, crēvī, crētus,** discern, see
* **canis, -is,** *m. and f.* dog
* **mōtus, -ūs,** *m.* movement, motion
* **abscēdō, -ere, -cessī, -cessum,** go away
* **longē,** far away

61-65

obsideō, -ēre, -sēdī, -sessus, hem in, besiege
sūdor, -ōris, *m.* sweat
frīgidus, cold, chilling
* **artus, -ūs,** *m.* joint, limb
* **caeruleus,** dark blue, dark
gutta, drop
mānō (1), drip, flow
lacus, -ūs, *m.* lake
rōs, rōris, *m.* dew, water
* **cito,** quickly
* **factum,** deed, action
* **renārrō** (1), tell again, relate
latex, -ticis, *m.* water
* **mūtō** (1), change

Arethusa. Woodcut by Aristide Maillol (1861-1944) from Virgil's *Eclogues,* **Weimar, 1926. Metropolitan Museum of Art, N.Y.C.**

The Metropolitan Museum of Art, Harris Brisbane Dick Fund, 1928

Per tamen et campōs, per opertōs arbore montēs,
saxa quoque et rūpēs et quā via nūlla, cucurrī.
Sōl erat ā tergō. Vīdī praecēdere longam
ante pedēs umbram, nisi sī timor illa vidēbat.
Sed certē sonitusque pedum terrēbat et ingēns   45
crīnālēs vittās adflābat anhēlitus ōris.

"My patron goddess Diana heard my call for help and hid me in a
cloud."

Fessa labōre fugae, "Fer opem, dēprēndimur," inquam,
"armigerae, Dictynna, tuae, cui saepe dedistī
ferre tuōs arcūs inclūsaque tēla pharetrā."
Mōta dea est, spissīsque ferēns ē nūbibus ūnam   50
mē super iniēcit.

"Though baffled, Alpheus did not give up the search."

Lūstrat cālīgine tēctam
amnis, et ignārus circum cava nūbila quaerit,
bisque locum, quō mē dea tēxerat, īnscius • ambit,
et bis, "Iō Arethūsa, iō Arethūsa!" vocāvit.
Quid mihi tunc animī miserae fuit? Anne quod agnae est,   55
sī qua lupōs audit circum stabula alta frementēs,
aut leporī, quī vepre latēns hostīlia cernit
ōra canum nūllōsque audet dare corpore mōtūs?
Nōn tamen abscēdit, neque enim vēstīgia cernit
longius ūlla pedum; servat nūbemque locumque.   60

"Metamorphosed into a stream, I flowed underground, joined by
Alpheus, and came to the surface at Ortygia."

Occupat obsessōs sūdor mihi frīgidus artūs,
caeruleaeque cadunt tōtō dē corpore guttae,
quāque pedem mōvī, mānat lacus, ēque capillīs,
rōs cadit, et citius quam nunc tibi facta renārrō,
in laticēs mūtor. Sed enim cognōscit amātās   65

---

41 arbore: collective singular for arboribus. 42 quā via nūlla (erat): *where there was no path.* 43 ā tergō: *at my back.* 44 umbram: i.e., Alpheus'. illa: *those things = that kind of thing.* 48 armigerae: indir. obj. of fer (dēprēndimur, *I am being overtaken,* is parenthetical). Dictynna: another name for Diana (v. I.P.N.). 49 ferre: dir. obj. of dedistī, *you have allowed to bear.*

50 ūnam (nūbem): dir. obj. of both ferēns and iniēcit. 51 mē super = super mē. tēctam: in agreement with mē implied, the object of both lūstrat and quaerit. 55 mihi: dat. of possession, like agnae and leporī below. animī: partitive genitive with Quid; *What feeling.* Anne quod: sc. id animī as antecedent for quod; *Or was it that feeling which a lamb has?* 56 qua = aliqua after sī: *if any lamb = any lamb which.* 60 longius: *farther away.* servat: *watches.* -que . . . -que: *both . . . and.*

63 quāque = quā + que: *and in whatever direction.* ēque = ē + que. 65 in laticēs mūtor: signifying the complete metamorphosis into a spring. 66 ōre: abl. abs. w. positō, and ante-

proprius, one's own, personal
* misceō, -ēre, -uī, mixtus, mix, join
Dēlius, Delian, of Delos
caecus, blind, dark
caverna, cave, cavern

* advehō, -ere, -vexī, -vectus, carry along
* cognōmen, -minis, n. surname, name
* dīva, goddess
superus, upper, above
* aura, air, breeze
hāctenus, so far, up to this point

cedent of quod. 68 Dēlia: *The goddess of Delos* (v. I.P.N.). caecīs cavernīs: *in dark caverns*, referring to the underground course of the water. 69 Ortygiam:·place to which without prep., Ortygia being a small island. 70 grāta with cognōmine, *welcome because of the name.*

aiō, *def.* I say; ait, he says
* immēnsus, unlimited, boundless
* potentia, power
* quisquis, quidquid, whoever, whatever
* superī (deī), the gods above
* peragō, -ere, -ēgī, -āctus, accomplish
* dubitō (1), doubt
tilia, linden tree
conterminus, sharing boundary with, next to
quercus, -ūs, f. oak
Phrygius, Phrygian
modicus, moderate, low
Pelopēius, of Pelops

6-10
arvum, field, land
quondam, once, formerly
* rēgnō (1), reign, rule (over)
* parēns, -entis, m. parent, father
* haud, not at all, not
hinc, from here
stāgnum, pool, pond
tellūs, -ūris, f. land

habitābilis, -e, habitable
celeber, -bris, -bre, crowded, frequented
mergus, duck, smew
fulica, coot
* palūster, -tris, -tre, marsh (*adj.*)
* unda, wave, water
* Iuppiter, Iovis, m. Jupiter
* speciēs, -ēī, f. look, appearance, shape
cādūcifer, -era, -erum, bearing the staff
āla, wing

11-15
requiēs, -ētis (*acc.* -em), f. rest
* claudō, -ere, clausī, clausus, shut, close
sera, bar
stipula, stalk, straw
canna, reed, cane
* tegō, -ere, tēxī, tēctus, cover, roof
* pius, pious, devout
Baucis, -idis (*acc.* -ida), f. Baucis
* anus, -ūs, f. old woman
parilis, -e, equal, like
Philēmōn, -onis (*acc.* -ona), m. Philemon
* iungō, -ere, iūnxī, iūnctus, join, unite
iuvenālis, -e, youthful

1 ait: the speaker is Lelex. 2 voluēre = voluērunt: Ovid uses the -ēre perfect ending sixteen times in this story and -ērunt only twice. 3 quōque minus dubitēs: *and so that you may be less uncertain.* Implied is something like *listen to this story.* tiliae: dat. w. contermina. *An oak sharing a tree trunk with a linden tree,* the symbol of unity between Philemon and Baucis, begins the story, and at the end the symbol is repeated, line 100. 5 Pittheus: the father of Lelex and the son of Pelops. 5-6 Pelopēia arva: Pelops' father, Tantalus, had been king of Phrygia. 6 suō parentī: dat. of agent w. rēgnāta; *ruled by his father,* i.e., by Pelops. 7 stāgnum: how this marshy pool came into being will be stated in lines 76-77. 7-8 tellūs, undae: in apposition w. stāgnum.

10 Atlantiadēs: *grandson of Atlas,* i.e., Mercury. positīs = dēpositīs. cādūcifer: an epithet of Mercury; the caduceus was the herald's staff which he bore as messenger of the gods. 11 adiēre: see note on voluēre above. locum requiemque: *a place to rest* (hendiadys). 15 illā, illā: modifying casā in the next line. 16 casā: abl. of place where without a prep.

amnis aquās, positōque virī quod sūmpserat ōre
vertitur in propriās, ut sē mihi misceat, undās.
Dēlia rūpit humum, caecīsque ego mersa cavernīs
advehor Ortygiam, quae mē cognōmine dīvae
grāta meae superās ēdūxit prīma sub aurās."   70
Hāc Arethūsa tenus.

METAMORPHOSES V. 572–

Ortygia was also a name for Delos; hence Ortygia = Dēlia. **71 Arethūsa:** sc. a verb of speaking. **tenus:** separated from its ablative **hāc.**

Philemon and Baucis

An old man, Lelex, tells the story of Philemon and Baucis, an elderly couple living in contented poverty in a village of Phrygia. When Jupiter and Mercury, disguised as humans, visit the village, all the other villagers shut their doors against the strangers, but they are warmly welcomed by Philemon and Baucis. The gods reward them by transforming their humble cottage into a magnificent temple and punish the others by converting the village into a swamp. In the fullness of time Philemon and Baucis, keepers of the temple, are metamorphosed into trees on the Phrygian hill, an oak and a linden, growing from a single trunk.

Jonathan Swift (1667–1745) has an amusing adaptation of the poem, "Philemon and Baucis."

Sīc ait: "Immēnsa est fīnemque potentia caelī
nōn habet, et quidquid superī voluēre, perāctum est,
quōque minus dubitēs—tiliae contermina quercus
collibus est Phrygiīs, modicō circumdata mūrō.
Ipse locum vīdī, nam mē Pelopēia Pittheus   5
mīsit in arva suō quondam rēgnāta parentī.
Haud procul hinc stāgnum est, tellūs habitābilis ōlim,
nunc celebrēs mergīs fulicīsque palūstribus undae.

Jupiter and Mercury find hospitality only with Philemon and Baucis, a poor couple who have learned to be contented with their lot.

Iuppiter hūc speciē mortālī cumque parente
vēnit Atlantiadēs positīs cādūcifer ālīs.   10
Mīlle domōs adiēre, locum requiemque petentēs,
mīlle domōs clausēre serae. Tamen ūna recēpit,
parva quidem, stipulīs et cannā tēcta palūstrī,
sed pia. Baucis anus parilīque aetāte Philēmōn
illā sunt annīs iūnctī iuvenālibus, illā   15

117

cōnsenēscō, -ere, -senuī, grow old together
* casa, hut, cottage
* paupertās, -ātis, f. poverty
* fateor, -ērī, fassus sum, admit, own, confess
* levis, -e, light, easy to bear
inīquus, unfair, resentful
rēfert, impers. it matters
* illīc, there, in that place
famulus, servant
requīrō, -ere, -quīsīvī, -quīsītus, look for
caelicola, -ae, m. dweller in heaven, god
* tangō, -ere, tetigī, tāctus, touch, reach
* Penātēs, -ium, m. pl. Penates, household gods

21-25

submissus, lowered, bowed
humilis, -e, low, humble
intrō (1), enter
vertex, -ticis, m. top, head
postēs, -ium, m. pl. doorway
* membrum, limb
* senex, senis, m. old man
relevō (1), relieve, rest
sedīle, -lis, n. seat, chair
* superiniciō, -ere, -iēcī, -iectus, throw on top
textum, woven coverlet, rug
rudis, -e, rough, plain
sēdulus, busy, considerate
* focus, hearth
tepidus, warm
cinis, -neris, m. ashes
* dīmoveō, -ēre, -mōvī, -mōtus, move apart, stir
suscitō (1), revive
* hesternus, of yesterday
* folium, leaf
cortex,- ticis, m. bark of trees
siccus, dry

26-30

nūtriō, -īre, -iī, -ītus, nurse, feed
* anima, breath
anīlis, -e, old woman's, aged
multifidus, split into many pieces
fax, facis, f. faggot, kindling

rāmālia, -ium, n. pl. twigs, branches
* tēctum, roof, ceiling, house
* dēferō, -ferre, -tulī, -lātus, take down
minuō, -ere, -uī, -ūtus, break into pieces
aēnum, bronze pot
* coniūnx, -iugis, m. and f. husband, wife
riguus, well-watered
* hortus, garden
truncō (1), cut off, strip
holus, -leris, n. vegetables
* furca, fork, pole
* levō (1), lighten, lift
bicornis, -e, two-pronged

31-35

sordidus, begrimed, darkened
* tergum, back, side (of bacon)
sūs, suis, m. and f. pig, hog, pork
* pendeō, -ēre, pependī, hang
tignum, beam, rafter
resecō, -āre, -uī, -sectus, cut off
tergus, -goris, n. back, chine
* exiguus, small, scanty
* secō, -āre, secuī, sectus, cut
domō, -āre, -uī, -itus, tame, cook
ferveō, -ēre, boil
* fallō, -ere, fefellī, falsus, deceive, while away
* sermō, -ōnis, m. conversation, talk
concutiō, -ere, -cussī, -cussus, shake up
torus, couch, mattress
mollis, -e, soft
ulva, sedge, marsh grass

36-40

* lectus, bed, couch
sponda, frame
salignus, of willow
* vestis, -is, f. cloth, covering
vēlō (1), cover, drape
fēstus, festive, special
* sternō, -ere, strāvī, strātus, spread, cover
* cōnsuēscō, -ere, -suēvī, -suētus, become accustomed; cōnsuēvī, be accustomed
vīlis, -e, cheap, of little value
indignor (dep. 1), think unworthy
accumbō, -ere, -cubuī, -cubitum, recline at table
succīnctus, girt up
tremēns, -entis, trembling

16-17 fatendō, ferendō: gerunds, abl. of means; paupertātem is the dir. obj. of both gerunds as well as of effēcēre. 17 levem: predicate acc. nec . . . ferendō: *and by bearing it with no resentful feelings.*

18 dominōs . . . requīrās: disjunctive indir. question, (utrum) . . . ne, *whether . . . or.* 20-33 These lines are intended as a whole, one long sentence to show how busy and eager the aged couple were in offering hospitality according to their means. 20 Penātēs = domum. A god's name is frequently put by metonymy for that over which he presides: so Mārs for bellum; Vulcānus for ignis; or Cerēs for frūmentum. 21 submissō: *stooping,* because the doorway was low. intrārunt = intrāvērunt. 22 iussit: sc. eōs, *bade them.* 23 quō = in

cōnsenuēre casā, paupertātemque fatendō
effēcēre levem nec inīquā mente ferendō.
Nec rēfert, dominōs illīc famulōsne requīrās;
tōta domus duo sunt, īdem pārentque iubentque.

Baucis bustles about to make the guests comfortable.

Ergō ubi caelicolae parvōs tetigēre Penātēs   *20*
submissōque humilēs intrārunt vertice postēs,
membra senex positō iussit relevāre sedīlī,
quō superiniēcit textum rude sēdula Baucis,
inque focō tepidum cinerem dīmōvit, et ignēs
suscitat hesternōs, foliīsque et cortice siccō   *25*
nūtrit, et ad flammās animā prōdūcit anīlī,
multifidāsque facēs rāmāliaque ārida tēctō
dētulit et minuit, parvōque admōvit aēnō,
quodque suus coniūnx riguō collēgerat hortō,
truncat holus foliīs; furcā levat inde bicornī   *30*
sordida terga suis, nigrō pendentia tignō, .
servātōque diū resecat dē tergore partem
exiguam, sectamque domat ferventibus undīs.

While the dinner is cooking, the old couple entertain their guests with
conversation, and prepare a dining couch as best they can.

Intereā mediās fallunt sermōnibus hōrās,
concutiuntque torum dē mollī flūminis ulvā   *35*
impositum lectō, spondā pedibusque salignīs.
Vestibus hunc vēlant, quās nōn nisi tempore fēstō
sternere cōnsuērant, sed et haec vīlisque vetusque
vestis erat, lectō nōn indignanda sālignō.

The meal is described in detail, beginning with the *gustatio* (appetizers).

Accubuēre deī. Mēnsam succīncta tremēnsque   *40*

---

quod: *over which.* 26 nūtrit, prōdūcit: the object is still **ignēs**. The fire had been kept alive
under the ashes. 27 tēctō: dat. of separation w. dētulit; *took down from the ceiling.* The
kindling was stored just under the ceiling to be dried by the heat of the fire. 29 quodque:
the antecedent for quod is holus in the next line. 30 foliīs: abl. of separation w. truncat.
31 terga: pl. for sing. tergum. 32 servātō diū: the bacon had long been kept for just such a
special occasion. 33 sectam: modifying partem. undīs = aquā.

34 mediās hōrās: *the intervening time (until the meal is ready).* fallunt: the same metaphor
appears in the English idiom *to beguile the time.* 35 concutiunt torum: *they smooth out a
cushion.* 36 spondā . . . salignīs: abl. of description; *with frame and legs of willow.* 38 cōnsuērant: (pronounced with three syllables) = cōnsuēverant. sed et haec: *even this.* 39 lectō
nōn indignanda: *not to be thought unworthy of the couch.*

40 Accubuēre deī: *The gods took their places on the dining couch.* succīncta: the usual
dress of the ancients consisted of a long loose robe (tunica in Latin) girt round the waist
with a cord. The length of the garment could be adjusted by pulling it up through this
girdle; one engaged, as Baucis is here, in some activity would shorten the tunica in this

119

impār, -paris, uneven

testa, piece of broken pottery

° subdō, -ere, -didī, -ditus, put beneath

° clīvus, slope, slant

° tollō, -ere, sustulī, sublātus, remove

menta, mint

tergeō, -ēre, tersī, tersus, wipe clean

virēns, -entis, green, fresh

bicolor, -ōris, of two colors

sincērus, pure, clean

bāca, berry, olive

conditus, stored, preserved

cornum, cornel berry, cornelian cherry

° autumnālis, -e, autumnal

faex, faecis, f. sediment, dregs

46-50

intiba, endive

rādīx, -īcis, f. root, radish

° lac, lactis, n. milk; lac coāctum, cottage cheese

massa, heap, amount

ōvum, egg

° leviter, lightly

versō (1), keep turning, turn

favīlla, ash, embers

fictile, -is, n. earthenware dish

° caelō (1), emboss, engrave, carve

sistō, -ere, stitī, status, put, place

° argentum, silver

° crātēr, -ēris, m. mixing bowl, winebowl

fabricō (1), make

fāgus, -ī, f. beechwood

pōculum, cup, goblet

flāvēns, -entis, yellow

inlitus, smeared, covered

cēra, wax

51-55

epulae, -ārum, f. feast

caleō, -ēre, -uī, -itum, be hot

° rūrsus, again

senecta, old age, age

° paulum, a little

° sēdūcō, -ere, -dūxī, -ductus, draw aside

nux, nucis, f. nut

° misceō, -ēre, miscuī, mixtus, mix, mingle

rūgōsus, wrinkled

cārica, fig

palma, date

prūnum, plum

patulus, wide, open

redolēns, -entis, fragrant

° mālum, apple

canistrum, basket

56-60

° vītis, -is, f. vine

ūva, grape

° candidus, clear, white

favus, honeycomb

° vultus, -ūs, m. face, expression

° accēdō, -ere, -cessī, -cessum, approach, be added

° iners, -ertis, inactive

° pauper, -eris, poor

° voluntās, -ātis, f. willingness

° totiēns, so many times

hauriō, -īre, hausī, haustus, drain, empty

° repleō, -ēre, -plēvī, -plētus, refill

sponte suā, of its own accord, automatically

succrēscō, -ere, grow up, increase

61-65

attonitus, amazed

° novitās, -ātis, f. novelty, strange event

paveō, -ēre, pāvī, tremble, be frightened

supīnus, palms upward, uplifted

° concipiō, -ere, -cēpī, -ceptus, form, utter

prex, precis, f. prayer

° venia, pardon, forgiveness

daps, dapis, f. food, meal

parātus, -ūs, m. preparation

ūnicus, single, just one

ānser, -eris, m. goose

° custōdia, guard, protection

° hospes, -pitis, m. and f. guest, stranger

mactō (1), sacrifice

manner to allow freedom of movement. **42 Quae = Et ea (testa). 43 aequātam: mēnsam** is understood; *the table, once it had been leveled.* **mentae:** to clean the table top and give it a pleasant odor. **44 bicolor:** i.e., both green and black. **baca:** sing. for pl.; *olives,* as Athena (Minerva) had created the olive tree. **45 faece:** in this thrifty household the undrinkable sediment-filled part of the wine was used for pickling. **47 ōvaque . . favīllā:** *and eggs lightly roasted in the warm ashes.* **48 fictilibus:** abl. of place; *on earthenware.* **48-49 eōdem argentō:** i.e., earthenware; abl. of material w. **caelātus.** Ovid here describes the dinnerware with a touch of irony. **50 quā cava sunt:** to be construed with **inlita;** the insides of the cups were waxed to keep the wine from soaking into the wood.

pōnit anus. Mēnsae sed erat pēs tertius impār;
testa parem fēcit. Quae postquam subdita clīvum
sustulit, aequātam mentae tersēre virentēs.
Pōnitur hīc bicolor sincērae bāca Minervae,
conditaque in liquidā corna autumnālia faece,   *45*
intibaque et rādīx et lactis massa coāctī
ōvaque nōn ācrī leviter versāta favīllā,
omnia fictilibus. Post haec caelātus eōdem
sistitur argentō crātēr fabricātaque fāgō
pōcula, quā cava sunt, flāventibus inlita cērīs.   *50*

The main course and the dessert.

Parva mora est, epulāsque focī mīsēre calentēs,
nec longae rūrsus referuntur vīna senectae
dantque locum mēnsīs paulum sēducta secundīs.
Hīc nux, hīc mixta est rūgōsīs cārica palmīs
prūnaque et in patulīs redolentia māla canistrīs   *55*
et dē purpureīs collēctae vītibus ūvae.
Candidus in mediō favus est. Super omnia vultūs
accessēre bonī nec iners pauperque voluntās.

Amazed that the wine bowl keeps being replenished of its own accord
and fearful that their preparations have been inadequate, Philemon
and Baucis apologize and prepare to kill their only goose.

Intereā totiēns haustum crātēra replērī
sponte suā per sēque vident succrēscere vīna.   *60*
Attonitī novitāte pavent, manibusque supīnīs
concipiunt Baucisque precēs timidusque Philēmōn,
et veniam dapibus nūllīsque parātibus ōrant.
Ūnicus ānser erat, minimae custōdia vīllae,
quem dīs hospitibus dominī mactāre parābant.   *65*

51 epulās: a dignified word for the simple main course of bacon with vegetables. A Roman meal consisted of three parts: 1. the **gustātiō** (appetizers); here olives, pickled cornelberries, endive, radishes, cheese, and eggs; 2. the **fercula** (the main course, here called **epulae**); and 3. the **secundae mēnsae** (dessert), usually fruits and nuts. A Roman table top was not attached to its legs and could be removed and replaced like a tray. **52 nec longae senectae:** gen. of description; the poor couple could not afford to let their wine age. **53 paulum sēducta:** *pushed a little to one side,* in order to make room on the small table for the dessert (**mēnsae secundae**). **54 cārica:** collective sing., *figs.* **57 Super:** *In addition to.* **58 nec:** with both adjectives; *and an eager, generous kindness.*

59 crātēra: Greek acc. sing. ending. They could afford only a small winebowl; hence the frequent replenishings. **61 manibus supīnīs:** in offering prayers the ancients stood with uplifted hands. **64 custōdia:** abstract for concrete **custōs.** So also **tūtēla** (l. 91) for **tūtōrēs.** Because of their excitable nature and loud cries, geese were sometimes used as watchdogs. **65 dīs:** dat. pl. of **deus.**

penna (pinna), feather, wing
* tardus, slow
* fatīgō (1), tire, weary
* ēlūdō, -ere, ēlūsī, ēlūsus, escape from
* cōnfugiō, -ere, -fūgī, flee for safety
* vetō, -āre, -uī, -itus, forbid
* necō (1), kill
  meritus, earned, deserved
  luō, -ere, luī, pay, suffer
  vīcīnia, neighborhood
  impius, wicked, ungodly, impious
  immūnis, -e, w. gen., free from, exempt

71-75
* modo, only, just
  comitō (1), accompany
* gradus, -ūs, m. step, pace
  arduum, height
* ambō, -ae, -ō, both
  baculus, stick, staff
  nītor, -ī, nīsus (nīxus) sum, struggle, strive
* vēstīgium, footstep
  tantum ... quantum, as far ... as
  semel, once

76-80
flectō, -ere, flexī, flexus, bend, turn
mergō, -ere, mersī, mersus, sink
* prōspiciō, -ere, -spexī, -spectus, look out and see
  tantum, only
* dēfleō, -ēre, -flēvī, -flētus, weep for
* vertō, -ere, vertī, versus, turn, change
  furca, fork, pole
  subeō, -īre, -iī, -itus, go under, replace
  columna, column, pillar

81-85
strāmen, -minis, n. straw, thatch
flāvēscō, -ere, grow yellow (golden)
aurātus, ornamented with gold, gilded
foris, -is, f. door
adoperiō, -īre, -operuī, -opertus, cover over
marmor, -oris, n. marble
* placidus, calm, peaceful
* ēdō, -ere, ēdidī, ēditus, put forth, utter
* ōs, ōris, n. mouth

* iūstus, just, righteous
* optō (1), yearn, pray for

86-90
* iūdicium, judgment, decision
  aperiō, -īre, -uī, -tus, open, reveal
* sacerdōs, -dōtis, m. and f. priest, priestess
  dēlūbrum, shrine, temple
  tueor, -ērī, tūtus sum, care for
* poscō, -ere, poposcī, demand, ask
* quoniam, since
  concors, -cordis, in agreement
* annōs agō, spend years
  auferō, -ferre, abstulī, ablātus, carry away
* umquam, ever
  bustum, funeral mound, tomb
  tumulō (1), bury, entomb

91-95
vōtum, vow, prayer, wish
* fidēs, -eī, f. faith, confidence, fulfillment
  tūtēla, guardianship, protection
  dōnec, while, as long as
  aevum, time, age
  solūtus, freed, weakened
* forte, by chance
* cāsus, -ūs, m. chance, fortune
  frondeō, -ēre, put forth leaves
* cōnspiciō, -ere, -spexī, -spectus, behold, view
  senior, -ōris, m. aged man

96-100
* geminī, -ōrum, m. pl. twins, two alike
* crēscō, -ere, crēvī, crētum, grow
  cacūmen, -minis, n. summit, top, treetop
  mūtuus, mutual, interchanged
* dictum, word
* valē: imper. of valeō, farewell
* abdō, -dere, -didī, -ditus, put away, hide
  frutex, -ticis, m. bush, foliage
* ostendō, -ere, -tendī, -tentus, show, point out
* adhūc, still, even now
  Cibyrēius, of Cibyra, a town in Phrygia
* incola, -ae, m. inhabitant
  geminus, shared by two
* vīcīnus, near, adjacent
  truncus, tree trunk

70 immūnibus: modifying vōbīs, although strict syntax would require immūnēs as a complement for esse. **70-71 huius malī:** w. immūnibus; *exempt from this punishment.*

75-76 quantum ... potest: the unnecessary addition of this exact detail adds verisimilitude to the story. **77 cētera:** *everything else.* **sua tēcta:** for suam casam. **78 dēflent:** they are more merciful than the gods. **79 illa vetus:** modifying casa. **80 Furcās:** the poles which supported the roof; they would be forked to hold the ridgepole and the rafters.

The gods reveal themselves and ask the couple to leave their home and climb the hill with them.

> Ille celer pennā tardōs aetāte fatīgat
> ēlūditque diū tandemque est vīsus ad ipsōs
> cōnfūgisse deōs. Superī vetuēre necārī,
> "Dī"que "sumus, meritāsque luet vīcīnia poenās
> impia," dīxērunt. "Vōbīs immūnibus huius   70
> esse malī dabitur. Modo vestra relinquite tēcta
> ac nostrōs comitāte gradūs et in ardua montis
> īte simul." Pārent ambō baculīsque levātī
> nītuntur longō vēstīgia pōnere clīvō.

When they reach the hilltop they discover that the village has disappeared into a marsh, and that their humble cottage has been transformed into a magnificent temple.

> Tantum aberant summō quantum semel īre sagitta   75
> missa potest. Flexēre oculōs et mersa palūde
> cētera prōspiciunt, tantum sua tēcta manēre.
> Dumque ea mīrantur, dum dēflent fāta suōrum,
> illa vetus dominīs etiam casa parva duōbus
> vertitur in templum. Furcās subiēre columnae,   80
> strāmina flāvēscunt, aurātaque tēcta videntur,
> caelātaeque forēs, adopertaque marmore tellūs.

Philemon and Baucis are granted their wish to be keepers of the temple and to die together; in death they are united through the metamorphosis into trees growing from a single trunk.

> Tālia tum placidō Sāturnius ēdidit ōre:
> "Dīcite, iūste senex et fēmina coniuge iūstō
> digna, quid optētis." Cum Baucide pauca locūtus   85
> iūdicium superīs aperit commūne Philēmōn:
> "Esse sacerdōtēs dēlūbraque vestra tuērī
> poscimus, et quoniam concordēs ēgimus annōs,
> auferat hōra duōs eadem, nec coniugis umquam
> busta meae videam neu sim tumulandus ab illā."   90
> Vōta fidēs sequitur. Templī tūtēla fuēre
> dōnec vīta data est. Annīs aevōque solūtī
> ante gradūs sacrōs cum stārent forte locīque
> nārrārent cāsūs, frondēre Philēmona Baucis,
> Baucida cōnspexit senior frondēre Philēmōn.   95
> Iamque, super geminōs crēscente cacūmine vultūs,
> mūtua dum licuit reddēbant dicta, "Valē"que
> "Ō coniūnx!" dīxēre simul, simul abdita tēxit
> ōra frutex. Ostendit adhūc Cibyrēius illīc
> incola dē geminō vīcīnōs corpore truncōs.   100

---

83 **Sāturnius:** *son of Saturn,* i.e., Jupiter. 89 **auferat:** subjv. in a wish; so too **videam** and sim. 94-95 **Philēmona, Baucida:** Greek acc. endings. 99 **Cibyrēius:** modifying **incola**. 100 **dē geminō corpore:** indicating that the trees were rooted together.

101-104

* **vānus**, empty, useless, unreliable
* **equidem**, indeed
  sertum, garland, wreath
* **rāmus**, branch
* **recēns, -entis**, fresh, new
* **colō, -ere, coluī, cultus**, cultivate, honor

101 nōn vānī: litotes for *quite reliable.* **neque . . . vellent:** *and there was no reason why they would want to deceive me.* **102 Equidem:** *I personally.* **103 recentia:** sc. **serta. 104 quī:** supply **eī** or **mortālēs** as antecedent.

1-5

* **optō** (1), choose, wish
* **mūnus, -neris**, n. gift
  arbitrium, decision, choice
* **gaudeō, -ēre, gāvīsus sum**, *semidep.* rejoice
  altor, -ōris, m. nourisher, foster father
* **aiō:** *def.* I say; **ait**, he says
  quisquis, quidquid, whoever, whatever
* **contingō, -ere, -tigī, -tāctus**, touch
* **fulvus**, yellow, tawny
* **aurum**, gold
  adnuō, -ere, -nuī, -nūtum, *w. dat.*, nod approval for, grant
  optātum, wish, desire
* **solvō, -ere, solvī, solūtus**, loosen, free, pay

6-10

* **Līber, -erī**, m. Liber, name of Bacchus
  indolēscō, -ere, -doluī, feel distress
* **laetus**, happy, glad
* **malum**, harm, evil
  Berecyntius, of Berecyntus
  hērōs, -ōis, m. hero
  pollicitum, promise
  singulus, individual, one by one
  frōns, frondis, f. bough, foliage
  vireō, -ēre, -uī, be green, be fresh
  īlex, īlicis, f. oak, ilex
* **dētrahō, -ere, -trāxī, -trāctus**, draw down
  virga, branch, twig
* **aureus**, golden

11-15

* **humus, -ī**, f. ground
* **palleō, -ēre, -uī**, be pale
* **glaeba**, clod, lump of earth
  contāctus, -ūs, m. touch
  massa, lump, mass, nugget
  āreō, -ēre, -uī, be dry
  Cerēs, Cereris, f. Ceres
  dēcerpō, -ere, -cerpsī, -cerptus, pluck off
  arista, ear of grain
  messis, -is, f. harvest
* **dēmō, -ere, dēmpsī, dēmptus**, take away
* **pōmum**, fruit, apple
  Hesperides, -um (*acc.* -as), f. Hesperides, daughters of Hesperus
  dōnō (1), give, present
  postis, -is, m. door post

16-20

* **digitus**, finger
  radiō (1), shine, radiate
* **palma**, palm
  lavō, -āre, lāvī, lavātus (lautus, lōtus), wash
* **unda**, wave, water
  fluō, -ere, flūxī, flūxum, flow
  Danaē, -ēs (*acc.* -ēn), f. Danaë
  ēlūdō, -ere, ēlūsī, ēlūsus, elude, deceive, trick
* **fingō, -ere, fīnxī, fictus**, mould, fashion
* **minister, -trī**, m. servant

1 Huic: Midas (so too **Ille**, l. 3). **deus:** Bacchus. **1-2 optandī mūneris:** gerundive; *of wishing for a gift.* **2 altōre receptō:** abl. of cause, depending on **gaudēns**; *glad because his foster father* (*Silenus*) *had been restored.* **3 male ūsūrus:** *destined to make ill use of;* the fut. active participle may indicate, besides mere futurity, either intention or destiny. **4 vertātur:** dependent on **Effice** (**ut**).

6 Līber: Bacchus. **petīsset = petīvisset:** subjv. in implied indir. discourse, i.e., giving the reason in Bacchus' mind. **7 Berecyntius hērōs:** Midas. **9 nōn altā:** litotes for **humilī**; *low.*

11 humō: **humus**, like **domus** and **rūs**, uses no prep. with abl. of place from which. **13 Cereris:** by a metonymy common in Latin verse, the name of the goddess often stands for food, fruit, or (as here) grain. **14 arbore:** abl. of separation w. **Dēmptum. 15 Hesperidas:** the guardians of the golden apples. **dōnāsse = dōnāvisse. putēs:** potential subjv.; *you would think.*

124

Evidence that the story is reliable.

Haec mihi nōn vānī (neque erat cūr fallere vellent)
nārrāvēre senēs. Equidem pendentia vīdī
serta super rāmōs pōnēnsque recentia dīxī:
"Cūra piī dīs sunt, et quī coluēre coluntur."   104
                    METAMORPHOSES VIII, 618–

Midas

Silenus, companion and foster father of Bacchus, has been missing for
ten days. When Midas, king of Phrygia, saw to his return, Bacchus in
gratitude offered to gratify any wish that Midas would make. The king
asked that anything he touched be turned to gold. As his food and
drink turned to gold, Midas was brought to the point of starvation.
When he asked that the "golden touch" be taken from him, Bacchus
instructed him to bathe in the Pactolus, a river where gold has been
found since that time.

Huic deus optandī grātum sed inūtile fēcit
mūneris arbitrium, gaudēns altōre receptō.
Ille, male ūsūrus dōnīs, ait, "Effice, quidquid
corpore contigerō, fulvum vertātur in aurum."
Adnuit optātīs, nocitūraque mūnera solvit   5
Līber, at indoluit quod nōn meliōra petīsset.
Laetus abit gaudetque malō Berecyntius hērōs,
pollicitīque fidem tangendō singula temptat.
Vixque sibī crēdēns, nōn altā fronde virentem
īlice dētrāxit virgam; virga aurea facta est.   10
Tollit humō saxum; saxum quoque palluit aurō.
Contigit et glaebam; contāctū glaeba potentī
massa fit. Ārentēs Cereris dēcerpsit aristās;
aurea messis erat. Dēmptum tenet arbore pōmum;
Hesperidas dōnāsse putēs. Sī postibus altīs   15
admōvit digitōs, postēs radiāre videntur.
Ille etiam liquidīs palmās ubi lāverat undīs,
unda fluēns palmīs Danaēn ēlūdere posset.

"Hard Food for Midas"

Vix spēs ipse suās animō capit, aurea fingēns
omnia. Gaudentī mēnsās posuēre ministrī   20

---

18 palmīs: abl. of separation. **Danaēn:** a princess of Argos whom Jupiter visited in the
form of a golden shower. **ēlūdere posset:** *could have deceived;* posset is a potential subjv.
19 capit: *grasps.* **20 Gaudentī:** dat. w. **eī** or **illī** implied. **posuēre** = posuērunt. **21 nec**

21-25

exstrūctus, piled high
* daps, dapis, *f.* feast, banquet
tostus, roasted, baked
frūx, frūgis, *f.* grain, meal
* egeō, -ēre, -uī, *w. gen.*, need
* sīve . . . sīve, whether . . . or, if . . . or if
Cereālis, -e, of Ceres
* rigeō, -ēre, be stiff
avidus, eager, hungry
* convellō, -ere, -vellī, -vulsus, tear apart
lammina, layer, leaf of metal

26-30

misceō, -ēre, -uī, mixtus, mix
* auctor, -ōris, *m.* author
fūsilis, -e, molten, liquid
rictus, -ūs, *m.* open jaw
fluitō (1), flow, float
attonitus, dumbfounded, amazed
* novitās, -ātis, *f.* strangeness, novelty
* dīves, -vitis, rich
* effugiō, -ere, -fūgī, escape from
opēs, -um, *f. pl.* wealth
modo, just now, recently
voveō, -ēre, vōvī, vōtus, vow, pray for
* ōdī, ōdisse, hate
famēs, -is, *f.* hunger
* relevō (1), lift up, relieve
sitis, -is, *f.* thirst
āridus, dry, parched
guttur, -uris, *n.* throat

31-35

ūrō, -ere, ussī, ustus, burn
invīsus, hated, detested
* meritus, deserving, deserved
torqueō, -ēre, torsī, tortus, twist, torture,
    torment
splendidus, shining, glistening
bracchium, arm
venia, pardon, forgiveness
Lēnaeus, Lenaean; epithet of Bacchus as
    god of the wine press

* peccō (1), err, sin
* misereor, -ērī, -itus sum, pity
* precor (*dep.* 1), pray
speciōsus, attractive, deceitful
* damnum, loss, ruin
mītis, -e, mild, gentle
nūmen, -minis, *n.* divine will, divinity
* fateor, -ērī, fassus sum, own, admit

36-40

* restituō, -ere, -stituī, -stitūtus, restore
pactus, agreed upon, stipulated
nēve, and in order that . . . not
circumlitus, besmeared
vādō, -ere, go
* vīcīnus, *w. dat.*, neighboring, near
Sardēs, -ium, *f. pl.* Sardis, capital of Lydia
* amnis, -is, *m.* river
iugum, yoke, ridge
Lȳdus, Lydian
lābor, -ī, lāpsus sum, glide, flow
obvius, *w. dat.*, facing, meeting
carpō, -ere, carpsī, carptus, pluck, pick
* dōnec, until
* ortus, -ūs, *m.* rising, source

41-46

spūmiger, -era, -erum, carrying foam,
    foaming
* fōns, fontis, *m.* fount, source
quā, where
* subdō, -ere, -didī, -ditus, put . . . under
ēluō, -ere, ēluī, ēlūtus, wash off
* crīmen, -minis, *n.* charge, guilt, crime
* succēdō, -ere, -cessī, -cessum, *w. dat.*, go
    up to
tingō, -ere, tīnxī, tīnctus, dye, color, stain
percipiō, -ere, -cēpī, -ceptus, grasp, re-
    ceive, take
sēmen, -minis, *n.* seed
vēna, vein
arvum, field
madidus, wet, drenched

Midas bathing in the Pactolus as Bacchus watches. Painting by Poussin
(1594-1665). Metropolitan Museum of
Art, N.Y.C.

*The Metropolitan Museum of Art,
Purchase, 1871*

exstrūctās dapibus nec tostae frūgis egentēs.
Tum vērō, sīve ille suā Cereālia dextrā
mūnera contigerat, Cereālia dōna rigēbant;
sīve dapēs avidō convellere dente parābat,
lammina fulva dapēs, admōtō dente, premēbat.　　　　　*25*
Miscuerat pūrīs auctōrem mūneris undīs;
fūsile per rictūs aurum fluitāre vidērēs.

The Bitter Truth

Attonitus novitāte malī, dīvesque miserque,
effugere optat opēs, et quae modo vōverat ōdit.
Cōpia nūlla famem relevat; sitis ārida guttur　　　　　*30*
ūrit, et invīsō meritus torquētur ab aurō,
ad caelumque manūs et splendida bracchia tollēns,
"Dā veniam, Lēnaee pater! Peccāvimus," inquit,
"sed miserēre, precor, speciōsōque ēripe damnō."

Release from the Wish

Mīte deum nūmen; Bacchus peccāsse fatentem　　　　　*35*
restituit. "Pactam"que "fidem, data mūnera, solvī;
nēve male optātō maneās circumlitus aurō,
vāde," ait, "ad magnīs vīcīnum Sardibus amnem,
perque iugum Lȳdum lābentibus obvius undīs
carpe viam, dōnec veniās ad flūminis ortūs;　　　　　*40*
spūmigerōque tuum fontī, quā plūrimus exit,
subde caput, corpusque simul, simul ēlue crīmen."
Rēx iussae succēdit aquae. Vīs aurea tīnxit
flūmen, et hūmānō dē corpore cessit in amnem.
Nunc quoque iam, veteris perceptō sēmine vēnae,　　　　　*45*
arva rigent aurō madidīs pallentia glaebīs.
 METAMORPHOSES XI. 100

egentēs: litotes for *and having plenty of.* tostae frūgis: *bread,* like Cereālia mūnera (dōna)
below. 26 Miscuerat: the ancients customarily mixed water with their wine. auctōrem
mūneris = Bacchum, which by metonymy stands for vīnum. 27 vidērēs: potential subjv.;
you would have seen.

28 novitāte: explained by the oxymoron dīvesque miserque. 29 quae: n. pl. w. implied
ea; *the things which.* 31 ab aurō: abl. of cause; the ab would not be used in prose.
32 splendida: suggesting the luster of the gold. 34 ēripe: sc. as object mē or nōs.

35 deum = deōrum. nūmen: sc. est. peccāsse: syncopated form of peccāvisse. Sc. sē as
acc. subject. fatentem: modifies the implied object of restituit (eum); *restored him when he
confessed that he had erred.* 36 Pactam . . . solvī: *I have paid the agreed pledge, the gifts
which I gave.* 38 amnem: the Pactolus. 39 iugum Lȳdum: *the Lydian mountain,* Mt.
Tmolus where the Pactolus begins. obvius undīs: i.e., upstream. 41 tuum: modifies caput.
fontī: dat. w. the compound verb subde.

43 iussae: transferred epithet; *as he had been ordered.* 45 Nunc quoque iam: *Even today.*
45-46 veteris . . . glaebīs: *receiving the seed of the ancient vein (of metal), the fields are
hard, growing pale when their clods have been saturated with gold.* 46 aurō: probably to
be taken with rigent, madidīs and pallentia; *are stiff with gold, saturated with gold,* and
growing pale with gold.

1-5

candidus, white, shining
folium, leaf
niveus, snowy
ligustrum, privet
° flōridus, flowery
prātum, meadow
prōcērus, tall
alnus, -ī, f. alder
° splendidus, shining, bright
vitrum, glass
lascīvus, playful
haedus, kid, young goat
° lēvis, -e, smooth
assiduus, constant, persistent
dētrītus, worn smooth
concha, mussel, shell
° aestīvus, of summer
° umbra, shade

6-10

° pōmum, fruit, apple
platanus, -ī, f. plane tree
cōnspectus, viewed, admired
° lūcidus, clear
glaciēs, -ēī, f. ice
° mātūrus, ripe
° ūva, grape
mollis, -e, soft, mild
cycnus, swan
plūma, feather, down
lac, lactis, n. milk; lac coāctum, cottage
  cheese
riguus, watered
° fōrmōsus, beautiful
° hortus, garden
saevus, cruel, fierce, wild
indomitus, untamed
iuvencus, bullock; iuvenca, heifer

11-15

° dūrus, unfeeling
annōsus, aged
° quercus, -ūs, f. oak tree
fallāx, -ācis, treacherous
lentus, pliant, flexible, tough
salix, -icis, f. willow
virga, twig, switch, wand
° vītis, -is, f. vine

° albus, white, pale
° immōbilis, -e, immovable
scopulus, crag, cliff
amnis, -is, m. river, stream
pāvō, -ōnis, m. peacock
° superbus, proud, haughty
° asper, -era, -erum, rough, harsh
tribulus, thorn, thistle
fētus, having given birth
truculentus, ferocious
° ursa, she-bear

16-20

surdus, deaf
calcātus, trodden upon
immītis, -e, ungentle, savage
hydrus, water snake, serpent
praecipuē, chiefly
dēmō, -ere, dēmpsī, demptus, take away
  . . . from
° nōn tantum . . . vērum etiam, not only . . .
  but also
cervus, stag, deer
° clārus, loud, clear
lātrātus, -ūs, m. barking
volucer, -cris, -cre, flying, swift
fugāx, -ācis, fleeting
° nōscō, -ere, nōvī, nōtus, get to know
piget, -ēre, uit, regret
mora, delay, reluctance

21-25

° damnō (1), condemn
° vīvus, living, natural
pendēns, -entis, hanging
antrum, cave
aestus, -ūs, m. heat
gravō (1), weigh down, burden
rāmus, branch
° aurum, gold

26-28

purpureus, purple, red
caeruleus, dark blue
nitidus, trim, pretty, sleek
exserō, -serere, -seruī, -sertus, put out
pontus, sea
° dēspiciō, -ere, -spexī, -spectus, scorn, despise

1-9 In this list of comparisons there are thirteen ingratiating adjectives; in the second part (lines 10-19) there are thirteen reproachful adjectives. The simple-minded giant knows only the comparative degree. His comparisons, though numerous, are drawn from his life on the mountains and make no appeal to the sea nymph.

1 Candidior: the name Galatea was thought to mean *milk-white*. 3 vitrō: Ovid's admiration for Horace (the phrase is from the *Odes*, III, 13) leads him to include a comparison not really appropriate to the rustic setting. 4 lēvior: do not confuse with levior (with a short e). 6 nōbilior: here probably in its agricultural sense; *better bred*. 9 fugiās: subjv. in a future less vivid condition; *if only you would not run away*. Here and in lines 18-19 the lumbering giant objects to the ease with which the nymph slips lightly away as he approaches.

The Song of Polyphemus

Before Odysseus and his men came to the land of the Cyclopes, Polyphemus was hopelessly in love with the sea nymph Galatea. Deciding to spruce up, he combed his matted hair with a rake, trimmed his shaggy beard with a pruning hook, and viewed with complacency his reflection in a pool. Part of the song with which Polyphemus attempted to woo Galatea is given below.

Candidior foliō niveī, Galatēa, ligustrī,
flōridior prātīs, longā prōcērior alnō,
splendidior vitrō, tenerō lascīvior haedō,
lēvior assiduō dētrītīs aequore conchīs,
sōlibus hībernīs, aestīvā grātior umbrā,   *5*
nōbilior pōmīs, platanō cōnspectior altā,
lūcidior glaciē, mātūrā dulcior ūvā,
mollior et cycnī plūmīs et lacte coāctō,
et (sī nōn fugiās!) riguō fōrmōsior hortō:
saevior indomitīs eadem Galatēa iuvencīs,   *10*
dūrior annōsā quercū, fallācior undīs,
lentior et salicis virgīs et vītibus albīs,
hīs immōbilior scopulīs, violentior amne,
laudātō pāvōne superbior, ācrior ignī,
asperior tribulīs, fētā truculentior ursā,   *15*
surdior aequoribus, calcātō immītior hydrō,
et (quod praecipuē vellem tibi dēmere possem!)
nōn tantum cervō clārīs lātrātibus āctō,
vērum etiam ventīs volucrīque fugācior aurā.
(At bene sī nōrīs, pigeat fūgisse morāsque   *20*
ipsa tuās damnēs et mē retinēre labōrēs!)
Sunt mihi, pars montis, vīvō pendentia saxō
antra quibus nec sōl mediō sentītur in aestū
nec sentītur hiems; sunt pōma gravantia rāmōs,
sunt aurō similēs longīs in vītibus ūvae,   *25*
sunt et purpureae; tibi et hās servāmus et illās. . .
Iam modo caeruleō nitidum caput exsere pontō,
iam, Galatēa, venī nec mūnera dēspice nostra!
METAMORPHOSES XIII. 789–

10 **eadem Galatēa:** balancing **Galatēa** of line 1, as the new set of comparisons begins.
13 **hīs scopulīs:** Polyphemus sings from a sea cliff near Mt. Etna in Sicily. 17 **vellem:**
potential subjv.; *I could wish.* **possem:** optative subjv.; *that I could.* Hence **quod vellem
dēmere possem:** *what I could wish I were able to take away.* **tibi:** dat. of reference; *from
you.* 18 **cervō:** abl. of comparison with **fugācior.**

20 **nōrīs** (= **nōverīs**): subjv. in a future less vivid condition; *if you were to know.*
20-21 **pigeat** (sc. **tē**), **damnēs, labōrēs:** subjvs. in future less vivid conclusion; *you would . . .*
22 **pars:** in apposition with **antra.** 23 **mediō in aestū:** *in the noonday heat.* 25 **aurō:** dat.
with **similēs.**

TRISTIA

1-5

* tener, -era, -erum, tender, soft, young
lūsor, -ōris, *m.* player, playful writer
* nōscō, -ere, nōvī, nōtus, get to know; *perf.*
nōvī, I know
* posteritās, -ātis, *f.* future time, posterity
Sulmo, -ōnis, *m.* Sulmo, modern Sulmona
gelidus, cool, chilling
ūber, -eris, fertile, rich
* unda, wave, water
noviēns, nine times
distō, -āre, be distant
ēdō, -ere, ēdidī, ēditus, put out, give birth
to

6-10

* fātum, fate, destiny
usque, all the way
proavus, great-grandfather
hērēs, -ēdis, *m. and f.* heir
modo, only, merely
* mūnus, -neris, *n.* function, service, gift
stirps, stirpis, *f.* stem, offspring
gignō, -ere, genuī, genitus, beget; *in pass.*
be born
creō (1) = gignō
quater, four times

11-15

* Lūcifer, -erī, *m.* morning star, planet Venus
* ambō, -ae, -ō, both
nātālis, -is, *m.* birthday
celebrō (1), throng, celebrate
lībum, cake
armifer, -era, -erum, armed, warrior

* fēstus, festive, festival
cruentus, bloody, gory
* soleō, -ēre, solitus sum, be accustomed
* prōtinus, straightway
excolō, -ere, -coluī, -cultus, train carefully
* parēns, -entis, *m. and f.* parent

16-20

īnsignis, -e, distinguished, outstanding
ars, artis, *f.* art, skill, profession
ēloquium, eloquence
viridis, -e, green, fresh, young
tendō, -ere, tetendī, tentus (tēnsus), direct, aim
* aevum, age
* verbōsus, wordy, noisy
* caelestis, -e, heavenly, divine
sacra, *n. pl.* sacred things, rituals, poems
fūrtim, secretly, stealthily

21-25

* inūtilis, -e, useless
Maeonidēs, -ae, *m.* man from Maeonia (in
Asia Minor), Homer
* opēs, opum, *f. pl.* wealth
* dictum, word, remark
Helicōn, -ōnis, *m.* Helicon, mountain sacred to Apollo and the Muses
* solvō, -ere, solvī, solūtus, set free
* modus, way, measure, meter
* sponte suā, of his (her, its, their) own
accord
* carmen, -minis, *n.* song, poem
numerus, number, verse, meter
* aptus, fit, suitable, right

1-2 **Ille . . . posteritās:** a less confusing order would be **Accipe, posteritās, ut nōrīs quī fuerim ego, ille tenerōrum amōrum lūsor quem legis.** 1 **Ille:** *The well-known;* the juxtaposition of **Ille** and **ego** suggests a secondary meaning, *I'm the one.* **quī fuerim:** indir. question, depending on **nōrīs** and **accipe. tenerōrum lūsor amōrum:** *playful poet of young love;* Ovid rests his reputation on his lighter works. 2 **nōrīs** = **nōverīs:** *so that you may know.* **accipe:** *listen.* **posteritās:** voc.; by addressing posterity Ovid shows his confidence that his works will survive. 3 **Sulmo . . . est:** the initials (S.M.P.E.) are still used in the coat of arms and official correspondence of modern Sulmona and appear on many public buildings. **mihi:** dat. of possession. 4 **mīlia:** acc. of extent of space; sc. **passuum. noviēns decem:** 9 x 10 = 90. **Urbe:** Rome. 5 **nec . . . nōrīs:** *yes, and so that you may know the time;* the clause does little more than fill out the meter. 6 **cum . . . parī:** 43 B.C., when the two consuls, Hirtius and Pansa, were killed in battle.

7 **Sī . . . est:** *If it is anything = For whatever it is worth.* **ōrdinis:** i.e., the equestrian order, consisting of the wealthiest citizens. 9 **Genitō frātre:** abl. abs. 10 **tribus quater** = **duodecim** (which cannot fit the meter). **mēnsibus:** abl. of degree of difference w. **ante.** 11 **Lūcifer īdem:** *The same morning-star = The same date.* **nātālibus:** dat. w. compound **adfuit.** 12 **lība:** *birthday cakes (offered in gratitude to the gods).* 13 **Haec:** sc. **diēs. fēstīs quīnque:** the Quinquatria, a five-day festival of Minerva, 19-23 March.

132

Autobiography

I, whose verses you read, was born at Sulmo, 90 miles from Rome, in the year when both consuls fell in battle. I had one brother, exactly one year older. Our birthdays fall on 20 March.

> Ille ego quī fuerim, tenerōrum lūsor amōrum,
>> quem legis, ut nōrīs, accipe, posteritās.
> Sulmo mihī patria est, gelidīs ūberrimus undīs,
>> mīlia quī noviēns distat ab Urbe decem.
> Ēditus hīc ego sum, nec nōn ut tempora nōrīs,   5
>> cum cecidit fātō cōnsul uterque parī.
> Sī quid id est, usque ā proavīs vetus ōrdinis hērēs
>> nōn modo fortūnae mūnere factus eques.
> Nec stirps prīma fuī. Genitō sum frātre creātus,
>> quī tribus ante quater mēnsibus ortus erat.   10
> Lūcifer ambōrum nātālibus adfuit īdem:
>> ūna celebrāta est per duo lība diēs.
> Haec est armiferae fēstīs dē quīnque Minervae,
>> quae fierī pugnā prīma cruenta solet.

We were given from early boyhood a good education in Rome. Despite my father's protests, I loved to write verses and had a natural aptitude.

> Prōtinus excolimur tenerī, cūrāque parentis   15
>> īmus ad īnsignēs Urbis ab arte virōs.
> Frāter ad ēloquium viridī tendēbat ab aevō,
>> fortia verbōsī nātus ad arma forī;
> at mihi iam puerō caelestia sacra placēbant,
>> inque suum fūrtim Mūsa trahēbat opus.   20
> Saepe pater dīxit, "Studium quid inūtile temptās?
>> Maeonidēs nūllās ipse relīquit opēs."
> Mōtus eram dictīs, tōtōque Helicōne relictō,
>> scrībere temptābam verba solūta modīs.
> Sponte suā carmen numerōs veniēbat ad aptōs   25

---

14 **pugnā**: explaining **cruenta**; the gladiatorial games began on the 2nd day of the Quinquatria, 20 March, the birthday of the two brothers.

15 **Prōtinus . . . tenerī**: *From an early age we are carefully educated.* 16 **īmus . . . virōs**: Ovid and his brother were sent to Rome for the best education available. **ab arte**: abl. of cause w. **īnsignēs**. 17 **Frāter . . . aevō**: the older brother found the training in rhetoric and law congenial. 18 **forī**: the forum was the center of the political activity of the empire; the brother could look forward to a career in politics, for which he was well suited. 20 **trahēbat**: sc. **mē**.

21 **quid**: *why;* the father was a man of practical common sense. 22 **Maeonidēs**: if "the man from Maeonia," who was the most famous of all poets, had made no money, there was small hope for any other poet. 23 **Helicōne**: metaphor for poetry. 24 **solūta modīs**: *freed from meters = in prose.* **modīs**: abl. of separation.

133

26-30

* versus, -ūs, *m.* line, verse
tacitus, silent, quiet
* lābor, -ī, lāpsus sum, slip, glide, pass
* toga, dress of the Roman citizen
induō, -ere, -duī, -dūtus, put on
* umerus, shoulder
purpura, purple, purple cloth
clāvus, nail, stripe

31-35

geminō (1), double, repeat
* pereō, -īre, -iī, -itum, perish, die
* careō, -ēre, -uī, -itum, *w. abl.* be without, miss, lack
* honor, -ōris, *m.* honor, public office

* quondam, once, formerly
* cūria, senate house
restō, -āre, -stitī, remain, be left
mēnsūra, measure, size
cōgō, -ere, coēgī, coāctus, bring together, limit

36-40

* onus, oneris, *n.* load, burden
sollicitus, troubled, worrying
fugāx, -ācis, *w. gen.* inclined to flee from
ambitiō, -ōnis, *f.* vote canvassing, ambition
Āonius, of Aonia (part of Boeotia)
* suādeō, -ēre, suāsī, suāsus, advise, counsel
* tūtus, safe, secure, prudent
* ōtium, leisure, peace

Parnassus. The Muses dance as Apollo and Mercury watch. The horse Pegasus belonged to the Muses. Mantegna. Louvre, Paris.

Archives Photographiques, Paris

1-5

* subeō, -īre, -iī, -itum, come up, occur
* trīstis, -e, sad, gloomy
* imāgō, -ginis, *f.* likeness, ghost, vision

* suprēmus, highest, last
* repetō, -ere, -iī, -ītus, seek again, recall
* cārus, dear
* lābor, -ī, lāpsus sum, glide, slip, fall
gutta, drop

In A.D. 8 Ovid was banished to Tomis, a frontier post on the Black Sea (v. p. xii). In this poem the poet describes the scene in his home as he prepared, on his last night, to set out into exile.

1 subit: *comes to me, enters my mind.* **4 nunc quoque:** *even now.* **5 Caesar:** Augustus.

134

et quod temptābam scrībere versus erat.

My brother died when I was nineteen. My love for poetry stayed with me and I renounced all prospect of a political career.

Intereā, tacitō passū lābentibus annīs,
    līberior frātrī sūmpta mihīque toga est,
induiturque umerīs cum lātō purpura clāvō,
    et studium nōbīs quod fuit ante manet.   30
Iamque decem vītae frāter gemināverat annōs,
    cum perit, et coepī parte carēre meī.
Cēpimus et tenerae prīmōs aetātis honōrēs
    ēque virīs quondam pars tribus ūna fuī.
Cūria restābat: clāvī mēnsūra coācta est;   35
    maius erat nostrīs vīribus illud onus.
Nec patiēns corpus, nec mēns fuit apta labōrī,
    sollicitaeque fugāx ambitiōnis eram,
et petere Āoniae suādēbant tūta sorōrēs
    ōtia, iūdiciō semper amāta meō.   40

TRISTIA IV. 10

27 **lābentibus annīs:** abl. abs. **28 līberior toga:** the wearing of the **toga virīlis** (commonly assumed at the age of 16, at the festival of Liber) indicated the coming of age, with greater freedom and greater responsibility. **frātrī mihīque:** dat. of agent w. **sūmpta. 29 cum . . . clāvō:** *the purple with the wide stripe;* the broad purple stripe (**lāticlāvium**) on the tunic indicated that the young men were preparing for a senatorial career. **30 studium:** *interest.* **33 prīmōs honōrēs:** *junior offices;* in the next line Ovid informs us that he had been a member of the **trēsvirī,** *three-man committee* (there were several minor offices by this name). **34 ēque:** prep. ē + encl. -que.

35 Cūria restābat: election to the quaestorship would have made Ovid a member of the senate, but he could not face the prospect; hence, *the measure of the stripe was narrowed* (i.e., he reverted to equestrian rank). **36 vīribus:** abl. of comparison; *greater than my strength = too great for my strength.* **39 petere:** in formal prose, **ut peterem. Āoniae:** Aonia was an ancient name for Boeotia, whose hills (especially Mt. Helicon) the Muses haunted. **39-40 tūta ōtia:** favorable to his literary interests.

Ovid's Last Night in Rome

I vividly recall the agony of that last night when, by the Emperor's edict, I was to leave Rome.

Cum subit illīus trīstissima noctis imāgō
    quā mihi suprēmum tempus in Urbe fuit,
cum repetō noctem quā tot mihi cāra relīquī,
    lābitur ex oculīs nunc quoque gutta meīs.
Iam prope lūx aderat quā mē discēdere Caesar   5

6-10

Ausonia, Italy
* aptus, fit, suitable, right
torpēscō, -ere, torpuī, become inactive or numb
* pectus, -toris, n. breast, heart
* comes, -mitis, m. and f. companion
* legō, -ere, lēgī, lēctus, pick, choose, read
profugus, fugitive, exile
* (ops), opis, f. help, support

11-15

stupeō, -ēre, -uī, be dazed, be stunned
* Iuppiter, Iovis, m. Jupiter
ictus, struck
nescius, ignorant, unaware
* nūbēs, -is, f. cloud
* sēnsus, -ūs, m. feeling, sense
* convalēscō, -ere, -valuī, get better, recover
* adloquor, -ī, -locūtus sum, address, speak to
* maestus, sad, sorrowful
* abeō, -īre, -iī, -itūrus, go away, depart

16-20

* modo, only, just, now
ūnus et alter, one or two
* fleō, -ēre, -ēvī, -ētus, cry, weep
* ācriter, bitterly
imber, -bris, m. shower, stream
indignus, unworthy, undeserving
usque, all the way, continually

gena, cheek
* nāta, daughter
Libycus, Libyan, African
* dīversus, different, remote
* ōra, coast
* fātum, fate
certior, -ius, w. gen., informed

21-25

* quōcumque, in whatever direction
* aspiciō, -ere, aspexī, aspectus, look, see
lūctus, -ūs, m. grief, sorrow
* gemitus, -ūs, m. groaning
sonō, -āre, -uī, -itum, sound, ring out
* fōrma, shape, appearance
* tacitus, silent, quiet
* fūnus, -neris, n. death, funeral
intus, inside, within
maereō, -ēre, sorrow, grieve
angulus, corner
* exemplum, example, pattern
grandis, -e, large, great

26-30

* faciēs, -ēī, f. face, appearance
quiēscō, -ere, quiēvī, quiētum, become quiet, rest
* canis, -is, m. and f. dog
nocturnus, of the night, nighttime
suspiciō, -ere, -spexī, -spectus, look up at
* Capitōlia, -ōrum, n. pl. the Capitol
cernō, -ere, crēvī, crētus, see, discern
* Lār, Laris, m. household god, home

6 fīnibus: abl. of separation w. discēdere. Ausoniae: strictly, southern Italy, but used by poets as a synonym for Italy in general.

7 Nec . . . parandī: *There had been no time, no thought for making really suitable preparations.* apta: n. pl., used as a substantive, the direct object of the gerund parandī. parandī: objective gen. w. spatium and mēns. 8 longā morā: referring to the tranquillity of his life up to this time. 9-10 servōrum, legendī, vestis, opis: objective genitives w. cūra; *concern for slaves, for choosing, for clothing, for means.* 9 comitēs: direct object of the gerund legendī. 10 profugō: dat. w. aptae; *suitable for an exile.* 11 Nōn aliter quam: *Not otherwise than* = *Just as.* quī: sc. is as antecedent; *one who.* Iovis ignibus: thunderbolts. 12 vītae nescius: in a coma; vītae is objective gen.

15 extrēmum: internal acc. w. adloquor; *I make a last speech to* (*I address for the last time*). abitūrus: *about to leave.* 16 modo: modifies multīs; *recently many.* ūnus et alter: *one and a second* = *one or two*; others had deserted him for fear of incurring the emperor's displeasure. 17 flēns ācrius ipsa: to be taken together; *weeping more bitterly herself.* 18 imbre cadente: abl. abs.; imbre is a metaphor for lacrimīs. 19 Nāta: his only child, who was with her husband in the province of Africa. 20 fātī . . . esse = dē fātō certior fierī.

21 aspicerēs: subjv. in rel. clause of characteristic, indef. 2nd person; *one might look.* 22 nōn tacitī: litotes for *with loud lamentation.* 23 Fēmina virque: i.e., Ovid and his wife. puerī: *the slaves.* 25 exemplīs: abl. w. deponent ūtor.

28 equōs: the moon-goddess here uses a chariot. 29 ab hāc: i.e., turning my eyes from her. Capitōlia: the Capitoline Hill, with the great temple of Jupiter Optimus Maximus, Juno, and Minerva, and several smaller temples. 30 frūstrā: *in vain;* not having prevented his banishment.

Sorcerer and Traveler. National Museum, Naples.

fīnibus extrēmae iusserat Ausoniae.
Nec spatium nec mēns fuerat satis apta parandī;
    torpuerant longā pectora nostra morā.
Nōn mihi servōrum, comitēs nōn cūra legendī,
    nōn aptae profugō vestis opisve fuit.   10
Nōn aliter stupuī quam quī Iovis ignibus ictus
    vīvit et est vītae nescius ipse suae.

Sharing my sorrow were my wife and the few friends who had remained
faithful to me.

Ut tamen hanc animī nūbem dolor ipse remōvit
    et tandem sēnsūs convaluēre meī,
adloquor extrēmum maestōs abitūrus amīcōs,   15
    quī modo dē multīs ūnus et alter erant.
Uxor amāns flentem flēns ācrius ipsa tenēbat,
    imbre per indignās usque cadente genās.
Nāta procul Libycīs aberat dīversa sub ōrīs
    nec poterat fātī certior esse meī.   20
Quōcumque aspicerēs, lūctūs gemitūsque sonābant,
    fōrmaque nōn tacitī fūneris intus erat.
Fēmina virque meō, puerī quoque fūnere maerent,
    inque domō lacrimās angulus omnis habet.
Sī licet exemplīs in parvō grandibus ūtī,   25
    haec faciēs Trōiae, cum caperētur, erat.

I bade farewell to all that I held dear, and solemnly protested my in-
nocence.

Iamque quiēscēbant vōcēs hominumque canumque,
    Lūnaque nocturnōs alta regēbat equōs.
Hanc ego suspiciēns et ab hāc Capitōlia cernēns,
    quae nostrō frūstrā iūncta fuēre Larī,   30

137

31-35

* nūmen, -minis, n. divine power, deity
* vīcīnus, neighboring, nearby
  sēdēs, -is, f. seat, dwelling
* inquam, def. say; inquit, says
* templum, temple
* deus, deī, (nom. pl. deī, diī, dī), m. god
  Quirīnus, the deified Romulus
* salūtō (1), greet
* quamquam, although
  sērō, late, too late
  clipeus, shield

36-40

attamen, yet, nevertheless
* odium, hatred, displeasure
  exonerō (1), unburden, relieve
* fuga, flight, exile
  caelestis, -e, heavenly, divine
* dēcipiō, -ere, -cēpī, -ceptus, deceive, betray
* error, -ōris, m. error, mistake
* culpa, blame, fault
* scelus, -leris, n. crime
  auctor, -ōris, m. author, promoter
  plācō (1), placate, appease

41-45

prex, precis, f. prayer
* adōrō (1), pray to
* superī (sc. deī), the gods above
* plūs, plūris, more
  singultus, -ūs, m. sobbing
  sonus, sound

passus, flowing, disheveled
prōstrātus, prostrate
* capillus, hair
* contingō, -ere, -tigī, -tāctus, touch
  exstīnctus, extinguished
* ōs, ōris, n. mouth, face
  tremēns, -entis, trembling
  focus, hearth, fireplace
  adversus, opposite, facing
* effundō, -ere, -fūdī, -fūsus, pour out
  Penātēs, -ium, m. pl. Penates, household
  gods

46-50

dēplōrātus, bewailed, wept over
praecipitātus, hurried, hurrying
* negō (1), deny, refuse
  axis, -is, m. axis, pole
  Parrhasis, -idis, Arcadian
  Arctos, -ī, f. constellation of the Great Bear,
  North
  blandus, enticing, alluring

51-55

* quotiēns, how many times
* properō (1), hurry, hasten
  urgeō, -ēre, ursī, force on, press, urge
  festīnō (1), hasten
  mentior, -īrī, -ītus sum, lie, say falsely
  prōpositus, planned, proposed
* ter, three times
* līmen, -minis, n. threshold

The emperor Augustus. Vatican Museum, Rome.

Alinari, Fototeca Unione

"Nūmina vīcīnīs habitantia sēdibus," inquam,
   "iamque oculīs numquam templa videnda meīs,
dīque relinquendī, quōs urbs habet alta Quirīnī,
   este salūtātī tempus in omne mihi!
Et quamquam sērō clipeum post vulnera sūmō,   35
   attamen hanc odiīs exonerāte fugam,
caelestīque virō, quis mē dēcēperit error,
   dīcite, prō culpā nē scelus esse putet,
ut quod vōs scītis, poenae quoque sentiat auctor.
   Plācātō possum nōn miser esse deō."   40

My wife too poured forth prayers in the agony of despair. Repeatedly
I tried to say farewell but my heart still prompted me to stay.

Hāc prece adōrāvī superōs ego; plūribus uxor,
   singultū mediōs impediente sonōs.
Illa etiam ante Larēs passīs prōstrāta capillīs
   contigit exstīnctōs ōre tremente focōs,
multaque in adversōs effūdit verba Penātēs   45
   prō dēplōrātō nōn valitūra virō.
Iamque morae spatium nox praecipitāta negābat,
   versaque ab axe suō Parrhasis Arctos erat.
Quid facerem? Blandō patriae retinēbar amōre,
   ultima sed iussae nox erat illa fugae.   50
Āh! Quotiēns aliquō dīxī properante, "Quid urgēs?
   Vel quō festīnēs īre, vel unde, vidē!"
Āh! Quotiēns certam mē sum mentītus habēre
   hōram, prōpositae quae foret apta viae!
Ter līmen tetigī, ter sum revocātus, et ipse   55

31-33 Nūmina, templa, dī: voc. case, as Ovid makes a solemn protest that he is innocent
of crime. **32 iam numquam:** *nevermore.* **34 este:** imper. mood; by coupling it with the perfect pass. participle Ovid creates a kind of perfect imperative, emphasizing that the action
of the verb is over; *be greeted for the last time.* **mihi:** dat. of agent w. **salūtātī. 35 sērō . . .
sūmō:** Ovid suggests that he is offering a defense even though he has already been sen-
tenced. **36 odiīs:** abl. of separation w. **exonerāte. 37 caelestī virō:** a flattering reference to
Augustus; so also **deō** in 1. 40. **quis** (for **quī**) **. . . error:** indir. question. **38 prō . . . putet:**
indir. command; both clauses depend on **dīcite;** *inform the godlike man as to what mistake
betrayed me, and that he is to consider it a fault, not a crime.* **prō:** *instead of.* **39 quod:** sc.
id as antecedent. **poenae auctor:** Augustus. **40 Plācātō deō:** abl. abs.

41 plūribus uxor: sc. **precibus adōrāvit. 42 singultū impediente:** abl. abs. **44 exstīnctōs
focōs:** because the hearth was the symbol of the continuity of the family, the fire was
allowed to go out on the hearths of exiles. **45 adversōs:** *turned toward her;* i.e., she offered
her prayers directly to their faces. **46 valitūra:** *destined to prevail.* **48 versa . . . erat:** an
indication that morning was near. **49 Quid facerem:** deliberative subjv.; *What was I to do?*
50 fugae: dat. of purpose w. **ultima nox. 51 aliquō properante:** abl. abs. **Quid urgēs:** *Why
are you hurrying me?* In lines 51-68 Ovid makes every excuse to delay his departure. **52 quō,
unde:** introducing indir. questions depending on **vidē.**

54 foret = esset: subjv. in subordinate clause in indir. discourse; *I lied, (saying) that I
had a definite time that was right for the journey before me.* **56 animō:** dat. with **indulgēns.**

indulgeō, -ēre, -dulsī, *w. dat.*, humor, give
    way to
tardus, slow, lingering, lame
* quasi, as if
* ōsculum, kiss
* summus, highest, last
mandātum, instruction
fallō, -ere, fefellī, falsus, deceive, trick
* respiciō, -ere, -spexī, -spectus, regard, con-
    sider, look back at
pignus, -noris, *n.* pledge, token

61-65

* dēnique, finally
Scythia, country north of the Black Sea
* aeternus, eternal; in aeternum, forever
vīvus, alive, living
* fīdus, faithful, loyal
* dulcis, -e, sweet, dear
* membrum, member
dīligō, -ere, -lēxī, -lēctus, love, cherish
* frāternus, brotherly
sodālis, -is, *m.* companion, friend

66-70

Thēsēus, *adj.* of Theseus, Thesean
* dum, *w. indic.*, while
amplector, -ī, amplexus sum, embrace
fortasse, perhaps
* amplius, more, further
lucrum, profit, gain
* sermō, -ōnis, *m.* conversation, talk
* imperfectus, unfinished
complector, -ī, -plexus sum, embrace

71-75

nitidus, bright, shining
* Lūcifer, -erī, *m.* morning star, planet
    Venus

dīvidō, -ere, -vīsī, -vīsus, divide, part,
    separate
* haud, not at all, not
* abrumpō, -ere, -rūpī, -ruptus, break off
tunc, then
* contrārius, opposite

76-80

ultor, -ōris, *m.* avenger
prōditiō, -ōnis, *f.* treachery
* vērō, truly, indeed
* exorior, -īrī, -ortus sum, rise up
feriō, -īre, strike
* coniūnx, -iugis, *m. and f.* husband, wife
* umerus, shoulder
inhaereō, -ēre, -haesī, -haesum, cling to
* misceō, -ēre, miscuī, mixtus, mix, mingle,
    join

81-85

āvellō, -ere, āvellī, āvulsus, tear away
* hinc, from here
exsul, -sulis, *m. and f.* exile
tellūs, -ūris, *f.* earth, country
profugus, outcast, exiled
sarcina, burden, load
* ratis, -is, *f.* raft, boat, ship

86-90

* pietās, -ātis, *f.* piety, devotion
* sīcut, just as
* ūtilitās, -ātis, *f.* expediency, advantage
sīve, or, or else
squālidus, unkempt, dirty
immissus, let loose, allowed to fall
hirtus, rough, unshaven
* coma, hair

mihi: dat. of reference; *my.* tardus: *lame;* Ovid means that his foot stumbled on the threshold of its own accord, thus forcing him to turn back, since to stumble at the beginning of a journey was such a bad omen that one would have to make a new start. **57 Valē:** used as a noun in abl. abs. construction; *after saying "Farewell."* **61 Quid:** Why. **62 Utraque mora =** Utraque causa morae: sc. **est. 63 Uxor:** his wife was to remain in Rome and intercede, Ovid hoped, with the emperor for his recall. vīvō, vīva: i.e., while they both were still alive. **65 quōsque sodālēs =** et sodālēs quōs. **66 Thēsēā fidē:** *with the loyalty of a Theseus,* of the friends who stood by him in adversity; the friendship between Theseus and Pirithous was proverbial.

68 In lucrō: *On the profit side of the ledger =* Counted as gain. **69 Nec mora:** sc. **est; =** Sine morā. **70 animō:** dat. w. proxima. proxima quaeque: *all that was most dear.* **75 prīmus:** the first to suffer this punishment was Mettius Fufetius, an Alban general; he was found guilty of treachery, and Tullus Hostilius, the Roman king, gave orders that he was to be made fast to two four-horse chariots, which were then driven in opposite directions (v. Livy, I. 28).

77 Tum vērō: repeated in line 79 to indicate that this is the final parting. **78 feriunt . . . manūs:** beating the breast was a part of Roman mourning customs. **79 abeuntis:** sc. meī. **84 sarcina:** in apposition w. the subject of Accēdam. ratī: dat. w. compound verb Accēdam. **86 Pietās . . . erit:** i.e., wifely devotion has the same effect as the imperial command. **88 dedit manūs:** *submitted;* metaphor of a captive who holds out his hands to be manacled. victās ūtilitāte: *persuaded by the useful course;* it would be more helpful if she remained in Rome

indulgēns animō pēs mihi tardus erat.
Saepe, "Valē" dictō, rūrsus sum multa locūtus,
    et quasi discēdēns ōscula summa dedī.
Saepe eadem mandāta dedī mēque ipse fefellī,
    respiciēns oculīs pignora cāra meīs.   60
Dēnique, "Quid properō? Scythia est quō mittimur," inquam;
    "Rōma relinquenda est. Utraque iūsta mora est.
Uxor in aeternum vīvō mihi vīva negātur,
    et domus et fīdae dulcia membra domūs,
quōsque ego dīlēxī frāternō mōre sodālēs,   65
    Ō mihi Thēsēā pectora iūncta fidē!
Dum licet, amplectar. Numquam fortasse licēbit
    amplius. In lucrō est quae datur hōra mihi."
Nec mora, sermōnis verba imperfecta relinquō,
    complectēns animō proxima quaeque meō.   70

The approach of dawn cut short my farewells but the anguish remained.

Dum loquor et flēmus, caelō nitidissimus altō,
    stella gravis nōbīs, Lūcifer ortus erat.
Dīvidor haud aliter quam sī mea membra relinquam,
    et pars abrumpī corpore vīsa meō est.
Sīc doluit prīmus tunc cum in contrāria versōs   75
    ultōrēs habuit prōditiōnis equōs.

It was only with difficulty that I dissuaded my wife, who insisted that she wanted to go into exile with me.

Tum vērō exoritur clāmor gemitusque meōrum
    et feriunt maestae pectora nūda manūs.
Tum vērō coniūnx umerīs abeuntis inhaerēns
    miscuit haec lacrimīs trīstia verba suīs: 80
"Nōn potes āvellī. Simul hinc, simul ībimus," inquit.
    "Tē sequar et coniūnx exsulis exsul erō.
Et mihi facta via est, et mē capit ultima tellūs.
    Accēdam profugae sarcina parva ratī.
Tē iubet ā patriā discēdere Caesaris īra,   85
    mē pietās. Pietās haec mihi Caesar erit."
Tālia temptābat, sīcut temptāverat ante,
    vixque dedit victās ūtilitāte manūs.

Friends later described to me the agony of her despair. I pray for her safety and her help.

Ēgredior—sīve illud erat sine fūnere ferrī—
    squālidus, immissīs hirta per ōra comīs.   90

and worked for his recall. The adj. **victās** has been transferred from the subject of **dedit** to **manūs**.

89 ferrī = efferrī: a Latin idiom for *to go to the grave* (Roman law required that corpses be carried outside the city for burial). **90 ōra:** pl. for sing. **91-92 Illa narrātur prōcubuisse:**

141

āmēns, -entis, wild, distracted, frantic
tenebrae, -ārum, *f. pl.* darkness
* oborior, -īrī, -ortus sum, rise up
sēmianimis, -e, half-dead
prōcumbō, -ere, -cubuī, -cubitum, fall
  prostrate
* resurgō, -ere, -surrēxī, -surrēctum, rise up
  again
foedō (1), befoul, dirty
* pulvis, -veris, *m.* dust
* crīnis, -is, *m.* hair
gelidus, cold, chilling
* levō (1), raise, lift
* humus, -ī, *f.* ground

modo . . . modo, now . . . now
dēserō, -ere, -seruī, -sertus, desert, abandon
complōrō (1), lament, bewail

gemō, -ere, gemuī, gemitus, groan, mourn
  for
* minus, less
* struō, -ere, strūxī, strūctus, build, erect
rogus, funeral pyre
respectus, -ūs, *m.* regard, respect
* pereō, -īre, -iī, -itum, die, perish
* absēns, -entis, absent, distant
* quoniam, since
sublevō (1), lighten, relieve, support

she is reported to have fallen = I am told that she fell. 95-100 complōrāsse, vocāsse, gemuisse, voluisse, and periisse: likewise depend on narrātur. 91 tenebrīs obortīs: abl. abs. 92 sēmianimis: the first i is here a consonant. 93 pulvere: she had fallen near the hearth (mediā domō). 94 humō: *from the ground.* 95 sē: sc. dēsertam esse, indir. statement w. complōrāsse (= complōrāvisse); *that she lamented now that she herself, now that the Penates (= her home) had been deserted.* 97 nātaeque virīque: both genitives depend on corpus (= corpora), which is the object of habēre. 98 vīdisset: subjv. in contrary-to-fact

Illa dolōre āmēns tenebrīs nārrātur obortīs
  sēmianimis mediā prōcubuisse domō,
utque resurrēxit, foedātīs pulvere turpī
  crīnibus, et gelidā membra levāvit humō,
sē modo, dēsertōs modo complōrāsse Penātēs,   95
  nōmen et ēreptī saepe vocāsse virī
nec gemuisse minus quam sī nātaeque virīque
  vīdisset strūctōs corpus habēre rogōs,
et voluisse morī, moriendō pōnere sēnsūs,
  respectūque tamen nōn periisse meī.   100
Vīvat, et absentem—quoniam sīc fāta tulērunt—
  vīvat, et auxiliō sublevet usque suō.

TRISTIA I. 3

---

condition. **99 moriendō:** abl. of means. **pōnere** (= **dēpōnere**) **sēnsūs:** *lay aside all aware-ness.* **100 respectū:** abl. of cause. **meī:** objective gen. w. **respectū;** *out of concern for me.*

101-102 Vīvat, sublevet: optative subjvs. **101 absentem:** sc. **mē,** object of **sublevet;** Ovid breaks off in the middle of the sentence to insert the parenthesis and then starts the sentence over again in the next line. **101 quoniam . . . tulērunt:** *since the fates have so willed.*

143

List of Abbreviations

abl. = ablative
abs. = absolute
acc. = accusative
adj. = adjective
adv. = adverb
cf. = confer (Lat.), compare
comp. = comparative
conj. = conjunction
dat. = dative
def. = defective verb
dep. = deponent
dim. = diminutive
encl. = enclitic
exclam. = exclamatory
f. = feminine
fut. = future
gen. = genitive
i.e. = id est, (Lat.) this is
imper. = imperative
impers. = impersonal
indecl. = indeclinable
indef. = indefinite
indic. = indicative
indir. = indirect
interj. = interjection

interr. = interrogative
intrans. = intransitive
l. = line
lit. = literally
loc. = locative
m. = masculine
n. = neut.
nom. = nominative
pass. = passive
perf. = perfect
pers. = personal
pl. = plural
prep. = preposition
pron. = pronoun
rel. = relative
sc. = scilicet (Lat.), supply,
    understand
semidep. = semideponent
sing. = singular
subjv. = subjunctive
superl. = superlative
trans. = transitive
voc. = vocative
w. = with

In the running vocabulary, gender and genitive singular are not given for regular nouns of the first and second declensions.

For third declension adjectives of one termination, the ending for the genitive singular is given.

Where the perfect tense ending is -īvī or -iī, the latter form is usually given. For non-deponent verbs, -us represents the ending of the perfect passive participle; but if the verb is normally intransitive, the supine ending (-um) is given or, occasionally, the future active participle ending (-ūrus).

GENERAL
VOCABULARY

A

ā, ab, abs *prep. w. abl.* by, from, away from

abeō, -īre, -iī, -itum go away, depart

absum, -esse, āfuī, āfutūrus be away, be missing, be lacking

ac = atque *conj.* and

accēdō, -ere, -cessī, -cessum come toward, approach, be added to

accidō, -ere, -cidī, fall to, happen, occur

accipiō, -ere, -cēpī, -ceptus receive, take on, hear

ācer, ācris, ācre sharp, keen, eager, fierce

aciēs, -ēī *f.* point, edge, battle line

acus, -ūs *f.* needle, pin

ad *prep. w. acc.* to, toward, for, at, about

addō, -ere, -didī, -ditus add, put to

addūcō, -ere, -dūxī, -ductus lead toward, draw, persuade, tighten

adeō, -īre, -iī, -itus go toward, approach

adferō (aff-), -ferre adtulī (att-), adlātus (all-) bring to, offer, report

adhūc *adv.* so far, as yet, hitherto

adiciō, -ere, -iēcī, -iectus throw to, add

adiuvō, -āre, -iūvī, -iūtus help

admoveō, -ēre, -mōvī, -mōtus move toward, apply

adōrō (1), pray to, worship

adstō, see astō

adsum, -esse, -fuī, -futūrus be present, be near, assist

adulēscēns, -entis *m.* youth

adventus, -ūs *m.* approach, arrival

aeger, -gra, -grum sick, feeble, weary

aequō (1), make equal, level

aequor, -oris *n.* level surface, sea, ocean

aequoreus, -a, -um of the sea, watery

aequus, -a, -um even, equal, fair, just; *adv.* aequē equally, in like manner

āēr, āeris *m.* air, weather

aestās, -ātis *f.* summer

aestus, -ūs *m.* heat, tide

aetās, -ātis *f.* age, life, generation

aethēr, -eris *m.* upper air, air, heaven

aetherius, -a, -um of the upper air, heavenly

ager, agrī *m.* field, farm, land

aggredior (adg-), -ī, -gressus sum move against, attack

agitō (1), drive, move, excite, agitate

agmen, agminis *n.* band, crowd, column

agna, -ae *f.* ewe lamb

agō, -ere, ēgī, āctus do, lead, drive, keep, conduct, spend; partēs agō play the role

agricola, -ae *m.* farmer

aiō *def. verb* say, speak

āla, -ae *f.* wing, armpit

albus, -a, -um white

aliquis, -qua, -quid (*adj.* -quod) someone, something, any, some

aliter *adv.* otherwise, differently; aliter quam otherwise than

alius, -a, -ud other, another, different

almus, -a, -um fostering, kind, gracious

alter, -era, -erum (*gen.* -ius) the other of two; alter . . . alter the one . . . the other, one . . . another

alternus, -a, -um alternate, by turns; alternīs *abl. pl. as adv.* alternately, by turns

altus, -a, -um high, deep; *as noun* altum, -ī *n.* the sea, the sky

amātor, -ōris *m.* lover

ambulō (1), walk, stroll

amīcitia, -ae *f.* friendship

amīcus, -a, -um friendly; *as noun* amīcus, -ī *m.* friend; amīca, -ae *f.* woman friend

āmittō, -ere, āmīsī, āmissus send away, let go, lose

amnis, -is *m.* river

amō (1), love

amor, -ōris *m.* love; Amor Cupid, god of love

amplus, -a, -um large, ample, spacious; amplius *adv. comp.* further, longer

an *or;* utrum (*or* -ne) . . . an whether . . . or; *sometimes* utrum *or* -ne *is omitted*

ancora, -ae *f.* anchor

anima, -ae *f.* breath, spirit, life

animal, -ālis *n.* living creature, animal

animus, -ī *m.* spirit, heart, mind, feeling

annus, -ī *m.* year

ante *adv. and prep. w. acc.* before, in front of, earlier

ante . . . quam *conj.* before

antīquus, -a, -um old, ancient, former

antrum, -ī *n.* cave

anus, -ūs *f.* old woman

aperiō, -īre, aperuī, apertus open, reveal

apertus, -a, -um open, exposed; apertē *adv.* openly

appellō (1), call, name

aptus, -a, -um fit, suitable, proper, appropriate; aptē *adv.* suitably

apud *prep. w. acc.* at, with, near, in, among

aqua, -ae *f.* water

Aquilō, -ōnis *m.* the North Wind

arātrum, -ī *n.* plow

arbor, -oris *f.* tree

arcus, -ūs *m.* bow, arch

ārdor, -ōris *m.* ardor, vehemence, eagerness

argentum, -ī *n.* silver

āridus, -a, -um dry

arma, -ōrum *n. pl.* weapons, tools, equipment

armō (1), arm, equip

ars, artis *f.* art, skill, science

arvum, -ī *n.* field, land

ascendō, -ere, ascendī, ascēnsus mount, climb

asper, -era, -erum rough, harsh, bristly

aspiciō, -ere, aspexī, aspectus look at, regard, see

assiduus, -a, -um constant, busy, ceaseless

astō (adstō), -āre, astitī stand near, stand up

at *conj.* but
atque ($=$ ac) and also, and
attonitus, -a, -um thunderstruck, frightened, bewildered
auctor, -ōris *m.* author, adviser, giver
audācia, -ae *f.* boldness, daring
audāx, -ācis daring, bold
audeō, -ēre, ausus sum *semi-dep.* be bold, dare, risk
audiō, -īre, -iī, -ītus hear, listen to
auferō, -ferre, abstulī, ablātus carry away
augeō, -ēre, auxī, auctus increase, grow
augustus, -a, -um august, revered
aura, -ae *f.* breeze, wind, air
aureus, -a, -um of gold, golden
auris, -is *f.* ear
aurum, -ī *n.* gold
aut *conj.* or; aut . . . aut either . . . or
autem *conj.* but, however, now
auxilium, -ī *n.* help, aid
avis, -is *f.* bird
avus, -ī *m.* grandfather

B

barba, -ae *f.* beard
barbarus, -a, -um foreign, barbarian
bellum, -ī *n.* war
bene *adv.* well; *comp.* melius; *superl.* optimē
bis *adv.* twice
bonus, -a, -um good; *comp.* melior; *superl.* optimus; *as noun* bonum, -ī *n.* blessing, advantage
bōs, bovis *m. and f.* ox, bull, cow; *gen. pl.* boum; *dat. and abl. pl.* būbus *or* bōbus
bracchium, -ī *n.* arm
brevis, -e short, brief

C

cacūmen, -minis *n.* peak, summit, top
cadō, -ere, cecidī, cāsum fall, perish, happen
caedēs, -is *f.* slaughter, bloodshed
caedō, -ere, cecīdī, caesus cut, strike, kill
caelestis, -e heavenly, divine; *as noun* caelestis, -is *m.* deity, god; caelestia, -ium *n. pl.* statues of the gods
caelō (1), engrave, emboss
caelum, -ī *n.* sky, heaven, climate
caeruleus, -a, -um dark blue, dark
campus, -ī *m.* plain, field, expanse
candor, -ōris *m.* whiteness, brightness, beauty
canis, -is *m. and f.* dog
canō, -ere, cecinī, cantus sing, chant, prophesy
canōrus, -a, -um melodious, musical
cantō (1), sing, chant, recite
capillus, -ī *m.* hair
capiō, -ere, cēpī, captus take, seize, grasp, deceive, feel
captīvus, -a, -um captured, captive

caput, capitis *n.* head, source, life
careō, -ēre, -uī, -itum *w. abl.* be without, lack, be free from
carīna, -ae *f.* keel
carmen, -minis *n.* song, poem, charm, prophecy
carpō, -ere, carpsī, carptus pick, pluck
cārus, -a, -um dear, loved, expensive
casa, -ae *f.* hut, cottage
castra, -ōrum *n. pl.* camp
castus, -a, -um pure, virtuous, chaste
cāsus, -ūs *m.* fall, chance, accident, misfortune
causa, -ae *f.* cause, reason, motive; causā *w. gen.* because of, for the sake of
cavus, -a, -um hollow
cēdō, -ere, cessī, cessum move, withdraw, give way to, result, yield
celer, -eris, -ere swift, speedy
centum *indecl.* one hundred
cēra, -ae *f.* wax, writing tablet
certāmen, -minis *n.* contest, struggle
certē *adv.* of course, at least
certus, -a, -um sure, certain, definite
cervīx, īcis *f.* neck
cēterus, -a, -um the other, the rest of
cibus, -ī *m.* food
cingō, -ere, cīnxī, cīnctus gird, surround
circum *adv. and prep. w. acc.* around, about
circumdō, -dare, -dedī, -datus surround, enclose
circus, -ī *m.* circle; Circus Maximus, race course for chariots
cīvis, -is *m. and f.* citizen
clāmō (1), shout, cry out
clāmor, -ōris *m.* shout, outcry
clārus, -a, -um clear, loud, bright, famous
classis, -is *f.* fleet, ships
claudō, -ere, clausī, clausus shut, close
clīvus, -ī *m.* slope, hill
coepī, -isse, coeptus have begun, began
coeptum, -ī *n.* beginning, task
coerceō, -ēre, -uī, -itus check, restrain
cognōscō, -ere, -nōvī, -nitus get to know, learn; *perf.* cognōvī know, be aware of
cōgō, -ere, coēgī, coāctus bring together, compel
cohors, cohortis *f.* band, company
colligō, -ere, -lēgī, -lēctus gather, collect
collis, -is *m.* hill
colloquium, -ī *n.* talk, conversation
collum, -ī *n.* neck
colō, -ere, coluī, cultus cultivate, cherish, respect, worship, groom, till
color, -ōris *m.* color
coma, -ae *f.* hair, foliage
comes, comitis *m. and f.* companion, attendant
committō, -ere, -mīsī, -missus commit, bring about, entrust, allow
commodus, -a, -um proper, fit, suitable; commodum, -ī *n.* convenience, advantage

147

commūnis, -e common, public, joint

comparō (1), bring together, provide, compare

compleō, -ēre, -plēvī, -plētus fill up, complete

concipiō, -ere, -cēpī, -ceptus take up, gather, conceive

conclāmō (1), cry out, exclaim

condiciō, -ōnis f. condition, agreement, lot

condō, -ere, -didī, -ditus build, found, store up, conceal

cōnferō, -ferre, -tulī, -lātus bring together, compare, match, unite

cōnficiō, -ere, -fēcī, -fectus complete, finish, use up

cōnfīdō, -ere, -fīsus sum semi-dep. w. dat. or abl. trust in, rely on, be confident

congredior, -ī, -gressus sum come together, meet

coniciō, -ere, -iēcī, -iectus throw together, hurl

coniungō, -ere, -iūnxī, -iūnctus join, unite

coniūnx, -iugis m. and f. marriage partner, husband, wife

cōnor dep. (1), try, attempt

cōnscendō, -ere, -scendī, -scēnsus climb up, mount, embark

cōnscrībō, -ere, -scrīpsī, scrīptus write, draw up, compose

cōnsequor, -ī, -secūtus sum follow, overtake, attain

cōnsīdō, -ere, -sēdī, -sessum sit down, settle, sink

cōnsilium, -ī n. plan, council, advice

cōnsistō, -ere, -stitī, -stitum stand, stop, stay, consist, depend on

cōnspiciō, -ere, -spexī, -spectus catch sight of, view

cōnstituō, -ere, -stituī, -stitūtus decide, determine, arrange

cōnsuēscō, -ere, -suēvī, -suētus become accustomed; perf. cōnsuēvī be accustomed

cōnsuētus, -a, -um customary, usual

cōnsul, cōnsulis m. consul

cōnsulō, -ere, -suluī, -sultus consult, advise; w. dat. look after, take thought for

contemnō, -ere, -tempsī, -temptus despise, disdain

contendō, -ere, -tendī, -tentus strive, assert, contend

contentus, -a, -um contained, content, satisfied

contineō, -ēre, -tinuī, -tentus hold together, contain, restrain, check

contingō, -ere, -tigī, -tāctus touch, come to, happen

contrā adv. and prep. w. acc. opposite, in reply, on the other hand, against, facing

contrahō, -ere, -trāxī, -trāctus draw together, contract

cōnūbium, -ī n. marriage, wedlock

conveniō, -īre, -vēnī, -ventus come together, meet; convenit impers. is agreed

convocō (1), call together, summon

cōpia, -ae f. supply, abundance, opportunity; in pl. means, wealth, forces

cor, cordis n. heart

cornū, -ūs n. horn, end, tip, wing (of an army)

corpus, -poris n. body

crās adv. tomorrow

crātēr, -ēris (Gk. acc. -ēra) m. mixing bowl, wine bowl

crēdibilis, -e believable, credible

crēdō, -ere, -didī, -ditus believe, trust

creō (1), produce, create

crēscō, -ere, crēvī, crētum grow

crīmen, crīminis n. accusation, charge, crime

crīnis, -is m. hair

culmen, culminis n. roof, top, summit

cultus, -a, -um cultivated, groomed, stylish

cultus, -ūs m. culture, civilization, good grooming, refinement, personal care

cum prep. w. abl. with

cum conj. w. indic. at the time when, whenever; w. subjv. when, since, although

cūnctus, -a, -um all, entire, the whole

cupidus, -a, -um desirous, eager, covetous

cupiō, -ere, -iī, -ītus wish, desire

cūr interr. why

cūra, -ae f. care, concern, worry, love

cūrō (1), care for, see to, cause (to be done)

currō, -ere, cucurrī, cursum run

currus, -ūs m. chariot, car, wagon

cursus, -ūs m. running, course, race, speed

curvus, -a, -um bent, curved, crooked

custōs, custōdis m. and f. guard, protector

D

damnum, -ī n. loss, harm, damage

daps, dapis f. feast, banquet

dē prep. w. abl. down from, from, out of, by, because of, about

dea, -ae f. goddess

dēbeō, -ēre, -uī, -itus owe, ought

decem indecl. ten

decet, -ēre, -uit impers. suits, is becoming to

dēcidō, -ere, -cidī fall down

decor, -ōris m. grace, beauty

dēdūcō, -ere, -dūxī, -ductus lead down, draw out, withdraw, conduct, uncover

dēfendō, -ere, -fendī, -fēnsus ward off, protect, defend

dēferō, -ferre, -tulī, -lātus carry down, remove, report, present

dēfessus, -a, -um tired, weary, exhausted

deinde adv. thence, then, next

dēlectō (1), delight

dēligō, -ere, -lēgī, -lēctus pick out, choose
dēmittō, -ere, -mīsī, -missus send down, let
  down, lower
dēnique adv. finally, in short
dēns, dentis m. tooth
dēnsus, -a, -um dense, thick, frequent
dēprēndō, -ere, -prēndī, -prēnsus seize, detect, surprise
dēscendō, -ere, -scendī, -scēnsum climb
  down, go down, descend
dēsistō, -ere, -stitī, -stitum leave off, cease,
  desist
dēsum, deesse, dēfuī, dēfutūrus w. dat. fail,
  lack, be missing
dētineō, -ēre, -tinuī, -tentus hold back, keep
  busy
deus, -ī m. god; nom. pl. deī, diī, dī
dexter, -tra, -trum right, skillful; dextra
  (manus implied) -ae f. right hand
dīcō, -ere, dīxī, dictus say, speak, tell, call,
  mean
dictum, -ī n. word, remark
diēs, -ēī m. and f. day, time
difficilis, -e hard, difficult
diffugiō, -ere, -fūgī scatter in flight, dis-
  perse
digitus, -ī m. finger, toe
dignus, -a, -um w. abl. worthy, deserving
dīligō, -ere, -lēxī, -lēctus esteem, love
dīmittō, -ere, -mīsī, -missus let go away,
  send out, dismiss, turn
discēdō, -ere, -cessī, -cessum depart, withdraw
discō, -ere, didicī learn, learn how
dispōnō, -ere, -posuī, -positus set out, arrange
dissimilis, -e unlike, different
diū adv. for a long time
diurnus, -a, -um daily, by day
dīva, -ae f. goddess
dīversus, -a, -um different, opposite, remote
dō, dare, dedī, datus give, allow, put, render
doceō, -ēre, docuī, doctus teach, inform,
  explain
doleō, -ēre, doluī, dolitus pain, grieve, be
  sorry
dolor, -ōris m. pain, grief
domina, -ae f. lady, mistress
dominus, -ī m. master, lord, owner
domus, -ūs f. house, home
dōnum, -ī n. gift
dōs, dōtis f. dowry, gift
dubitō (1), doubt, be uncertain, hesitate
dūcō, -ere, dūxī, ductus lead, draw, consider, hold
dulcis, -e sweet, dear, kind
dum conj. w. indic. while, as long as; w.
  subjv. until, provided that, if only
duo, -ae, -o two
dūrus, -a, -um hard, rough, stern, harsh
dux, ducis m. and f. leader, guide, chieftain

E

ē see ex
ecce interj. lo! behold! see!
ēdūcō, -ere, ēdūxī, ēductus lead out, extend
efficiō, -ere, -fēcī, -fectus bring about, effect,
  finish
effundō, -ere, -fūdī, -fūsus pour out
ego gen. meī pers. pron. I
ēgredior, -ī, ēgressus sum go out, depart
ēligō, -ere, ēlēgī, ēlēctus pick out, choose
enim postpositive conj. for, in fact
eō adv. to that place, there, on that account
eō, īre, iī (īvī), itum go
epistula, -ae f. letter
eques, equitis m. horseman, rider, knight
equus, -ī m. horse
ergō adv. therefore
ēripiō, -ere, ēripuī, ēreptus snatch away,
  carry off, rescue
errō (1), wander, stray, err
error, -ōris m. error, wandering, mistake
ērudiō, -īre, -iī, -ītus train, instruct
et conj. and, also, even; et . . . et both . . .
  and
etiam adv. also, even, yet, still
etsī conj. although, even if
ex (= ē) prep. w. abl. out of, from, since,
  according to
excēdō, -ere, -cessī, -cessum go out, leave,
  depart, exceed
excidō, -ere, -cidī fall out, faint
exclāmō (1), cry out
excūsō (1), excuse, apologize for
excutiō, -ere, -cussī, -cussus shake off, rouse
exemplum, -ī n. example, pattern, precedent
exeō, -īre, -iī, -itum go out, depart, result
exerceō, -ēre, -uī, -itus train, keep busy,
  exercise, worry
exiguus, -a, -um small, short, limited, scanty
exitus, -ūs m. way out, event, end, result,
  death
exōrō (1), prevail upon, entreat
expellō, -ere, -pulī, -pulsus drive out, banish
explōrō (1), search, examine, ascertain
expōnō, -ere, -posuī, -positus place out, expose
exprimō, -ere, -pressī, -pressus force out,
  squeeze out
exspectō (1), wait for, expect
extrēmus, -a, -um furthest, last, end of

F

fābula, -ae f. story
faciēs, -ēī f. face, appearance
facilis, -e easy, ready; adv. facile easily
faciō, -ere, fēcī, factus make, do, bring
  about
factum, -ī n. action, deed
facultās, -ātis f. ability, opportunity, means
fallō, -ere, fefellī, falsus deceive, cheat, fail

149

falsus, -a, -um false, deceitful; falsum, -ī n. deceit, falsehood; falsō adv. falsely

fāma, -ae f. talk, rumor, report, reputation, fame

fātum, -ī n. fate, destiny

faveō, -ēre, fāvī, fautum w. dat. favor, be kind to, approve

fēlīx, -īcis happy, fortunate

fēmina, -ae f. woman

fēmineus, -a, -um of a woman, womanly

fera, -ae f. wild beast

ferē adv. almost, about, usually

ferō, ferre, tulī, lātus bear, carry, endure, lead, tend, say, report

ferrum, -ī n. iron, sword

fidēlis, -e loyal, faithful

fidēs, -eī f. trust, faith, belief, protection

fīgō, -ere, fīxī, fīxus fix, fasten, pierce, imbed

figūra, -ae f. shape, form, appearance

fīlia, -ae f. daughter

fīlius, -ī m. son

fīniō, -īre, -īī, -ītus limit, end, finish

fīnis, -is m. end, limit, border

fīnitimus, -a, -um neighboring, bordering; as noun fīnitimus, -ī m. neighbor

fīō, fierī, factus sum become, be made, be done, happen

flamma, -ae f. flame, fire

flectō, -ere, flexī, flexus turn, bend, direct

fleō, -ēre, flēvī, flētus cry, weep (for)

flōs, flōris m. flower

flūctus, -ūs m. wave, billow

flūmen, flūminis n. river, stream

fluō, -ere, flūxī, flūxum flow

focus, -ī m. hearth, fireside

folium, -ī n. leaf

fōns, fontis m. fountain, spring

fōrma, -ae f. form, shape, beauty, appearance

fōrmōsus, -a, -um well-shaped, pretty, beautiful, handsome

fors, fortis f. chance; forte, by chance

fortis, -e brave, strong, energetic; adv. fortiter bravely, vigorously

fortūna, -ae f. fortune, chance, fate

forum, -ī n. forum, market-place

fossa, -ae f. ditch, trench

fragilis, -e fragile, frail

frangō, -ere, frēgī, frāctus break, smash, weaken

frāter, frātris m. brother

frāternus, -a, -um brotherly, of a brother

frequēns, -entis frequent, crowded, in great numbers; as adv. (= frequenter) often

frōns, frondis f. leaf, foliage

frōns, frontis f. brow, forehead, front

frūmentum, -ī n. grain

frūstrā adv. in vain

fuga, -ae f. flight, escape, exile

fugiō, -ere, fūgī, fugitūrus flee, flee from, escape, shun, avoid, go into exile

fugō (1), cause to flee, rout, repel

fulmen, fulminis n. thunderbolt

fulvus, -a, -um yellow, tawny

fūnus, -neris n. funeral, death

furca, -ae f. fork, prop

furō, -ere rave, rage

G

Gallicus, -a, -um of Gaul, Gallic

gaudeō, -ēre, gāvīsus sum semi-dep. rejoice, be glad

gaudium, -ī n. joy, delight

gemitus, -ūs m. sigh, groan, moan

gena, -ae f. cheek

gener, -erī m. son-in-law

generōsus, -a, -um noble, generous

genitor, -ōris m. begetter, father

gēns, gentis f. race, tribe, clan, people

genus, generis n. birth, descent, family, kind

Germānus, -a, -um German

gerō, -ere, gessī, gestus bear, wear, carry, conduct, do

gestus, -ūs m. gesture, act, manner

gladius, -ī m. sword

glaeba, -ae f. clod of earth, lump

glōria, -ae f. fame, renown, pride

gracilis, -e thin, slight, meager

gradus, -ūs m. step, pace, rank, tread

grātia, -ae f. grace, beauty, favor, kindness, gratitude, influence

grātus, -a, -um dear, pleasing, grateful, welcome

gravis, -e heavy, burdened, severe, oppressive, grave, offensive

gremium, -ī n. bosom, lap

guttur, -uris n. throat

H

habeō, -ēre, -uī, -itus have, hold, consider, regard

habitō (1), inhabit, dwell in, live

haereō, -ēre, haesī, haesus stick, cling, stay close

harēna, -ae f. sand, seashore, arena, desert

hasta, -ae f. spear

haud adv. not at all, not

herba, -ae f. herb, grass

heri (here) adv. yesterday

heu, interj. oh! alas!

hībernus, -a, -um of winter, wintry, stormy; hīberna, -ōrum n. pl. winter camp

hīc adv. here

hic, haec, hoc pron. and adj. he, she, it, this, the latter, the one

hiems, hiemis f. winter, cold, storm

hinc adv. from here, hence, from this

hodiē adv. today

homō, hominis m. and f. mortal, man, human being

hōra, -ae f. hour, time

hortor dep. (1), urge, encourage

hortus, -ī *m.* garden
hospes, -pitis *m.* stranger, guest, host
hostis, -is *m.* (*rarely f.*) enemy, foe
hūc *adv.* hither, here, this way, so far
hūmānus, -a, -um human, kind, courteous
humus, -ī *f.* ground, soil; humī *or* humō on the ground

I

iaceō, -ēre, -uī lie, be neglected, be uncared for
iaciō, -ere, iēcī, iactus throw, hurl, lay
iactō (1), keep throwing, hurl, toss
iaculum, -ī *n.* javelin, spear
iam *adv.* now, already, presently
iānua, -ae, *f.* door, entrance
ibi *adv.* there, in that place, thereupon
ictus, -ūs, *m.* stroke, blow
īdem, eadem, idem (*gen.* eiusdem) same
idōneus, -a, -um fit, suitable, proper, appropriate
iēiūnium, -ī *n.* fasting, fast
ignis, -is, *m.* fire, flame, brightness, fire of love, passion
ignōtus, -a, -um unknown, strange
ille, illa, illud (*gen.* illīus) *pron. and adj.* he, she, it, that, the former
illīc *adv.* there, in that place
imitor *dep.* (1), imitate, pretend
immēnsus, -a, -um vast, measureless
immortālis, -e immortal
impediō, -īre, -īī, -ītus hamper, hinder, prevent
impellō, -ere, -pulī, -pulsus drive, urge, push, encourage
imperium, -ī *n.* command, authority, empire
imperō (1), order, command, rule, control
impetus, -ūs *m.* attack, rush, charge, impetus, impulse
impleō, -ēre, -plēvī, -plētus fill
impōnō, -ere, -posuī, -positus place on, impose
īmus, -a, -um *superl. of* īnferus lowest, bottom of
in *prep. w. acc.* into, to, toward, against, for; *prep. w. abl.* in, on, among, in the case of
inānis, -e empty, unavailing
incendō, -ere, -cendī, -cēnsus set on fire, burn, inflame
incertus, -a, -um uncertain, undecided
incipiō, -ere, -cēpī, -ceptus begin
incitō (1), spur, urge on, encourage
incolō, -ere, -coluī inhabit, live in
inde *adv.* from there, then, next
indūcō, -ere, -dūxī, -ductus lead in, spread
ineō, -īre, -īī, -itus go into, enter, begin
iners, -ertis inactive, lazy
īnfēlīx, -īcis unhappy, unfortunate
īnferior, -ius *comp. of* īnferus lower, too low, rather low

īnferō, -ferre, -tulī, -lātus (illātus) bring upon, inflict, cause, introduce
īnfimus, -a, -um lowest, bottom of
ingenium, -ī, *n.* talent, ability, ingenuity, mind
ingēns, -entis huge, mighty
ingenuus, -a, -um freeborn, noble, frank
inimīcus, -a, -um unfriendly, hostile; *as noun* inimīcus, -ī *m.* enemy
inīquus, -a, -um uneven, unfair, unjust, cruel
initium, -ī *n.* beginning
iniūria, -ae *f.* injustice, wrong, injury
inopia, -ae *f.* want, lack, scarcity
inops, -opis weak, poor, needy, destitute
inquam *def. verb* I say
īnscrībō, -ere, -scrīpsī, -scrīptus write on, inscribe
īnsequor, -ī, -secūtus sum pursue
īnsidiae, -ārum *f. pl.* ambush, trap, plot, treachery
īnstituō, -ere, -uī, -ūtus build, begin, train, organize
īnstruō, -ere, -strūxī, -strūctus draw up, arrange, inform, equip
īnsula, -ae *f.* island
īnsum, inesse, īnfuī be in
integer, -gra, -grum whole, uninjured, intact, fresh, upright
intellegō, -ere, -lēxī, -lēctus perceive, discern, understand
inter *prep. w. acc.* between, among, in, during
intereā *adv.* meanwhile
interior, -ius inner; *adv.* interius inwardly
intermittō, -ere, -mīsī, -missus break off, intervene, cease, interrupt
intrō (1), enter
inūtilis, -e useless
inveniō, -īre, -vēnī, -ventus come upon, find
ipse, ipsa, ipsum *intensive pron.* -self, myself, yourself, etc. *often rendered by* even, very
īra, -ae *f.* anger, rage, fury
is, ea, id (*gen.* eius) *pron. and adj.* he, she, it, this, that
iste, ista, istud (*gen.* -īus) he, she, it, that of yours, that, your
ita *adv.* so, thus, to such an extent
item *adv.* likewise
iter, itineris *n.* way, journey, route, course
iterum *adv.* again, a second time
iubeō, -ēre, iussī, iussus order
iūdex, iūdicis *m. and f.* judge
iūdicium, -ī *n.* judgment, decision, opinion
iūdicō (1), judge, decide
iungō, -ere, iūnxī, iūnctus join, unite, yoke
Iuppiter, Iovis *m.* Jupiter
iūs, iūris *n.* justice, right, law, authority
iussum, -ī *n.* order
iūstus, -a, -um just, fair, right, proper

iuvenis, -is young, youthful; *as noun,* iuvenis, -is *m.* and *f.* youth, young man, young woman

iuvō, -āre, iūvī, iūtus help, aid, delight, please

L

lābor, -ī, lāpsus sum slip, glide, fall

labor, -ōris *m.* work, toil, hardship, exertion, suffering

labōrō (1), toil, work, suffer, care

lac, lactis, *n.* milk

lacertus, -ī *m.* (upper) arm

lacrima, -ae *f.* tear

lacrimō (1), weep, shed tears

laedō, -ere, laesī, laesus hurt, harm, injure

laetus, -a, -um happy, joyful

lapis, lapidis *m.* stone

latebra, -ae *f.* hiding place, retreat

lateō, -ēre, -uī lie hidden, escape notice, lurk

lātus, -a, -um wide, broad; *adv.* lātē widely, far and wide

latus, lateris *n.* side, flank

laudō (1), praise

laurus, -ī, *f.* laurel, bay tree

laus, laudis *f.* praise, glory, fame

lavō, -āre, lāvī, lavātus (lautus, lōtus) wash, bathe

lectus, -ī *m.* bed, couch

lēgātus, -ī *m.* envoy, deputy

legō, -ere, lēgī, lēctus pick, choose, read

lentus, -a, -um slow, tough, pliant; *adv.* lentē slowly

leō, leōnis *m.* lion

lētum, -ī *n.* death

levis, -e light, nimble, fleet, easy, trivial, fickle; *adv.* leviter

levō (1), raise, lighten, support

lēx, lēgis *f.* law, order

libellus, -ī *m.* small book

līber, -era, -erum free

liber, librī *m.* bark of a tree, book

līberī, -ōrum *m. pl.* children

līberō (1), set free, release

lībertās, -ātis *f.* freedom

licet, -ēre, licuit (licitum est) *impers.* is allowed, is permitted; one may; *sometimes as conj.* although

lingua, -ae *f.* tongue, language

liquidus, -a, -um liquid, fluid, clear

littera, -ae *f.* letter (of the alphabet); *pl.* letter, document

lītus, lītoris *n.* shore, coast

locus, -ī *m.* (*pl.* locī *or* loca) place, position, occasion, matter

longus, -a, -um long; *adv.* longē far

loquor, -ī, locūtus sum speak, talk, say

lūctus, -ūs *m.* grief, sorrow

lūdō, -ere, lūsī, lūsus play, make fun of, cheat

lūdus, -ī *m.* play, sport, game, gambling; *pl. often* public performances

lūmen, lūminis, *n.* light, eye

lūna, -ae *f.* moon, (*personified*) Diana, goddess of the moon

lupa, -ae *f.* she-wolf

lupus, -ī *m.* wolf

lūx, lūcis *f.* light, daylight, dawn

lyra, -ae *f.* lyre

M

madidus, -a, -um wet, soaked

maestus, -a, -um sad, sorrowful

magis *adv.* more, rather

magister, -trī *m.* master, teacher, pilot

magnus, -a, -um great, large; *comp.* maior, *superl.* maximus

maior, maius larger, greater, older; *comp. of* magnus

mālō, mālle, māluī prefer

mālum, -ī *n.* apple

malus, -a, -um bad; *comp.* peior, *superl.* pessimus; *as noun* malum, -ī *n.* evil, harm, wrong, what is bad; *adv.* male badly

mandō (1), hand over, instruct, command

maneō, -ēre, mānsī, mānsum wait, stay, remain, wait for

manus, -ūs *f.* hand, touch, band, company

mare, maris *n.* sea

marmoreus, -a, -um of marble

māter, mātris *f.* mother

māteria, -ae (māteriēs, -ēī) *f.* matter, material

māternus, -a, -um maternal, of a mother

medius, -a, -um middle, middle of; medium, -ī *n.* the middle

melior, -ius *comp. of* bonus better

membrum, -ī *n.* member, limb

memor, -oris mindful, remembering, thoughtful

mēns, mentis *f.* mind, feeling, heart

mēnsa, -ae *f.* table, course (of a meal)

mēnsis, -is *m.* month

mercātor, -ōris *m.* trader, merchant

mereō, -ēre, -uī, -itus *also as dep.* mereor, -ērī, meritus sum earn, deserve, win

mergō, -ere, mersī, mersus dip, plunge, sink

metus, -ūs *m.* fear

meus, -a, -um my, mine

mīles, mīlitis *m.* soldier

mīlle *indecl. in sing.* thousand; *in pl.* mīllia (mīlia) -ium *n.*

minimus, -a, -um *superl. of* parvus least, smallest, very little; *adv.* minimē least, very little

minor, minus *comp. of* parvus smaller, less, younger; *adv.* minus; sī minus if not

mīror *dep.* (1), marvel, wonder at, admire

mīrus, -a, -um strange, wonderful, marvelous

misceō, -ēre, -uī, mixtus mix, mingle, confuse

miser, -era, -erum wretched, unhappy, unfortunate

mītis, -e mild, gentle

mittō, -ere, mīsī, missus let go, send, throw

modo *adv.* only, now, just; **modo . . . modo** now . . . now; sometimes . . . sometimes

modus, -ī *m.* way, manner, style, limit; tune, music

mollis, -e soft, gentle, delicate

moneō, -ēre, -uī, -itus warn, advise, remind

mōns, montis *m.* mountain

mōnstrō (1), show, indicate, point out

mora, -ae *f.* pause, delay

morbus, -ī *m.* sickness, disease

morior, -ī, mortuus sum die

moror *dep.* (1), delay, linger, hinder

mors, mortis *f.* death

mortālis, -e mortal, human

mōs, mōris *m.* way, manner, custom, habit

moveō, -ēre, mōvī, mōtus move, arouse, trouble, disturb, stir, challenge

mox *adv.* soon

mulceō, -ēre, mulsī, mulsus soothe

mulier, mulieris *f.* woman

multus, -a, -um much, many; *adv.* **multum, multō**

mūniō, -īre, -iī, -ītus build, fortify, protect

mūnus, mūneris *n.* service, duty, task, gift, public show, function

murmur, murmuris *n.* murmur, rumbling, roar

mūrus, -ī *m.* wall

Mūsa, -ae *f.* Muse

N

nam *conj.* for; **namque** for indeed, for example

nārrō (1), relate, tell

nāscor, -ī, nātus sum be born, arise

nātūra, -ae *f.* nature

nātus, -a, -um born; *as noun,* nātus, -ī *m.* son; nāta, -ae *f.* daughter

nauta, -ae *m.* sailor

nāvigō (1), sail, put to sea

nāvis, -is *f.* ship

nē *adv.* not; **nē . . . quidem** not . . . even; *as conj.* nē in order that . . . not, lest, for fear that

-ne *encl. introducing a question; in indir. question* -ne . . . -ne whether . . . or

nebula, -ae *f.* mist, cloud

nec *see* neque

necesse *indecl. adj.* necessary

neglegō, -ere, -lēxī, -lēctus neglect, treat with indifference

negō (1), refuse, deny, say that . . . not

negōtium, -ī *n.* business, affair, trouble

nēmō (*dat.* nēminī; *acc.* nēminem) no one, nobody

nemus, nemoris *n.* grove

nepōs, -ōtis *m.* grandson, descendant

neque (= nec) and not, nor; **neque . . . neque** neither . . . nor

nesciō, -īre, -iī, -ītus not know, be ignorant of

nescioquis, -qua, -quid (*adj.* -quod) I know not what (who), some or other

neuter, -tra, -trum (*gen.* -trīus) neither

nēve (= neu) and not, and in order that . . . not

niger, -gra, -grum black, dark

nihil (= nīl) nothing; *as adv.* not at all, by no means

nimbus, -ī *m.* storm cloud, cloud

nimium *adv.* too, too much

nisi *conj.* if not, unless, except

niveus, -a, -um snowy, snow white

nōbilis, -e well-known, famous, noble

nocēns, -entis harmful, guilty

noceō, -ēre, -uī, -itum *w. dat.* hurt, harm, injure

nōlō, nōlle, nōluī wish not, be unwilling, refuse

nōmen, nōminis *n.* name, title, fame, account

nōn *adv.* not, no

nōndum *adv.* not yet

nōnne *interr. expecting affirmative answer; in indir. question* whether . . . not

nōnus, -a, -um ninth; **Nōnae, -ārum,** *f. pl.* the Nones

nōscō, -ere, nōvī, nōtus get to know, learn; *perf.* nōvī I know

noster, -tra, -trum our, ours

nōtus, -a, -um known, well-known, famous

Notus, -ī *m.* the South Wind

novem *indecl.* nine

novus, -a, -um new, strange, early

nox, noctis *f.* night

nūbēs, -is *f.* cloud

nūbilum, -ī *n.* cloud

nūdus, -a, -um bare, naked, exposed, defenseless

nūllus, -a, -um (*gen.* -īus) nobody, none, no

num *interr. expecting negative answer; in indir. question* whether

nūmen, nūminis *n.* nod, divine will, divinity, power, approval

numerus, -ī, *m.* number, rank, meter, verse, part

numquam *adv.* never

nunc *adv.* now

nūntiō (1), announce, report

nūntius, -ī *m.* messenger, report

nympha, -ae *f.* nymph, bride

O

ob *prep. w. acc.* on account of

observō (1), watch over, tend

obses, obsidis *m. and f.* hostage, security

obstō, -āre, -stitī w. dat. prevent, resist

obtineō, -ēre, -tinuī, hold, get, obtain

occāsus, -ūs m. fall, setting of the sun, west

occidō, -ere, -cidī, -cāsum fall, perish, die, set (of the sun)

occīdō, -ere, -cīdī, -cīsus kill, slay

occupō (1), seize, surprise, attack

ōcior, ōcius swifter, rather swift, swift

octāvus, -a, -um eighth

octō indecl. eight

oculus, -ī m. eye

ōdī, -isse, ōsūrus hate

odor, odōris m. smell, odor

offendō, -ere, -fendī, -fēnsus offend, annoy

officium, -ī n. duty, service, favor, loyalty

ōlim adv. once, formerly, some time

omnīnō adv. at all, altogether

omnis, -e all, every

onus, oneris n. load, burden

oportet, -ēre, -uit impers. is necessary; one ought

oppidum, -ī n. town

opprimō, -ere, -pressī, -pressus oppress, crush, overwhelm, surprise

oppugnō (1), attack

(ops), opis f. help, aid, power; pl. opēs wealth, means, resources

optō (1), choose, desire, pray for

opus, operis n. work, labor; opus est w. abl. there is need of

ōrāc(u)lum, -ī n. oracle, prophecy

orbis, -is m. ring, circle, disc, world

ōrdō, ōrdinis m. line, rank, class, order

orīgō, orīginis f. origin, source, parentage

orior, -īrī, ortus sum rise, spring up; oriēns, -entis m. the rising sun, morning, east

ōrnātus, -ūs m. dress, adornment, style

ōrnō (1), adorn, equip, fit out, dress up

ōrō (1), pray, plead

ōs, ōris n. mouth, face

os, ossis n. bone

ōsculum, -ī n. kiss

ostendō, -ere, -tendī, -tentus show, reveal, point out

P

pacīscor, -ī, pactus sum bargain, agree; pactum, -ī n. agreement; pactus, -a, -um agreed on

paelex, paelicis f. mistress, rival, paramour

paene adv. nearly, almost

palleō, -ēre, -uī be pale

palūs, palūdis f. swamp, marsh

palūster, -tris, -tre marshy

papāver, papāveris n. poppy

pār, paris equal, fair, alike

parātus, -a, -um prepared, ready

parcō, -ere, pepercī, parsum w. dat. spare, forgive

parēns, -entis m. and f. parent, father, mother

pāreō, -ēre, -uī, -itum w. dat. obey

parō (1), make ready, prepare

pars, partis f. part, some

parvus, -a, -um small, humble; comp. minor; superl. minimus

pāscō, -ere, pāvī, pāstus (also as dep. pāscor, -ī, pāstus sum) feed, graze

passus, -ūs m. step, pace

pāstor, -ōris m. shepherd

pateō, -ēre, -uī be open, extend, be exposed

pater, patris m. father

patior, -ī, passus sum suffer, endure, allow

patria, -ae f. native land

patrius, -a, -um of a father, ancestral

paucus, -a, -um little, scanty; pl. few

paulum, paulō adv. a little, somewhat

paveō, -ēre, pāvī quake with fear, dread

pavidus, -a, -um trembling, frightened

pāx, pācis f. peace

peccō (1), err, do wrong, sin

pectus, pectoris n. breast, chest, heart, mind

pecūnia, -ae f. money

pedes, peditis m. foot soldier; as adj. on foot

pellis, -is f. skin, hide

pendeō, -ēre, pependī hang

penna, -ae f. feather, wing

per prep. w. acc. through, among, by, during, because of

percutiō, -ere, -cussī, -cussus hit, strike, smite

perdō, -ere, -didī, -ditus lose, destroy, ruin, waste

pereō, -īre, -iī, -itum perish, die, be lost

perficiō, -ere, -fēcī, -fectus finish, complete, bring about

perīculum, -ī n. trial, attempt, danger

perpetuus, -a, -um constant, continuous, perpetual

persuādeō, -ēre, -suāsī, -suāsus w. dat. of person, persuade

perterreō, -ēre, -uī, -itus terrify, frighten

pertineō, -ēre, -tinuī reach, apply to, concern

perveniō, -īre, -vēnī, -ventum come through to, reach, arrive

pēs, pedis m. foot; pede or pedibus on foot

pessimus, -a, -um superl. of malus worst, very bad

petō, -ere, -iī, -ītus seek, ask, request, aim, chase, attack, court, woo

pharetra, -ae f. quiver, case for arrows

pīlum, -ī n. javelin

pilus, -ī m. hair

pingō, -ere, pīnxī, pictus paint, color, depict

pinna (= penna), -ae f. feather, wing

piscis, -is m. fish

placeō, -ēre, -uī, -itum w. dat. please; impers. placet it is agreed

plēbs, plēbis, f. the common people

plēnus, -a, -um full

plūrimus, -a, -um superl. of multus most, very much, very many

plūs, plūris *comp. of* multus more
poena, -ae *f.* penalty, punishment, loss
poēta, -ae *m.* poet
polliceor, -ērī, -licitus sum promise
polus, -ī *m.* pole, north pole, sky
pōmum, -ī *n.* fruit, apple
pōnō, -ere, posuī, positus place, put, arrange, put aside
pōns, pontis *m.* bridge
pontus, -ī *m.* sea
populus, -ī *m.* a people, nation
porta, -ae *f.* gate, entrance
portō (1), bring, bear, carry
portus, -ūs *m.* harbor, port
poscō, -ere, poposcī demand, ask for
possideō, -ēre, -sēdī, -sessus own, possess
possum, posse, potuī be able, can, be strong
post *adv. and prep. w. acc.* after, behind
posteā *adv.* afterwards
posterus, -a, -um next, following; posterī, -ōrum *m. pl.* descendants; *comp.* posterior; *superl.* postrēmus last, lowest
postquam *conj.* after, when
postulō (1), demand, ask, request
potēns, -entis powerful
potestās, -ātis *f.* power, authority, opportunity
potior, -īrī, -ītus sum *w. abl. or gen.* get possession of
praebeō, -ēre, -uī, -itus provide, offer, furnish
praeceptum, -ī *n.* teaching, instruction
praecipuē *adv.* especially
praeda, -ae *f.* booty, prey
praeficiō, -ere, -fēcī, -fectus appoint, put in charge
praemium, -ī *n.* reward
praesidium -ī *n.* protection, defense
praesum -esse, -fuī, -futūrus *w. dat.* be in charge of, protect
praeter *adv. and prep. w. acc.* past, beyond, besides, except
praetereā *adv.* besides, furthermore
precor *dep.* (1), pray, entreat
premō, -ere, pressī, pressus oppress, lie on, weigh down, urge, close, check, crush
pretium, -ī *n.* price, reward
prex, precis *f.* prayer
prīmus, -a, -um first, foremost; *adv.* prīmum in the first place, first; prīmō first, at first
prīnceps, -cipis *m.* chief, prince, emperor; *as adj.* first, chief
prior, -ius former, earlier, previous; prius *adv.* earlier
prīscus, -a, -um of an earlier age
prīvātus, -a, -um private, individual
prō *prep. w. abl.* for, in front of, in behalf of, according to, in place of, compared to
probō (1), test, prove, approve
prōcēdō, -ere, -cessī, -cessum move forward, appear
procul *adv.* far off, at a distance

prōcumbō, -ere, -cubuī, -cubitum fall forward
prōdeō, -īre, -iī, -itum come forward, appear
prōdūcō, -ere, -dūxī, -ductus lead forward, draw out
proelium, -ī *n.* fight, battle
proficīscor, -ī, -fectus sum set out, depart
prōgredior, -ī, -gressus sum advance, proceed
prohibeō, -ēre, -uī, -itus hold off, hinder, prevent, forbid
prōmittō, -ere, -mīsī, -missus let grow, promise
prope *adv. and prep. w. acc.* near, nearby
properō (1), hurry, hasten
propinquus, -a, -um near, related
propior, -ius nearer, closer
propter *adv. and prep. w. acc.* near, because of
prōsum, prōdesse, prōfuī *w. dat.* help, be useful to
prōtinus *adv.* at once, straightway
prōveniō, -īre, -vēnī, -ventum come forth, grow
prōvideō, -ēre, -vīdī, -vīsus provide, foresee, take care
proximus, -a, -um nearest, next, latest
prūdēns, -entis wise, shrewd, prudent
pūblicus, -a, -um of the people, public, common
puella, -ae *f.* girl
puer, puerī *m.* boy, child, slave
pugna, -ae *f.* fight, battle
pugnō (1), fight
pulcher, -chra, -chrum lovely, beautiful, handsome, fine
pulsō (1), hit, strike, beat
puppis, -is *f.* stern of a ship, ship
purpureus, -a, -um purple
pūrus, -a, -um pure, plain, unadorned
putō (1), think, suppose, believe

Q

quā *adv.* where, by what way, which way
quadrupēs, -pedis *m. and f.* quadruped, horse
quaerō, -ere, quaesīvī, quaesītus ask, seek, miss, inquire, examine
quam *adv.* how, as, as much as; *after a comp.* than; *w. superl.* as . . . as possible
quamquam *conj.* although
quamvīs *conj.* although, however much
quantus, -a, -um how much, how great; *w.* tantus as much as
quārtus, -a, -um fourth
quattuor *indecl.* four
-que *encl.* and, also; -que . . . -que both . . . and
quī, quae, quod (*gen.* cuius) *rel. pron.* who, which, that, what; *interr. adj.* which, what

quia *conj.* because, the fact that

quīcumque, quae-, quod- whoever, whatever

quid *as interr. adv.* why? how?

quīdam, quaedam, quoddam (quiddam) *adj. and pron.* a certain, a, some, someone, something

quidem *adv.* indeed, to be sure, at least; nē . . . quidem not . . . even

quiēs, -ētis *f.* rest, quiet, sleep

quīlibet, quae-, quod- (*pron.* quid-) any you like, any at all

quīnque *indecl.* five

quīntus, -a, -um fifth

quis, quid *interr. pron.* who? which? what?

quis, quid *pron.* quī, qua, quod *adj.* anyone, anything, any (*replacing* aliquis *usually after* nē, nisi, num, sī, cum)

quisquam, quaequam, quidquam *indef. pron.* anyone, anything, any

quisque, quaeque, quidque (*as adj. n.* quodque) *pron. and adj.* each one, everyone, each, every

quō *conj.* (*usually w. comp.*) in order that; *adv.* whither, where to, where, why; *w. comp.* the

quod *conj.* because, the fact that, that

quoniam *conj.* since

quoque *adv.* also, too, even

quot how many; tot quot as many as

R

rāmus, -ī *m.* branch

rapiō, -ere, rapuī, raptus seize, snatch, carry off, sweep along

ratiō, -ōnis *f.* reckoning, account, reason, manner, means

ratis, -is *f.* raft, boat, ship

recēns, -entis recent, new, fresh

recipiō, -ere, -cēpī, -ceptus take back, recover, receive, welcome

reddō, -ere, reddidī, redditus give back, render, restore, repeat, pronounce

redeō, -īre, -iī, -itum go back

redūcō, -ere, -dūxī, -ductus lead back, draw back, restore

referō, -ferre, rettulī, relātus bring back, restore, relate, report, answer, repeat

reficiō, -ere, -fēcī, -fectus restore, renew, repair

rēgīna, -ae *f.* queen

regiō, -ōnis *f.* boundary, district, region

rēgnum, -ī, *n.* kingdom, royal power, rule

regō, -ere, rēxī, rēctus guide, rule, govern

reiciō, -ere, -iēcī, -iectus throw back, reject, refuse

relinquō, -ere, -līquī, -lictus leave behind

reliquus, -a, -um remaining, rest of; reliquī the rest

remaneō, -ēre, -mānsī, -mānsum remain, stay behind

rēmigium, -ī *n.* rowing, oars

removeō, -ēre, -mōvī, -mōtus move back, remove, clear away

rēmus, -ī *m.* oar

repellō, -ere, reppulī, repulsus drive back, repel, reject

repente *adv.* suddenly, hastily

reperiō, -īre, repperī, repertus find, discover

rēs, reī *f.* thing, matter, affair, fact, event, state, property

resistō, -ere, -stitī *w. dat.* resist, oppose

respiciō, -ere, -spexī, -spectus look behind, look back at, consider

respondeō, -ēre, -spondī, -spōnsus reply, answer, agree

retineō, -ēre, -tinuī, -tentus hold back, restrain, keep

retrō *adv.* backward, behind

revertor, -ī reversus sum (revertō, -ere, revertī, reversus) turn back, return

revocō (1), call back, recall

rēx, rēgis *m.* king

rīdeō, -ēre, rīsī, rīsus laugh (at)

rigeō, -ēre be stiff, be hardened

rīpa, -ae *f.* river bank, edge

rīsus, -ūs *m.* laughing, laughter

rōbur, rōboris *n.* hardwood, oak, strength, power

rogō (1), ask, ask for

rōrō (1), drip moisture

rosa, -ae *f.* rose

rubeō, -ēre be red, blush

ruber, -bra, -brum red

rudis, -e rough, unfinished, untrained, crude

rūmor, -ōris *m.* report, rumor, gossip

rumpō, -ere, rūpī, ruptus break, burst through, tear

ruō, -ere, ruī, rutum rush, run

rūrsus *adv.* again, back, in turn

rūs, rūris *n.* country; rūrī *or* rūre in the country

S

sacer, sacra, sacrum holy, sacred; sacra, -ōrum *n. pl.* rites, ceremonies, sacrifice

saepe *adv.* often

saevus, -a, -um fierce, cruel

sagitta, -ae *f.* arrow

salūs, -ūtis *f.* safety, health, life, greeting

sanguis, sanguinis *m.* blood, race, family

sānus, -a, -um healthy, sane

satis *indecl. noun and adv.* enough, very

saxum, -ī *n.* rock

scaber, -bra, -brum rough, mangy

scelus, sceleris *n.* crime, wickedness

scīlicet *adv.* of course, to be sure

sciō, -īre, -īvī, -ītus know, know how

scrībō, -ere, scrīpsī, scriptus write

scūtum, -ī *n.* shield

sē (*gen.* suī; *dat.* sibi) *reflexive pronoun* himself, herself, itself, themselves

secundus, -a, -um second, favorable
sed *conj.* but; sed enim but indeed
sedeō, -ēre, sēdī, sessum sit down, settle
seges, segetis *f.* field of grain
semper *adv.* always
senātus, -ūs *m.* senate
senex, senis *m.* old man
sēnsus, -ūs *m.* feeling, sense, awareness
sententia, -ae *f.* opinion, view, proposal
sentiō, -īre, sēnsī, sēnsus feel, perceive, think
septem *indecl.* seven
septimus, -a, -um seventh
sequor, -ī, secūtus sum follow
serpēns, -entis *m. and f.* serpent, snake
sērus, -a, -um late, withered; *adv.* sērō late, too late
servō (1), save, keep, guard, observe
servus, -ī *m.* slave, servant
sex *indecl.* six
sextus, -a, -um sixth
sī *conj.* if
sīc *adv.* thus, so, in this way
signō (1), mark, indicate, note, seal
signum, -ī *n.* mark, sign, seal, statue, constellation, figure, military standard
silentium, -ī *n.* silence
silva, -ae *f.* wood, forest
similis, -e *w. gen. or dat.* like, similar
simul *adv.* at once, at the same time, together; simul ac (atque) *or* simul *alone* as soon as
sine *prep. w. abl.* without
sinister, -tra, -trum left, on the left, unlucky, unfavorable
sinus, -ūs *m.* hollow, bay, fold, curve, bosom
socer, socerī *m.* father-in-law
socius, -ī *m.* helper, comrade, ally
sōl, sōlis *m.* sun
soleō, -ēre, solitus sum *semi-dep.* be accustomed
solitus, -a, -um usual, customary
sollicitus, -a, -um troubled, worried, uneasy, unruly
sōlus, -a, -um (*gen.* -īus) only, alone, lonely
solvō, -ere, solvī, solūtus release, free, pay, acquit, finish
somnus, -ī *m.* sleep
sonō, -āre, -uī, -itus sound, speak
sonus, -ī *m.* sound, noise
sopor, -ōris *m.* sleep
soror, sorōris *f.* sister
sors, sortis *f.* lot, destiny, fate, oracle
sōspes, sōspitis safe, unhurt, fortunate
spargō, -ere, sparsī, sparsus scatter, spread
spatium, -ī *n.* space, extent, period, time
speciēs, -ēī *f.* look, sight, appearance, view, kind, form
spectō (1), look at, face, watch, observe
speculum, -ī *n.* mirror
spērō (1), hope, hope for, expect
spēs, speī *f.* hope

spīritus, -ūs *m.* breath, air, spirit
squāma, -ae *f.* scale (of fish *or* serpent)
stella, -ae *f.* star
sternō, -ere, strāvī, strātus lay low, spread
stō, stāre, stetī, statum stand
studeō, -ēre, -uī *w. dat.* be eager for, favor, support, study
studium, -ī *n.* eagerness, zeal, interest
sub *prep. w. acc. and abl.* under, below, near
subeō, -īre, -iī, -itus go under, undergo
subitus, -a, -um sudden; *adv.* subitō suddenly
subsidium, -ī *n.* help, support
sulcus, -ī *m.* furrow, trench
sum, esse, fuī, futūrus be, exist, be able
summus, -a, -um highest, top of, utmost, last
sūmō, -ere, sūmpsī, sūmptus take, assume, use
super *adv.* over, above, besides; *prep. w. acc. and abl.* over, above, in addition to
superbus, -a, -um proud, haughty
superī (dī *implied*) -ōrum *m. pl.* the gods above
superō (1), rise above, surpass, defeat, conquer
suprā *adv.* above, earlier; *prep. w. acc.* above, beyond, more than
surgō, -ere, surrēxī, surrēctum rise, get up
suscipiō, -ere, -cēpī, -ceptus take up, undertake
suspiciō, -ere, -spexī, -spectus suspect, look up at
sustineō, -ēre, -tinuī, -tentus hold up, sustain, support, endure
suus, -a, -um his own, her own, its own, their own, his, her, its, their, one's own

T

tacitus, -a, -um silent
tālis, -e such, of such a kind; tālis . . . quālis such . . . as
tam *adv.* so, so much; tam . . . quam so . . . as
tamen *adv.* yet, however
tandem *adv.* at length
tangō, -ere, tetigī, tāctus touch
tantus, -a, -um so great, so much; tantus . . . quantus so much . . . as; *adv.* tantum so much, only, merely
tēctum, -ī *n.* covering, protection, roof, house
tegmen (tegimen, tegumen), -minis *n.* covering, protection
tegō, -ere, tēxī, tēctus hide, cover
tellūs, -ūris *f.* earth, ground
tēlum, -ī *n.* javelin, missile
tempestās, -ātis *f.* storm, weather, season, time
templum, -ī *n.* temple, sanctuary
temptō (1), try, test, attempt

tempus, temporis *n.* time, season, occasion, temple (of the head)

teneō, -ēre, -uī, tentus hold, keep, check, guard

tener, -era, -erum tender, young, dainty, delicate

tenuis, -e thin, slight, humble, poor

tepidus, -a, -um warm

ter *adv.* three times, thrice

tergum, -ī *n.* back, rear, skin, hide

terra, -ae *f.* earth, land

terreō, -ēre, -uī, -itus frighten

terribilis, -e terrifying, terrible

terror, -ōris *m.* fright, alarm, terror

tertius, -a, -um third

theātrum, -ī *n.* theater

thyrsus, -ī *m.* Bacchic wand

tigris, -is *m. and f.* tiger, tigress

timeō, -ēre, -uī fear, be afraid of

timidus, -a, -um timid, fearful; *adv.* timidē

timor, -ōris *m.* fear, dread

toga, -ae *f.* toga, dress of the Roman citizen

tollō, -ere, sustulī, sublātus raise, lift, remove

torus, -ī *m.* couch, bed

tot *indecl.* so many; tot . . . quot so many . . . as

tōtus, -a, -um (*gen.* -īus) the whole, entire, all

trādō, -ere, -didī, -ditus hand over, hand down, entrust, relate

trahō, -ere, trāxī, trāctus draw, assume, attract, influence, delay, prolong

trāns *prep. w. acc.* across, over

trānseō, -īre, -iī, -itus go across, pass over

trecentī, -ae, -a three hundred

tremor, -ōris *m.* trembling, shaking

trepidō (1), tremble, be alarmed

trēs, tria three

tribuō, -ere, -uī, -ūtus assign, bestow, distribute

trīstis, -e sad, gloomy, unpleasant

tū (*gen.* tuī) *pers. pron.* you

tum *adv.* then; cum . . . tum both . . . and; tum cum at the time when

tumeō, -ēre swell, be puffed up

tunc *adv.* then, at that time, accordingly

tunica, -ae *f.* tunic

turba, -ae *f.* confusion, crowd, throng, band of followers

turpis, -e ugly, shameful, base

turris, -is *f.* tower

tūtus, -a, -um safe, protected

tuus, -a, -um your, yours

tyrannus, -ī *m.* tyrant, ruler

U

ubi *adv. and conj.* where, when

ūllus, -a, -um (*gen.* -īus) any

ulterior, -ius farther

ultimus, -a, -um farthest, last

umbra, -ae *f.* shadow, shade

umerus, -ī *m.* shoulder

ūmidus, -a, -um wet, damp

ūmor, ūmōris *m.* moisture, liquid

umquam *adv.* ever

unda, -ae *f.* wave, water

unde *adv.* whence, from where

ūndecimus, -a, -um eleventh

undique *adv.* on all sides, from everywhere

unguis, -is *m.* fingernail

ūnus, -a, -um (*gen.* ūnīus) one, only, alone

urbs, urbis *f.* city; Urbs the City, Rome

usque *adv.* all the way, right to, ever, constantly

ūsus, -ūs *m.* need, enjoyment, use, service, experience

ut, utī *adv.* how, as; *conj. w. indic.* when, as, as soon as; *w. subjv. of purpose* in order that, that; *w. subjv. of result* that, so that; *after verb of fearing* that . . . not

uter, utra, utrum (*gen.* utrīus) which (of two)

uterque, utraque, utrumque (*gen.* utrīusque) each (of two), either

ūtilis, -e useful, expedient

ūtor, -ī, ūsus sum *w. abl.* use, enjoy

ūva, -ae *f.* grape, bunch of grapes

uxor, uxōris *f.* wife

V

vacuus, -a, -um empty, void, deserted, open

vadum, -ī *n.* shallow place, ford

valeō, -ēre, -uī, -itum be well, be strong, prevail, be able; *imperative* valē (valēte) farewell, good-bye

validus, -a, -um strong, powerful, able

vallēs, -is *f.* valley, hollow

vāllum, -ī *n.* rampart, wall

varius, -a, -um various, varied, diverse

vāstō (1), lay waste, destroy

vāstus, -a, -um desolate, vast

vātēs, -is *m.* poet, bard, prophet

vehemēns, -entis eager, impulsive, vigorous, violent

vehō, -ere, vexī, vectus carry, convey; *pass.* be carried, ride, sail

vel *conj.* or; vel . . . vel either . . . or

vēlō (1), cover up, veil

vēlum, -ī *n.* sail, awning, curtain, veil

venēnum, -ī *n.* poison

veniō, -īre, vēnī, ventum come

ventus, -ī *m.* wind

Venus, Veneris *f.* Venus, goddess of love

verbum, -ī *n.* word

vereor, -ērī, -itus sum fear, respect

vertō, -ere, vertī, versus turn, change

vērus, -a, -um true, truthful, real, proper; *adv.* vērō truly, indeed, but; vērē truly

vēsānus, -a, -um mad, insane

vester, -tra, -trum your, yours

vēstīgium, -ī *n.* track, footprint, trace

vestis, -is *f.* clothing, dress

vetus, veteris old, former

vetustās, -ātis f. long time, antiquity
via, -ae f. road, way
(vicis), -is f. change, turn, place
victor, -ōris m. victor
victōria, -ae f. victory
videō, -ēre, vīdī, vīsus see
videor, -ērī, vīsus sum seem, appear, seem
  right
vīgintī indecl. twenty
vigor, -ōris m. energy, vigor
vīlla, -ae f. farmhouse, villa
vincō, -ere, vīcī, victus defeat, conquer, surpass
vinculum (vinclum), -ī n. chain, bond
vīnum, -ī n. wine
violēns, -entis raging, vehement
vir, virī m. man, husband
virga, -ae f. twig, rod, wand
virgō, virginis f. girl, young woman, virgin
viridis, -e green, fresh, young
virtūs, -ūtis f. manliness, courage, ability,
  worth, quality, virtue

vīs (acc. vim; abl. vī) f. force, power, violence; vīrēs, vīrium f. pl. strength, forces
vīta, -ae f. life
vītis, -is f. vine
vitium, -ī n. fault, defect, vice
vīvō, -ere, vīxī, vīctum live
vix adv. hardly, scarcely
vocō (1), call, call upon, name, summon,
  invite
volō (1), fly
volō, velle, voluī wish, be willing, intend,
  mean
voluntās, -ātis f. will, wish, inclination, favor
vōtum, -ī n. vow, prayer
vōx, vōcis f. voice, sound, remark, word
vulnerō (1), wound
vulnus, vulneris n. wound
vultus, -ūs m. expression, face, look

Z

Zephyrus, -ī m. West Wind, Zephyr

INDEX OF
PROPER NAMES

A

Acarnania. Westernmost district of central Greece. (See map, p. xxix.)

Acca Larentia. Wife of the shepherd Faustulus. She nursed Romulus and Remus after they were taken from the she-wolf.

Achaea (Achais). A country on the northern coast of the Peloponnesus. (See map, p. xxix.)

Achaemenius. Persian.

Achelous. 1. The largest river in Greece, rising on Mt. Pindus and flowing south between Acarnania and Aetolia to the Ionian Sea. (See map, p. xxix.) 2. The god of this river.

Achilles. A Thessalian hero who fought and died in the Trojan War, recognized as the most valiant of the Greeks at the war.

Acis. A son of Faunus who was loved by the nymph Galatea. Polyphemus, who loved Galatea, crushed him under a rock. Galatea changed him into the River Acis, which rises on the northern slopes of Mt. Aetna and flows into the Sicilian Sea. (See map, p. xxv.)

Adonis. A youth who was beloved by Venus but killed by a boar. Because of Venus' grief he was allowed to return to the upper world for six months each year.

Aegean Sea. The sea east of Greece, dotted with many islands. (See map, p. xxviii.)

Aegisthus. A cousin of Agamemnon. During the Trojan War he seduced Agamemnon's wife Clytemnestra and helped her to kill her husband on his return.

Aeneas. A Trojan hero, the son of Venus, renowned for his *pietas*: his loyalty to gods, country, and family. At the fall of Troy he escaped and landed at Carthage, where Queen Dido fell in love with him. Following the command of the gods, he left Carthage and finally reached Latium in Italy. He was the ancestor of the Roman race and especially of the Julian family.

Aeolus. The god of the winds, which he kept imprisoned in a cavern on the floating island of Aeolia.

Aequi. An ancient people of Italy. With the Volsci they fought several wars with Rome but were finally conquered in 302 B.C. (See map, p. xxv.)

Aethiopia. A name applied by the Romans to several places which were inhabited, as they thought, by dark-skinned peoples: 1. the area south of Egypt, 2. an area extending from the mouth of the Tigris up the valley of the Choaspes, 3. an area farther east, toward India. King Cepheus and his daughter Andromeda were Aethiopians.

Aetna. An active volcano in the east of Sicily. (See map, p. xxv.)

Aetolia. A wild and mountainous district of central Greece. (See map, p. xxix.)

Agenor. King of Phoenicia and father of Cadmus and Europa, a maiden abducted by Jupiter in the form of a bull. Agenor ordered Cadmus to find his sister or not return.

Alba Longa. A city founded on the Alban mountain in Latium by Ascanius, Aeneas' son. It was the city of his descendants, Romulus and Remus.

Alcaeus. A Theban hero and the father of Amphitryon, who was the husband of Alcmene, the mother of Hercules.

Alpheus. 1. The chief river of the Peloponnesus, flowing through Arcadia and Elis into the Ionian Sea. (See map, p. xxix.) 2. The god of this river. Enamored of the nymph Arethusa, he pursued her; when she was changed into a river herself and plunged underground, he continued to follow her, mingling his waters with hers.

Amor. Cupid.

Amulius. A brother of Numitor, the king of Alba Longa. Deposing his brother he seized the throne and forced Numitor's daughter Rhea Silvia to become a Vestal Virgin. Nevertheless, made pregnant by Mars, she gave birth to Romulus and Remus. Amulius then ordered the twins thrown into the Tiber; but they were rescued and raised by the shepherd Faustulus. Reaching maturity, they killed Amulius and restored their grandfather Numitor to his throne.

Andromeda. An Aethiopian princess exposed by her father as a placatory offering to a sea monster that was devastating the kingdom. She was rescued by Perseus on his way back from killing Medusa. He killed the monster, married Andromeda, and took her with him to Seriphos and then to Argos.

Aonia. An old name for Boeotia.

Aonii. The ancient inhabitants of Boeotia.

Aphrodite. The Greek name for Venus.

Apollo. A god, the son of Jupiter and Latona; his twin sister was Diana. He was depicted as a long-haired beautiful youth. As the god of light, in both the physical and the spiritual sense, he was the divinity of the sun and also the chief god of prophecy. His principal oracular shrine, Delphi, he won by killing Python, a huge serpent guarding it. Delos (his birthplace), Claros, Tenedos, and Patara were also sacred to him. His attributes were the bow and the lyre, symbols of his powers as god of disease, medicine and music. He had many human loves, of whom the first was Daphne. He was a patron god of the Emperor Augustus, who built a temple to him on the Palatine Hill in Rome.

Aquilo. The North Wind, often personified as a god.

Appia. See **Via Appia.**

Arcadia. A country of mountains and lakes in the middle of the Peloponnesus. (See map, p. xxix.)

Arctos. 1. The constellation of the Great Bear (Ursa Major), a metamorphosis of the Arcadian nymph Callisto. 2. The Lesser Bear (Ursa Minor).

Arethusa. A nymph of Elis who, pursued by the river god Alpheus, was changed into a river which plunged underground and ran under the sea to Sicily. There it emerged as a spring on the island of Ortygia at Syracuse.

Argo. The first ship built in Thessaly under the guidance of Athena for Jason's expedition to Colchis to fetch the Golden Fleece. Its helmsman was Tiphys.

Ariadne (Ariadna). Daughter of King Minos of Crete and his wife Pasiphae; she was the sister of Phaedra and the half-sister of the Minotaur. When Theseus came to Crete to bring the Athenian tribute, she fell in love with him, helped him to escape from the Labyrinth, and accompanied him when he left Crete. He promised to marry her but abandoned her on the island of Naxos (Dia) while she slept. Rescued by Bacchus, she became his bride. He placed her marriage-diadem in the sky as the constellation Corona Borealis.

Arion. A lyric poet and cithara-player. After touring Sicily and south Italy he was returning to Corinth when the sailors planned to murder him for the presents he had gathered on his tour. Receiving permission to play and sing one last time, he invoked the gods in his song and leapt into the sea. He was rescued by a music-loving dolphin and brought to Taenarus, whence he returned to Corinth to confront his would-be slayers.

Armenius. Of Armenia. The Armenians were allied with the Parthians in the Parthian War of Augustus' reign.

Asia Minor. The great peninsula east of the Aegean. (See map, p. xxvii.)

Astypalaea. An island in the south Aegean north of Crete, noted for its fisheries. (See map, p. xxviii.)

Atalanta. A famous huntress of Arcadia, the daughter of Schoeneus.

Athena. The goddess of wisdom, and hence the patroness of all arts, crafts, and sciences. She is usually depicted as helmeted and armed. She was the inventress of the olive-tree; her bird was the owl. Though the patron goddess of Troy, with a temple in the citadel, she supported the Greeks in the Trojan War because the Trojan prince Paris had not awarded her the prize as the most beautiful of goddesses. Athena had a temple on the Aventine Hill in Rome, the central shrine of craftsmen, as Mercury's temple nearby was that of merchants.

Athens. Capital of Attica, a district of central Greece; the city of Theseus sacred to Athena. (See map, p. xxix.)

Atlantiades. "Descendant of Atlas," Mercury.

Atlas. A Titan, condemned to bear the heavens on his shoulders. His daughter Maia was the mother (by Jupiter) of Mercury.

Attica. A district in the southeast of central Greece. (See map, p. xxix.)

Augustus. Roman Emperor, 30 B.C.-A.D. 14, the adopted son of Julius Caesar. He instituted an extensive program of urban renewal and moral rearmament, attempting especially to restore Roman religious feeling and the sanctity of the family. He exiled Ovid for reasons which remain obscure. (See Introduction, p. vii.)

Ausonia. An old name for southern Italy, sometimes applied to the whole peninsula.

Automedon. The charioteer of Achilles, known for his skill.

Aventine. One of the hills of Rome. Overlooking the valley of the Circus Maximus, it was the site of the temples of Mercury and Minerva. (See Plan, p. xxvi.)

B

Bacche (Bacchante). A Maenad.

Bacchus. The god of wine, pictured as a beautiful long-haired youth. A son of Jupiter, left motherless in infancy, he was raised by Silenus. After his discovery of wine he traveled over the world in a chariot drawn by tigers or pards, accompanied by Silenus and the Thiasus, a rout of Maenads and Satyrs, teaching the cultivation of the vine and instituting the rites of his worship. The chief centers of his cult were Boeotia (the land of his birth), Phocis, Argos, Laconia, and Naxos (where he found his bride, Ariadne).

Baucis. The wife of Philemon.

Berecyntus. A mountain in Phrygia, sacred to Cybele. Her son Midas is called Berecyntius.

Boeotia. A country of central Greece. It was thought to have been named from the cow (**bos**) which led Cadmus to the spot where he founded Thebes, the chief city. The whole district, and especially Mt. Helicon, was a favorite haunt of the Muses. (See map, p. xxix.)

Bootes. The Plowman, a constellation of the northern sky which never sets below the horizon. It is near Ursa Major.

C

Cadmea. The citadel of Thebes, named for Cadmus, its founder.

Cadmus. A prince of Phoenicia, son of Agenor and brother of Europa, a maiden carried off by Jupiter in the form of a bull. Agenor sent Cadmus to find her. Upon consulting the Delphic oracle he was told to abandon his search, to follow a cow and to found a city on the spot where she would lie down. Near this site Cadmus slew a dragon, the offspring of Mars, which had killed his men, and on Athena's advice planted its teeth. A race of warriors sprang up from them and fell to killing each other until only five were left. These helped Cadmus to found Cadmea, the citadel of the future city of Thebes; their descendants were the aristocracy of Thebes, and Cadmus' descendants were its kings. For having killed Mars' dragon, Cadmus was visited with many misfortunes and finally was granted his wish to be changed into a serpent himself, since a serpent's life was so dear to the gods. Cadmus was believed to have brought the alphabet from Phoenicia to Greece.

Caduceus. The magical herald's staff borne by Mercury.

Caducifer. "Bearer of the Caduceus," Mercury.

Caesar. 1. Gaius Julius Caesar, the conqueror of Gaul. A leader of the popular party, he seized power at Rome in 49 B.C. and ruled until 44 when he was assassinated by a group of aristocrats who feared he would make himself King. After his death he was deified. 2. Gaius Julius Caesar Octavianus, Augustus.

Callisto. An Arcadian nymph and a companion of Diana, she was loved by Jupiter and changed into a she-bear. When she was killed, Jupiter placed her among the stars as the constellation Ursa Major.

Calydonian Boar. A monstrous boar laying waste the territory of Calydon in Aetolia was hunted by a large party of heroes, among whom were Theseus, Pirithous, and Atalanta. (See map, p. xxix.)

Calymne. A wooded island near Rhodes, famous for its honey. (See map, p. xxviii.)

Calypso. A nymph, the daughter of Atlas, living on the remote island of Ogygia, where Ulysses was shipwrecked. Although Calypso fell in love with him and promised him immortality if he would stay and be her husband, Ulysses wanted to go home. At the command of Jupiter he was allowed to leave in the eighth year of his stay.

Campania. Coastal plain of western central Italy. (See map, p. xxv.)

Campus Martius. The "Field of Mars," the northwest part of the plain lying in the bend of the Tiber at Rome. It was used by Roman youths for gymnastic exercises and military training.

Capena. See **Porta Capena.**

Capitolium. 1. The temple of the Capitoline Triad: Jupiter Optimus Maximus, Juno, and Minerva. It was the chief cult center of Roman worship. 2. The hill at Rome on which the temple stood, including the Arx or citadel, and several other temples. The hill was ascended by a street zigzagging up from the Forum; a triumphing general would drive up this street to make offerings to Jupiter.

Capua. Chief city of Campania. (See map, p. xxv.)

Carmentis. A Roman goddess of childbirth, the mother of Evander. A gate in the fortifications of old Rome, near the river, was named for her.

Cassandra. A daughter of King Priam of Troy. She was loved by Apollo, who gave her the gift of prophecy; but when she spurned his love he decreed that her prophecies would never be believed. At the fall of Troy she was dragged from the temple of Athena, where she had taken refuge and was brought by Agamemnon to Mycenae, where she was murdered by Clytemnestra.

Castalia. A spring on the slopes of Mt. Parnassus, near Delphi. It was sacred to Apollo and the Muses.

Caucasus. A mountain range extending from the east shore of the Black Sea to the west shore of the Caspian, an area wild, inaccessible, and uncivilized in classical times.

164

Celer. Romulus' lieutenant. Celer slew Remus when he leaped over the wall of Romulus' new city.

Celeus. A poor farmer (in some accounts the King) of Eleusis. He received Ceres hospitably during her search for Proserpina. In return she made him the first priest of her cult at Eleusis and showered favors on his son Triptolemus.

Cephisus. A river of Phocis and Boeotia. (See map, p. xxix.)

Cerealis. Of Ceres. **Cerealia**, the feast of Ceres, 10 April.

Ceres. Goddess of agriculture and all the fruits of the earth (her name is often used by metonymy to mean *food*). She was the sister of Jupiter and the mother by him of Proserpina. When Proserpina was carried off by Pluto, Ceres wandered the earth disconsolately in search of her. Received kindly by Celeus of Eleusis, she taught his son Triptolemus the arts of agriculture. She was finally informed of her daughter's whereabouts by the sun or by the nymph Arethusa. Many places in Sicily, particularly along the eastern coast, were sacred to her. She appears crowned with wheat, riding in a chariot drawn by dragons.

Chalcidice. A peninsula of Thrace. (See map, p. xxviii.)

Cibyra. A small city of Phrygia. (See map, p. xxviii.)

Cilicia. A district in the southeast of Asia Minor. (See map, p. xxvii.)

Circe. An enchantress who turned Ulysses' men into swine. Overcoming her spells, Ulysses restored his men and spent a year on her island.

Circus Maximus. Rome's course for horse-races, situated in the valley between the Palatine and Aventine Hills. (See Plan, p. xxvi.)

Clarus. A town of Asia Minor, famous for its temple and oracle of Apollo, who was sometimes called "Clarius deus."

Cnossus. Chief city of Crete, the capital of Minos.

Consus. The god of the stream which flowed through the valley between the Palatine and Aventine Hills at Rome. He was called Consus ("the buried one") because the stream was put underground when the race-course was laid out there. He was worshipped at a subterranean altar in the Circus Maximus. In his honor Romulus held the games at which the Sabine women were abducted. Because of his connection with water and with horses he was sometimes identified with Neptune; he was also a god of secret plans (because of a supposed connection of his name with **consilia**). His feasts, the Consualia, were held on 19 August and 15 December.

Corinth. A Greek city on the isthmus between central Greece and the Peloponnesus. (See map, p. xxix.)

Corona. See **Cressa.**

Corycides. Nymphs, the daughters of Plistus, so called from the Corycian Cave on Mt. Parnassus, their favorite haunt.

Cremera. A small river of Etruria, which joins the Tiber a little above Rome. (See map, p. xxv.)

Cressa. Cretan. As noun, the Cretan woman (Ariadne). **Cressa Corona**, a constellation, the Corona Borealis, Ariadne's diadem, placed in the sky by Bacchus after his marriage to her.

Cronus. The leader of the Titans and the father of the Olympian gods. Because of a prophecy that one of his children would overthrow him, he devoured each child as it was born. His wife Rhea gave birth to Jupiter on Mt. Dicte in Crete and left him hidden there. When he grew up he deposed his father and made him disgorge the other Olympians.

Cupid (Cupido). The god of love and the son of Venus, he was a temperamental and capricious boy, feared by all gods and men, armed with a bow and a burning torch, his instruments for inspiring love.

Cures. An ancient town of the Sabines. (See map, p. xxv.)

Cybele. A Phrygian nature goddess who roamed the woodlands of Mt. Ida and Mt. Berecyntus in a chariot drawn by lions; she was the mother of Midas.

Cyclopes. A race of one-eyed giants in Sicily. Some were smiths who forged Jupiter's thunderbolts in workshops under Mt. Aetna and other volcanoes. Others, like Polyphemus, were herdsmen.

Cydnus. A river of Cilicia. (See map, p. xxvii.)

Cyllene. A high mountain on the borders of Arcadia and Achaea, the birthplace of Mercury and sacred to him. (See map, p. xxix.)

Cyllenius. Of Cyllene; of Mercury. Used as a noun, **Cyllenius**, Mercury.

Cyprus. An island of the eastern Mediterranean sacred to Venus. (See map, p. xxvii.)

Cythera. An island off the southeast point of Laconia. Near the island Venus was born from the sea. (See map, p. xxix.)

Cytherea. Venus, so called from the island of Cythera, which was sacred to her.

D

Daedalus. Athenian inventor and artist. When his nephew, who was his apprentice, appeared likely to surpass him in skill he threw him from the Acropolis. Condemned for the murder, he fled to Crete and entered the service of King Minos. He built the wooden cow for Pasiphae,and when she had given birth to the Minotaur he built the Labyrinth at Cnossus, where the monster was kept. Although Daedalus was imprisoned with his son Icarus, they escaped on wings he had made of wax and feathers. Icarus fell into the sea, but Daedalus safely reached Italy; he ended his life in Sicily.

Danae. Daughter of the King of Argos, who shut her up in a bronze tower because an oracle had predicted that he would be killed by her son. After Jupiter visited her in the form of a shower of gold, she gave birth to Perseus. Although her father put her, with her son, into a chest and threw it into the sea, they drifted to Seriphos, where they were kindly received.

Daphne. Daughter of the Thessalian river-god Peneus. Apollo fell in love with her and pursued her. Just as he was about to overtake her she was changed, at her own wish, into a laurel tree. From that time, the laurel was sacred to Apollo.

Delos. The smallest of the Cyclades. Originally a floating island, it was fastened down by Jupiter so that Latona might there give birth to Apollo and Diana. The island remained sacred to the twin gods, especially to Apollo. Delos was sometimes called Ortygia, "Island of Quails." (See map, p. xxviii.)

Delphi. A city on the slopes of Mt. Parnassus in Phocis, the site of the most important oracular shrine of antiquity. The oracle was originally that of Tellus, the Earth, and her daughter Themis; but Apollo won it from them by slaying the serpent Python. The oracles of Delphi, usually couched in somewhat ambiguous terms, were of great importance in ancient myth and history. (See map, p. xxix.)

Demeter. Greek name for Ceres.

Deucalion. Son of Prometheus, married to his cousin Pyrrha, the daughter of Epimetheus. When Jupiter determined to destroy mankind by a universal flood, Deucalion (by his father's advice) shut himself and Pyrrha into a chest, which floated on the flood and came to rest, when the waters subsided, on Mt. Parnassus. Consulting the oracle of Themis at Delphi, Deucalion and Pyrrha were told that they could restore the human race by throwing the bones of their mother behind their backs. They complied, using stones (the bones of mother Earth); those thrown by Deucalion became men; those thrown by Pyrrha, women.

Dia. Another name for Naxos.

Diana. Daughter of Jupiter and Latona and twin sister of Apollo. She was armed, like her brother, with the bow, and as a nature goddess was both the protectress and the huntress of wild beasts. Allowed by Jupiter to remain unwed, she enforced chastity on the band of huntress-nymphs who were her companions. Delos, her birthplace, was sacred to her and to her brother.

Dicte. A mountain in Crete where Jupiter was reared without the knowledge of his father, Cronus.

Dictynna. A name of Diana, as goddess of the hunting-net (**dictyon** in Greek). A Cretan promontory where Diana had a temple was called Dictynnaeus Mons.

Diomedes. King of Argos. One of the bravest heroes at Troy, he wounded even Mars and Venus when they took the field in person. He was Ulysses' companion in the killing of Dolon and Rhesus and in the capture of Rhesus' horses.

Dione. Another name for Venus.

Dis. Brother of Jupiter and Neptune. When the three drew lots for the control of the universe, Dis was made the ruler of the Lower World, the land of the dead. He fell in love with his niece Proserpina, abducted her and made her his consort.

Dolon. A Trojan who volunteered to spy out the Greek camp in return for Hector's promise that he would receive Achilles' horses when the booty was shared after a Trojan victory. Caught by Ulysses and Diomedes on their scouting expedition, he was forced to reveal the disposition of the Trojan forces and was then killed.

E

Eleusis. A town in Attica, near Athens, famous for the celebration of the mystery cult of Demeter (Ceres). Little is known of the Eleusinian Mysteries, but they may have commemorated the annual return of Proserpina from the Lower World, thereby offering hope of human resurrection and immortality as well. Ceres is said to have chosen Eleusis for her cult center because of the hospitality shown her by Celeus. (See map, p. xxix.)

Elis. 1. A country on the west coast of the Peloponnesus. (See map, p. xxix.) 2. The chief city of this country.

Ennius. Quintus Ennius (239-169 B.C.), a Roman poet of Greek birth, was thought of as the father of Latin poetry. He wrote tragedies, comedies, and didactic poems, but his most important work was the *Annales,* an epic treatment of Roman history from the beginnings to his own day. Though his works exercised a great influence over later Latin literature, they are now mostly lost.

Epimetheus. A Titan, brother of Prometheus and Atlas, the father of Pyrrha who was the wife of Deucalion.

Erymanthus. A mountain of Arcadia. (See map, p. xxix.)

Esquiline Hill. The largest of the hills of Rome, it was added to the city by King Servius Tullius, who built his own house there in order to attract others to reside in that area.

Ethiopia. Aethiopia.

Etna. Aetna.

Etruria. District north of Latium in Italy, the land of the Etruscans, who had come to Italy from Lydia and early attained a high level of civilization. The Romans borrowed from the Etruscans many features of their arts and religion. (See map, p. xxv.)

Euhius. Another name for Bacchus.

Euphrates. A river of Asia, roughly the western boundary of Parthian territory.

Europa. Daughter of Agenor of Phoenicia, and sister of Cadmus, she was abducted and brought to Crete by Jupiter in the form of a bull. She became by Jupiter the mother of Minos.

Evander. An Arcadian, the son of Mercury, he led a colony to Italy before the Trojan War and there founded a city, Pallanteum, on the Palatine Hill. When Hercules, returning with the cattle of Geryon, passed through Italy, Evander received him hospitably. By Evander's daughter Hercules became the father of the founder of the Fabian clan.

F

Fabii. An ancient patrician family of Rome, which traced its descent from Hercules and a daughter of Evander. In 479 B.C. the Fabians undertook to manage the war against Veii, without help from the government of Rome. For two years they devastated the fields of Veii, but in 477 they fell into an ambush and the entire tribe, except for one man, was massacred by the people of Veii. The most famous of the later Fabii was Fabius Maximus, the general of the Hannibalic War.

Fabius Maximus. Quintus Fabius Maximus Verrucosus Cunctator. He was Consul five times, Dictator twice; his second dictatorship was in 217 B.C., during the Hannibalic War. He fought a brilliant war of attrition, continuing this policy through his third, fourth, and fifth consulships. Because of his reluctance to engage in pitched battles he was given the nickname, at first derogatory, later honorific, of *Cunctator,* "Delayer."

Faunus. An old Italian divinity, an oracular god of forests and of herdsmen, he was later identified with the Greek Pan and pictured with a goat's horns and hoofs.

Faustulus. Finding Romulus and Remus being suckled by a she-wolf after their rescue from the Tiber, where they had been cast at Amulius' command, the shepherd raised the twins as his own sons.

Fors. An ancient Italian goddess of good luck.

Forum. An open space at Rome between the Palatine and Capitoline Hills. Originally only a market-place, it gradually acquired many functions. The law courts and the stock-market were there; meetings were held and political speeches delivered there. It was the scene of gladiatorial shows and dramatic performances, and was a favorite loitering-place for idlers.

Furies. Goddesses of vengeance. Snakes served as hair and wound around their limbs; blood dripped from their eyes. They carried torches and scourges with which they punished evil-doers in the Lower World or emerged into the Upper World to strike the guilty with madness. They punished particularly crimes against parents, guests, and suppliants. They maddened and pursued Orestes for the murder of his mother. One of the Furies was the mother, by Mars, of the dragon killed by Cadmus.

G

Gabii. A town in Latium taken by Tarquin the Proud by a ruse. At his instigation, his son won the confidence of its citizens and then undermined its defenses. (See map, p. xxv.)

Gaius Caesar. A son of Julia, daughter of Augustus, he was adopted by Augustus at the age of three. In 1 B.C., at the age of nineteen, he was sent to command the campaign against the Parthians. He died of wounds received in this war in A.D. 4.

Gallicus. Of Gaul. **Canis Gallicus,** a kind of hunting dog.

Gargara. A city at the foot of Mt. Ida in the Troad famous for the fertility of its land and the size of its grain harvests. (See map, p. xxviii.)

Genius Loci. The spirit of a particular place, a being either associated or identified with the Lar, sometimes represented in the form of a large serpent.

Germania. The land of the Germans, separated from Roman lands by the Rhine and the Danube, where several campaigns were fought during the reign of Augustus.

Graius. Greek.

H

Hades. 1. Greek name for Dis. 2. In modern usage, the kingdom of Dis, the Lower World, the land of the dead.

Haemonius. Of Haemon (father of Thessalus, the ancestor of the Thessalians); of Thessaly. **Haemonia aqua,** a drug or poison brewed by Thessalian witches. **Haemonii equi,** the horses of Achilles. **Haemonia puppis,** the Argo.

Hector. Eldest son of King Priam of Troy and Troy's greatest hero. He was killed by Achilles.

Helice. 1. The constellation Ursa Major, so called because it revolved closely around the Pole (**helice** = winding, twisting). 2. Callisto.

Helicon. A mountain or range of Boeotia, a favorite haunt of the Muses.

Henna. An ancient town of central Sicily, surrounded by fertile plains, sacred to Ceres. It was from the fields of Henna that Dis carried off Proserpina.

Hercules. Son of Jupiter and Alcmene, he was the greatest hero of classical myth, performing many marvelous feats which include the famous Twelve Labors. After completing these, he went to Oechalia, where King Eurytus had promised his daughter Iole to anyone who could defeat him and his sons in archery. Hercules won the contest but was refused the girl on the grounds that he had murdered his children by a previous wife. He later invaded Oechalia, killed Eurytus and his sons, and carried Iole off as a prisoner. It was Hercules also who buried the body of Icarus on the island of Icaria. Hercules was worshipped by the Romans, who claimed that he had visited the site of Rome in the time of Evander. At Rome Hercules was associated with the Muses, with whom he shared a temple at the foot of the Capitoline Hill. (See Plan, p. xxvi.)

Hersilia. A Sabine woman, the wife of Romulus, who persuaded the other abducted Sabine women to interrupt the final battle between the Romans and the Sabines.

Hesperides. The daughters of Atlas and Hesperis, they guarded the golden apples which Earth had given Juno as a wedding present. These they kept in their garden, hanging on a tree and guarded by a never-sleeping serpent. To fetch these apples was one of the Labors of Hercules.

Hippolytus. Son of Theseus and Hippolyte the Amazon. Because he scorned women and was interested only in hunting, Venus punished him by causing his stepmother Phaedra to fall in love with him. When he rejected her advances, she falsely accused him to Theseus, who caused his death by a curse. Phaedra then committed suicide in remorse.

Hirtius. Consul with Pansa in 43 B.C. Both consuls fell fighting against Antony at Mutina.

Homer. The great epic poet, author of the *Iliad* and the *Odyssey,* was thought to have been blind and a beggar. His birthplace, though in dispute, was usually given as Lydia.

Hybla. A town in Sicily, famous for its honey. (See map, p. xxv.)

Hymen. The god of marriage, depicted as a handsome youth carrying a marriage-torch; he was invoked in wedding-hymns.

I

Icaria. An island of the Icarian Sea named for Icarus, who was buried there. (See map, p. xxviii.)

Icarian Sea. A part of the Aegean Sea named for Icarus, who fell into this sea when he had destroyed his wings by venturing too near the sun. (See map, p. xxviii.)

Icarus. Son of Daedalus. When he and his father had escaped from the Labyrinth on wings of wax and feathers, he flew (despite his father's warning) too near the sun, which melted the wax. He fell into the sea and his body was washed ashore on the island of Icaria and buried there by Hercules.

Ida. 1. A mountain of the Troad, sacred to Cybele. (See map, p. xxviii.) 2. A mountain of Crete, also sacred to Cybele.

168

Idalium. A town in Cyprus sacred to Venus. (See map, p. xxvii.) **Dea Idalia,** Venus.

Idus. The Ides, the 15th of March, May, July, and October; the 13th of the other months. A date before the Ides is indicated by how many days it is before, counting both ends of the series: e.g., **V Id. Mart. = quinto die ante Idus Martias** = 11 March.

Indi. Inhabitants of India, a term used loosely for any part of southeast Asia. India was occasionally treated as identical with, or as part of, the Aethiopia of the Choaspes Valley. The Indians exported perfumes, pepper, pearls, and Chinese silk to Rome.

Ionian Sea. The sea between the Peloponnesus and southern Italy. (See map, p. xxix.)

Iris. The goddess of the rainbow, a messenger of the gods, particularly of Juno.

Ithaca. Island of the Ionian Sea, the home of Ulysses. (See map, p. xxix.)

Itys. Son of King Tereus of Daulis and his wife, the Athenian princess Procne. Tereus had ravished Procne's sister Philomela and had cut out her tongue to prevent her accusing him; in revenge Procne killed Itys and she and Philomela cooked him and served him to his father. When Tereus sought to kill them they were metamorphosed into a swallow and a nightingale, birds which still mourn Itys.

Iuppiter. Jupiter.

J

Janus. 1. The name given to a magical bridge or gateway. It was the Roman custom when founding a city to mark its boundaries with a bronze plow. This furrow, along with natural water boundaries, formed a magic barrier over which the *imperium* of an enemy could not pass. In order to allow the Roman *imperium* to be carried out against the enemy, gaps were left in the furrow, and magical bridges made over the water, the Jani. At Rome there were three such bridges over the stream Cloaca, the original water boundary of the city, one in the Forum Romanum, one in the Forum of Nerva, and one (still marked by a quadruple arch of the time of Constantine) in the Forum Boarium or Cattle Market. Some gates in the city wall were also Jani. 2. The god of gateways and beginnings, originally the spirit of the Jani, was also called Janus.

Juno. Sister and wife of Jupiter, she was the protectress of women and goddess of the sanctity of marriage. Iris, the rainbow, was her messenger; the peacock, her bird. She was famous for her fierce resentment of slights, cruelly persecuting Jupiter's paramours and their children. She never forgave the Trojans for Paris' failure to give her the prize as the most beautiful goddess. Juno shared the Capitolium with Jupiter and Minerva and had a temple of her own on the Arx nearby.

Jupiter. King of gods and father of men. Drawing lots with his brothers Dis and Neptune for the rule of the universe, he was allotted the sky and the general overlordship. His bird was the eagle. Though he punished malefactors by hurling thunderbolts, he himself was an unfaithful husband, often deceiving his wife Juno. By Danae he was the father of Perseus; by Maia, of Mercury; by Leda, of Helen; by Alcmena, of Hercules; by Europa, of Minos. As Jupiter Optimus Maximus he was the chief god of the Romans, worshipped with his sister-wife Juno and his daughter Minerva in the Capitolia of Rome and other cities.

K

Kalendae. Kalends, the first day of the month. The dates of the latter half of a month are indicated by how many days they are from the Kalends of the next month, counting (as was the Roman custom) both ends of the series: e.g., **VI Kal. Feb. = sexto die ante Kalendas Februarias** = 27 January.

L

Labyrinth. A complex building built by Daedalus for King Minos at Cnossus for keeping the Minotaur. Its windings were so complicated that no one could escape from it without help. Daedalus (who had been imprisoned there) escaped with his son Icarus on wings which he had made of wax and feathers; Theseus escaped with the aid of a ball of thread given him by Ariadne.

Laconia. A district of the southeast Peloponnesus. (See map, p. xxix.)

Lar. A Roman family god, a divinity of the house or farm. Unlike the Penates, the Lares were spirits of the place, rather than of the family. There were also Lares of crossroads and street corners, and of the state in general. A Lar is depicted as a young man in a girt-up tunic and high boots, usually pouring wine from a drinking-horn into a small pail. Lares in paintings often appear to be dancing and are often accompanied by the tutelary spirit of the head of the family, the Genius.

Latium. The plain of the Tiber Valley, where Rome is situated. (See map, p. xxv.)

Latona. A Titaness, mother by Jupiter of Apollo and Diana. Persecuted by Juno, she fled from land to land until she came to Delos, where she gave birth to the twin gods.

Latonia. "Daughter of Latona," Diana.

Lebinthus. An island of the Aegean.

Lelex. King of the Locrians and the maternal uncle of Theseus.

Lenaeus. "God of the Wine-Press," Bacchus.

Lesbos. An island of the Aegean.

Liber. A Roman wine-god identified with Bacchus. The name is often used by metonymy for "wine."

Libya. The Roman name for the continent of Africa, usually excluding Egypt.

Lucifer. The morning star, a name given to the planet Venus when it appeared in the morning.

Lucius Tarquinius Superbus. Tarquin the Proud.

Lycia. A district of Asia Minor. (See map, p. xxviii.)

Lydia. A district of western Asia Minor. (See map, p. xxviii.)

M

Macedonia. A district north of Greece. (See map, p. xxviii.)

Maenads. Female companions of Bacchus in his wanderings, clothed in the skins of animals and crowned with vine-leaves. They carried the Thyrsis, vine-wreathed staffs tipped with pine cones, with which they goaded each other and the other participants in the Thiasus to wild and frenzied actions.

Maenalus. A mountain of Arcadia.

Maeonia. An old name for Lydia.

Mars (Mavors). The Roman god of agriculture and warfare, the two functions being connected since in early Italian warfare the chief target was the enemy's crops. As the father of Romulus, the founder of

the city, Mars, whose name is often used by metonymy to mean "war" or "battle," was an important deity of Rome. The Romans identified Mars with the Greek war-god Ares, the lover of Aphrodite (Venus) and the father, by one of the Furies, of the dragon killed by Cadmus.

Maximus. See **Fabius Maximus.**

Mercury. God of trade and commerce, also the messenger and herald of the gods, as is indicated by his winged cap and sandals, and the herald's staff (the Caduceus) which he carried and used as his magic wand. He was the son of Jupiter by Maia and was born on Mt. Cyllene in Arcadia. A few hours after his birth he stole some of the oxen of Apollo from Pieria in Macedonia. Returning to Cyllene, he found a tortoise shell; placing strings across it, he invented the lyre, which Apollo accepted in repayment for the cattle. A sly trickster, Mercury often aided his father in his love affairs. Mercury had a temple on the Aventine Hill at Rome, which became the chief shrine of merchants and traders.

Metanira. The wife of Celeus, mother of Triptolemus. When she and Celeus received Ceres in her wanderings, Ceres in gratitude was going to make Triptolemus immortal by placing him in the fire on the hearth. Metanira in terror snatched him away and so frustrated Ceres' plans.

Methymna. A city of Lesbos famous for its wine.

Mettius Fufetius. Dictator of Alba Longa and an ally of Tullus Hostilius, the third king of Rome. He behaved treacherously in a battle; and so, at Tullus' command, he was torn asunder by being tied to chariots driven in different directions.

Midas. A king of Phrygia, son of the goddess Cybele. In return for his kindness to Silenus, Bacchus offered to grant him a wish. His wish that anything he touched would be turned to gold was granted, but when his food became gold, he asked Bacchus to revoke the gift. A bath in the Pactolus removed the golden touch, but the river from then on had gold in its sand.

Mimallonides. A Macedonian name for the Maenads.

Minerva. A Roman name for Athena.

Minois. "Daughter of Minos," Ariadne.

Minos. The son of Jupiter and Europa. On the death of Europa's husband King Asterion of Crete, he seized the kingship from Asterion's sons with the aid of Neptune. Having no animal worthy to sacrifice, he prayed for help and received a beautiful white bull from the sea. When

Minos kept the bull for himself, Neptune as punishment caused Minos' wife Pasiphae to fall in love with the bull, by which she became the mother of the Minotaur. Minos imprisoned it in the Labyrinth, which Daedalus had built for him. To avenge the death at Athens of his son Androgeos, Minos required the Athenians to send a yearly tribute of seven youths and seven maidens, to be devoured by the Minotaur. When Theseus came as one of these youths, Minos' daughter Ariadne fell in love with him and helped him; and when he escaped, after having killed the Minotaur, she accompanied him. Legend regarded Minos as a just king, so much so that after his death he became a judge of the dead in the Lower World. His navies controlled the seas; his temporal power has prompted archaeologists to date an era of early civilization by his name.

Minotaur. The monstrous son of Pasiphae, wife of King Minos of Crete, by a bull. He was half man and half bull, and was a man-eater; he was imprisoned in the Labyrinth, where he yearly devoured seven youths and seven maidens, Athens' tribute to Crete. He was finally killed by Theseus.

Muses. Nine sisters, daughters of Jupiter, the goddesses who inspired poetry and song. They often accompanied Apollo, god of poets.

N

Naxos. Also called Dia, a small island in the Aegean famous for its wine and hence sacred to Bacchus. It was the scene of Theseus' desertion of Ariadne and of her rescue by Bacchus. (See map, p. xxviii.)

Neptune. The god of the seas and all other bodies of water, received as his share of the universe when he drew lots with his brothers Jupiter and Dis. He is depicted as armed with the trident, a huge three-pronged fishing spear. He was the creator of the first horse.

Nilus. The Nile, the great river of Egypt, flowing into the sea through seven mouths.

Nonae. The Nones, the seventh day of March, May, July, and October; the fifth of the other months. A date before the Nones is indicated by its distance from them, counting both ends of the series: e.g., **IV Non. Apr. = quarto die ante Nonas Apriles =** 2 April.

Notus. The South Wind personified, a warm wind which often brought rain. The plural **Noti** may stand for winds in general.

Numitor. King of Alba Longa. He was expelled by his brother Amulius, who seized his throne and forced his daughter to become a Vestal Virgin. When she gave birth, by Mars, to twin sons, Romulus and Remus, Amulius ordered that they be cast into the Tiber. However, the twins were rescued and reared as shepherds. On reaching maturity they killed Amulius and restored their grandfather Numitor to the throne.

O

Octavian. Octavianus, the cognomen taken by Gaius Octavius when he was adopted by his great-uncle Gaius Julius Caesar as Gaius Julius Caesar Octavianus; later, the Emperor Augustus.

Odrysae. A people of Thrace.

Oeta. A mountain of southern Thessaly. (See map, p. xxix.)

Orchomenos. A town of Arcadia. (See map, p. xxix.)

Orestes. Son of King Agamemnon of Mycenae and Clytemnestra. When Clytemnestra and Aegisthus murdered Agamemnon, Orestes fled to his uncle in Phocis. Having grown up, he returned and killed his mother and Aegisthus. In punishment for the murder of his mother, the Furies drove him mad and pursued him from country to country. With the help of Apollo, he was finally rescued and cured.

Orion. A gigantic hunter of Boeotia, who on his death was placed among the stars as a constellation, with a belt, a sword, a lion's skin, and a club.

Ortygia. "Island of Quails." 1. A small island off Syracuse in Sicily, the site of the spring of Arethusa. (See map, p. xxv.) 2. Old name for Delos. 3. Adjective, as feminine noun, "The Ortygian," Diana.

P

Pactolus. A river of Lydia, rising on Mt. Tmolus and flowing past Sardes to the Hermus. Its sands were a source of gold in antiquity.

Paean. "The Healer," a name for Apollo.

Palatine Hill. One of the hills of Rome, the site of Pallanteum, the city of Evander, and later of Romulus' newly-founded city. In the historical period it was the residence of the ruling families of Rome. The Emperor Augustus also took up residence there and built a temple to Apollo, one of his patron gods.

Pales. A Roman goddess (or god) of herds and flocks. Her feast, 21 April, was celebrated as the foundation-day of Rome, perhaps because Romulus and Remus were herdsmen.

Panope. A town in the south of Phocis.

Pallas. A name or title of Athena.

Pansa. Consul with Hirtius, 43 B.C. Both consuls fell fighting against Antony at Mutina.

Parnassus (Parnasus). A mountain with two summits near Delphi, sacred to Apollo and the Muses. (See map, p. xxix.)

Paros. An island of the Aegean famous for its white marble. (See map, p. xxviii.)

Parrhasia. A town of Arcadia.

Parrhasis. Of Parrhasia; of Arcadia. **Parrhasides stellae**, the constellation Ursa Major, a metamorphosis of the Arcadian nymph Callisto.

Patara. A city of Lycia in Asia Minor, a center of the worship of Apollo and the site of one of his oracles. (See map, p. xxviii.)

Peloponnesus. The southern part of the Greek peninsula, connected with central Greece by the narrow Isthmus of Corinth. It was named for Pelops, who once was king there. (See map, p. xxix.)

Pelops. Son of the king of Phrygia. When he reached manhood he went to Elis and won its kingship in a chariot race. He then extended his power from Elis over most of the peninsula, so that it was called Peloponnesus, "Island of Pelops."

Penates. Roman household gods, worshipped in the **penetralia**, the inmost part of the house. They were gods of the family, rather than of the place and moved with the family if it changed residence. *Penates* is often used by metonymy for "house" or "home."

Peneus. 1. A river of Thessaly, rising on Mt. Pindus and flowing into the sea. (See map, p. xxix.) 2. The god of the river, the father of Daphne. **Peneia.** "Daughter of Peneus," Daphne.

Pergama. The citadel of Troy, a term often used to refer to the whole city.

Persephone. Greek name of Proserpina.

Perses. The ancestor of the Persians, son of Perseus and grandson of Danae.

Perseus. Son of Jupiter and Danae. When he opposed the suit of King Polydectes of Seriphos for his mother's hand, Polydectes sent him to fetch the head of the Gorgon Medusa, whose glance could turn living creatures to stone. Having obtained the head, he was returning when he saw the Aethiopian princess Andromeda bound to a rock in the sea as an offering to a sea-monster. Killing the monster, he rescued the princess, married her, and took her with him to Seriphos, thence to Argos and finally to Tiryns, where he became king.

Persis. The Greek and Roman name for Persia, derived, as they thought, from the name of Perses, the grandson of Danae.

Phaedra. Daughter of King Minos of Crete and his wife Pasiphae, married to King Theseus of Athens. She became enamored of her stepson Hippolytus, a hunter who scorned love and was devoted to the goddess Diana. When he repulsed her advances, she accused him falsely to his father Theseus, who then caused his death by a curse. In remorse, she killed herself.

Phasis. A river of Colchis, the land of Medea.

Philemon. An aged Phrygian who, with his wife Baucis, hospitably received Jupiter and Mercury, traveling the earth in disguise. In gratitude the gods granted the old couple their wish to be priest and priestess of Jupiter's temple and to die at the same moment. In death they were metamorphosed into two trees growing from a single trunk.

Phocis. A country of central Greece, north of the Gulf of Corinth, famous as the site of Delphi. (See map, p. xxix.)

Phoebe. "Bright One," a name of Diana, the virgin goddess of the moon.

Phoebus. "Bright One," another name for the sun god Apollo.

Phoenicia. A mountainous land on the east shore of the Mediterranean, the birthplace of Cadmus and Europa. (See map, p. xxvii.)

Phrygia. A country of Asia Minor. (See map, p. xxvii.)

Phrygius. Of Phrygia; Trojan.

Pieria. A country on the southeast coast of Macedonia, an early center for the worship of the Muses. (See map, p. xxviii.)

Pindus. A mountain of Thessaly, a favorite haunt of the Muses. (See map, p. xxix.)

Pirithous. King of the Lapiths in Thessaly, a close friend of Theseus. The two were comrades in many adventures, including the Calydonian Boar hunt. Theseus' regard for his friend was so great that he even joined Pirithous in his attempt to carry off Proserpina from the Lower

World. Both were caught and imprisoned by Dis, but Theseus was afterward released by Hercules.

Pittheus. King of Troezen in the Peloponnesus. He was the son of Pelops, the father of Lelex and Aethra, and the grandfather of Theseus.

Plistus (Pleistus). 1. A small river of Phocis, near Delphi. 2. The god of the river, the father of the Corycidae.

Pluto. "God of Wealth," another name for Dis.

Polyphemus. One of the Cyclopes who fell in love with the Nereid Galatea. Repulsed, he crushed her lover Acis under a boulder.

Porta Capena. A city gate of Rome, leading to the Via Appia, near the east end of the Circus Maximus. Close by was a spring or fountain sacred to Mercury. (See Plan, p. xxvi.)

Priam. King of Troy at the time of the Trojan War. He was the father of fifty sons, including Hector and Paris, and fifty daughters, including Cassandra. He was the father-in-law of Aeneas and Andromache.

Priamides. "Son of Priam," e.g., Paris.

Procne. An Athenian princess, married to King Tereus of Daulis in Thrace. When Tereus went, at her request, to Athens to escort her sister Philomela to Thrace for a visit, he became enamored of Philomela, violated her, and cut out her tongue to keep her from telling. Procne discovered the truth from a tapestry which Philomela had woven and in revenge killed Itys, her own son by Tereus; the two sisters then cut the boy up, cooked him, and served him to his father. When Tereus discovered the truth he attempted to kill the sisters, but was metamorphosed into a hoopoe, while they became a swallow and a nightingale.

Prometheus. A Titan, brother of Epimetheus and Atlas. He was the creator of mankind, breathing life into a figure he had made of earth and water, and giving it some parts of the qualities of all other animals. Deucalion, King of Phthia in Thessaly, was his son.

Promethides. "Son of Prometheus," Deucalion.

Proserpina. Daughter of Jupiter and Ceres. She was carried off to the Lower World from the meadows of Henna by her uncle, Dis, who wanted to make her his wife. When Ceres found out where she was and appealed to Jupiter for her return, he promised that she could leave the Lower World if she had taken no food

there. Because she had eaten only part of a pomegranate, Jupiter allowed her to spend half of each year with her mother.

Psophis. A town of Arcadia. (See map, p. xxix.)

Pyrrha. Daughter of the Titan Epimetheus and wife of her cousin Deucalion. She and her husband were the only mortals preserved in the universal flood sent by Jupiter to punish the sins of mankind. On the advice of an oracle, they re-created the human race by throwing behind their backs stones which became people.

Pythia. The Pythian Games were held at Delphi every fourth year in commemoration of Apollo's victory over Python. The most important competitions were in instrumental music, singing, drama, and recitation, but there were also athletic contests and chariot races. The victors were crowned with laurel.

Python. A huge serpent, generated from the mud left by the universal flood, it lived in a cave on Mt. Parnassus and guarded the oracle of Earth and Themis at Delphi. Apollo killed Python and took the oracle for himself.

Q

Quinquatria. A five-day festival in honor of Minerva, 19-23 March. The first day, the anniversary of the founding of the temple of Minerva on the Aventine Hill, was celebrated with public sacrifices; the other four days were celebrated with gladiatorial combats.

Quirinus. The name given to Romulus, the founder of Rome, after he became a god.

Quirites. A term meaning *Roman citizens* (in a civil, not a military sense). It came into use after the union of the Romans and the Sabines, which followed the abduction of the Sabine women.

R

Remus. Grandson of King Numitor of Alba Longa, son of Mars, and twin brother of Romulus. Amulius had robbed his brother Numitor of his kingship and ordered the infant twins cast into the Tiber. They were rescued by a she-wolf and raised by the shepherd Faustulus. When they came of age they killed Amulius and restored Numitor. They then planned to found a city on the Palatine Hill for the band of shepherds which they led. Romulus was given by augury the right to be the founder; when his walls were partly finished Remus leaped over them in scorn and was killed by Celer, Romulus' lieutenant.

Rhesus. The king of the Odrysians or Thracians, who came to the aid of Troy in the Trojan War. Soon after his arrival he was killed, and his horses carried off by Ulysses and Diomedes, who feared a prophecy that Troy would never be taken if Rhesus' horses once drank the water of its rivers.

Roma. Rome, capital of the Roman Empire. Its two founders were Aeneas, son of Venus, who brought the gods of Troy to Latium, and Romulus, son of Mars, who actually founded the city.

Romulus. Son of Mars, grandson of Numitor, King of Alba Longa. Numitor was driven from the throne by his brother Amulius, who also forced Numitor's daughter to become a Vestal Virgin to prevent the birth of rival claimants. When she became, by Mars, the mother of twin sons, Romulus and Remus, Amulius ordered that the twins be cast into the Tiber. They were rescued by a she-wolf and raised by the shepherd Faustulus. When they were grown, they became the leaders of the shepherds and, with their aid, killed Amulius and restored Numitor. They then decided to found a city for their followers on the Palatine Hill; by augury Romulus was chosen as the founder. To make up for the lack of women in the new city Romulus invited the neighboring Sabines to a set of games, giving his men instructions to carry off the Sabine women at a signal. War followed, but eventually peace was made; and Romulus and the Sabine king ruled jointly over the combined peoples. After a reign of thirty-seven years Romulus was taken up to heaven, where he became the god Quirinus.

S

Sabines. An ancient people of central Italy. Under the leadership of Romulus the Romans carried off a number of Sabine women to be their wives. The seizure brought on a war between the Romans and Sabines, which was brought to an end by the intercession of the Sabine women, pleading for peace between their husbands and fathers. The two peoples were then united and lived under joint rule.

Samos. An Island of the Aegean. (See map, p. xxviii.)

Sardes. A city on the Pactolus river, the ancient capital of Lydia. (See map, p. xxviii.)

Saturn. A Roman god identified with the Greek Cronos.

Saturnia. "Daughter of Saturn," Juno.

Saturnius. "Son of Saturn," Jupiter.

Satyrs. Attendants of the god Bacchus, pictured by the Romans as men with the horns, ears, tails, and feet of goats. They were woodland creatures playful, amorous, mischievous, but cowardly.

Sceleratus Vicus. See **Vicus Sceleratus.**

Schoeneis. "Daughter of Schoeneus," Atalanta.

Schoeneus. King of Boeotia, the father of Atalanta.

Seres. The Chinese, from whom the Romans imported manufactured silk.

Seriphos. An island in the Aegean. (See map, p. xxix.) Danae and her infant son Perseus drifted to Seriphos after they had been cast into the sea in a chest. Perseus returned to Seriphos with Andromeda after he had rescued her, and took Danae with him to Argos.

Servius Tullius. The sixth king of Rome. He was born in the palace of Tarquinius Priscus and brought up by the king and his wife Tanaquil. The sons of the fourth king, Ancus Martius, assassinated Tarquin because they felt that he had deprived them of their father's kingdom. Tanaquil arranged the choice of Servius Tullius as Tarquin's successor. Fearing that Tarquin's two sons would resent his accession, he gave his two daughters to them in marriage. The daughter who was married to Arruns Tarquinius conspired with his brother Lucius Tarquinius to murder his wife (her sister) and her husband (Arruns, Lucius' brother). She then married him and together they conspired to overthrow Servius Tullius, her father. Lucius entered the Senate House, sat on the royal throne, and convened the Senate. When Servius attempted to eject him Lucius seized him and threw him down the steps of the Senate House. Covered with blood, Servius went home, but was overtaken and killed by Lucius Tarquinius' servants.

Sicily. A large island off the Italian peninsula, the home of the Cyclopes and sacred to the goddess Ceres. (See map, p. xxv.)

Sidon. A city of Phoenicia. (See map, p. xxvii.)

Silenus. Foster-father and constant companion of Bacchus, depicted as a drunken old man or Satyr riding on an ass.

Simois. A river near Troy. (See map, p. xxviii.)

Sithonia. The central point of the Chalcidice in Thrace. (See map, p. xxviii.)

Sparta. The capital of Laconia. (See map, p. xxix.)

Stymphalus. A town in Arcadia, near Lake Stymphalis. (See map, p. xxix.)

Styx. A river of the Lower World, over which the souls of the dead were ferried to the realm of Dis.

Sulmo. A town in the Sabine country of Italy and Ovid's birthplace. (See map, p. xxv.)

Superbus. See **Tarquinius Superbus.**

Sygambrus. Of the Sygambri, a powerful people of Germany, conquered during the reign of Augustus.

Syracuse (**Syracusae**). A city of eastern Sicily. (See map, p. xxv.)

T

Taenarius. Of Taenarum; of the Lower World.

Taenarum. 1. A promontory of Laconia in the Peloponnesus where there was a cave thought to be an entrance to the Lower World, the realm of Dis. (See map, p. xxix.) 2. A town on the promontory.

Tarquinius Priscus. Lucius Tarquinius Priscus, the Roman name adopted by Lucumo, a man of Tarquinii who migrated to Rome with his wife Tanaquil, a woman skilled in augury. Through her advice he succeeded in having himself elected the fifth king of the Romans. Foreseeing a brilliant future for Servius Tullius, a child born in the palace, Tanaquil persuaded Tarquin to adopt him as his successor, setting aside his own sons Lucius and Arruns. Tarquinius Priscus was assassinated by the sons of the fourth king of Rome, Ancus Martius, who felt that he had deprived them of the kingship.

Tarquinius Superbus. Tarquin the Proud. Lucius Tarquinius Superbus, seventh and last king of Rome, obtained the kingship by conspiring with his wife Tullia to murder her father Servius Tullius, the reigning king. He was eventually expelled by a group of citizens who were outraged at the violation of a virtuous Roman matron by Tarquin's son, Sextus Tarquinius. The taking of the town of Gabii by treachery was one of Tarquin's exploits.

Tartara. (**Tartarus.**) That part of the kingdom of Dis reserved for the punishment of sinners. Their torments were presided over by the Furies.

Tegea. A city of Arcadia. (See map, p. xxix.)

Tegeaeus. Of Tegea. **Tegeaea virgō,** Callisto.

Tellus. The goddess Earth, the mother of the Titans, and so of all gods and men.

Tenedos. An island of the Aegean just off the Troad, sacred to Apollo. (See map, p. xxviii.)

Thalia. The Muse who presided over comedy, pastoral poetry, and elegiac verse.

Theatrum Balbi. The theater of Cornelius Balbus, built in Rome in 13 B.C. (See Plan, p. xxvi.)

Theatrum Marcelli. A theater built in Rome by Augustus and dedicated in the name of his deceased nephew Marcellus in 11 B.C. (See Plan, p. xxvi.)

Theatrum Pompeii. A theater built in Rome by Pompey the Great in 55 B.C. (See Plan, p. xxvi.)

Thebes. Chief city of Boeotia, founded by Cadmus, the birthplace of Bacchus and Hercules. (See map, p. xxix.)

Themis. A Titaness, the goddess of divine justice, law and order. Together with her mother Earth she held the oracle at Delphi until Apollo won it by killing Python, its guardian.

Thesus. King of Athens. As a young man he accompanied the youths and maidens sent by his father as tribute to King Minos of Crete, to be devoured by the Minotaur. Minos' daughter Ariadne fell in love with him and gave him a ball of thread to enable him to find his way out of the Labyrinth. In return he promised to marry her. When he escaped from Crete after having killed the Minotaur, he took her with him but abandoned her, while she slept, on the island of Dia (Naxos). He later married her sister Phaedra. His friendship with Pirithous, king of the Lapiths, was proverbial.

Thessaly. A district of Greece, the home of Achilles and of Jason; it was also the abode of witches. (See map, p. xxix.)

Thrace. A vast territory north of the Aegean, a center of the Bacchic cult. (See map, p. xxviii.)

Tiber. A river of Latium, on which Rome is situated. (See map, p. xxv.)

Tigris. A great river of the Parthian empire.

Tiphys. The steersman of the Argo.

Titania. "Daughter of the Titan," Pyrrha.

Titans. The pre-Olympian gods, the offspring of Heaven and Earth whose king was Cronus (Saturn). Their power was overthrown by the Olympian gods, led by Jupiter, son of Cronus. Those attempting to rebel were cast into Tartarus.

Tmolus. A mountain of Lydia, the source of the Pactolus River. (See map, p. xxviii.)

Tonans. "Thunderer," a name of Jupiter as the god of the sky.

Trinacris. "With three promontories," an old name for Sicily.

Triptolemus. Son of Celeus and Metanira of Eleusis. When his parents entertained Ceres on her wanderings, she wished to repay them by making Triptolemus immortal. She put him on the fire to burn away his mortality; but Metanira, in terror, snatched him away and so frustrated Ceres' plan. Ceres then promised that Triptolemus would be a great benefactor of mankind; and when he was grown she gave him a chariot drawn by dragons and sent him over the earth to teach mankind the arts of agriculture.

Triton. A sea-god, the son of Neptune, he served his father by blowing his trumpet, a conch-shell, to raise or calm the waves. He was pictured as having the upper body of a man and the tail of a fish.

Tritonis. A name for Athena, derived from her birthplace, Lake Tritonis in Libya.

Troezen. A city in the northeast of the Peloponnesus. (See map, p. xxix.)

Troia (Troy). A city of Asia Minor. The abduction of Helen, Queen of Sparta, by Paris, prince of Troy, brought on the Trojan War. Troy, although aided by many allies, was finally taken and destroyed by the Greeks. (See map, p. xxviii.)

Tullia. Daughter of Servius Tullius, sixth king of Rome, who conspired with her husband Lucius Tarquinius (son of Tarquinius Priscus, the fifth king) to murder her father and seize the throne. When Servius Tullius had been killed by Tarquinius' men, Tullia, on her way to the palace, made her charioteer drive over her father's body lying in the street; she felt no remorse even though splashed with her father's blood.

Tydides. "Son of Tydeus," Diomedes.

Tyre. An important city of Phoenicia. Near Tyre were the most important fisheries for the murex, the shellfish from which the expensive "purple" dye was extracted. (See map, p. xxvii.)

Tyrrhenia. Etruria.

U

Ulixes. Ulysses.

Ulysses. King of Ithaca, renowned for his cleverness and skill in speaking. He led the Ithacan contingent to Troy, where he performed many exploits during the ten-year siege. Because of the enmity of Neptune (whose son, Polyphemus, he had killed), his homecoming also took ten years. He stayed for a year on the island of Circe, the enchantress, who had changed his men into swine. He forced her to restore them and received her advice about the rest of his journey. Sailing past the island of the Sirens, he saved his ship from shipwreck by plugging his companions' ears with wax so that they could not hear the alluring song and by having himself bound to the mast, so that he could neither countermand his own orders nor throw himself into the sea. When he had lost his ship and his companions in a storm, he was cast ashore on the island of Calypso, a goddess who promised him immortality if he would marry her. He refused, since his only desire was to go home; but she kept him with her for eight years. Then, at Jupiter's command, she let him go and showed him how to build a boat or raft. When this sank he was saved by the sea-goddess Leucothea. Finally, reaching Ithaca after twenty years' absence, he found that his wife Penelope had remained faithful to him, although she had been courted by many suitors, who had taken up residence in his house and were wasting his property. He killed the suitors and restored order.

Umber. An Umbrian, an inhabitant of Umbria. To the Romans the Umbrians seemed rustic, old-fashioned, stingy, and narrow-minded.

Umbria. A district of northeast Italy. (See map, p. xxv.)

Urbs. "The City," a word often used by the Romans without qualification to mean *Rome;* in their writings they often seem to display a certain reluctance to apply the word *urbs* to other cities.

Ursa Major. The constellation of the Great Bear or Big Dipper. This bear was thought to be a metamorphosis of the Arcadian nymph Callisto.

V

Veii. An Etruscan city on the river Cremera, about twelve miles from Rome. The Romans fought fourteen wars with the inhabitants of Veii, finally taking the city in 396 B.C. (See map, p. xxv.)

Venus. Goddess of Love, thought to have been born of the sea near the island of Cythera. She was the mother of Cupid

176

(**Amor**) the god of love, and of Aeneas, the founding hero of Rome.

Via Appia. A highway, built in 312 B.C., running south from the Porta Capena at Rome to Capua; the first major Roman Road.

Vesta. Goddess of the hearth, both of the individual home and of the community as a whole. She was associated with or was one of the Penates. Since her presence was important at the founding of cities, Aeneas had brought her sacred fire from Troy to Italy.

Vicus Cyprius. A street on the Esquiline Hill in Rome.

Vicus Sceleratus. "Wicked Street," a street on the Esquiline Hill in Rome, so called because it was here that Tullia ran her carriage over the corpse of her father.

Virtus. The goddess of manly valor, usually represented as armed.

Volsci. An ancient people of Latium. Hostile to the Romans, they were subdued in 338 B.C. (See map, p. xxv.)

Z

Zephyrus. The personification of the warm, gentle West Wind.